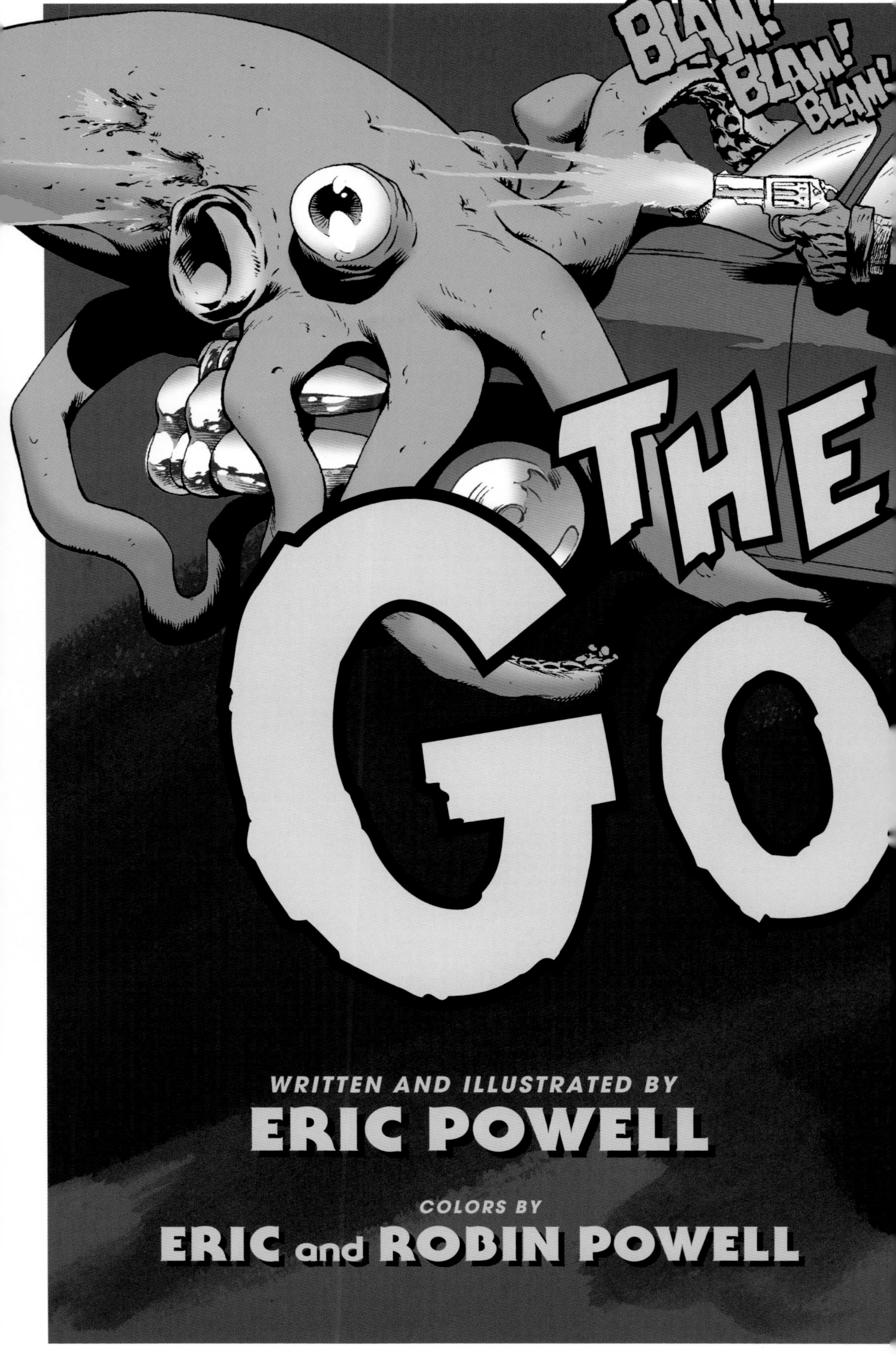
BLAM!
BLAM!
BLAM!
THE
GO

WRITTEN AND ILLUSTRATED BY
ERIC POWELL

COLORS BY
ERIC and ROBIN POWELL

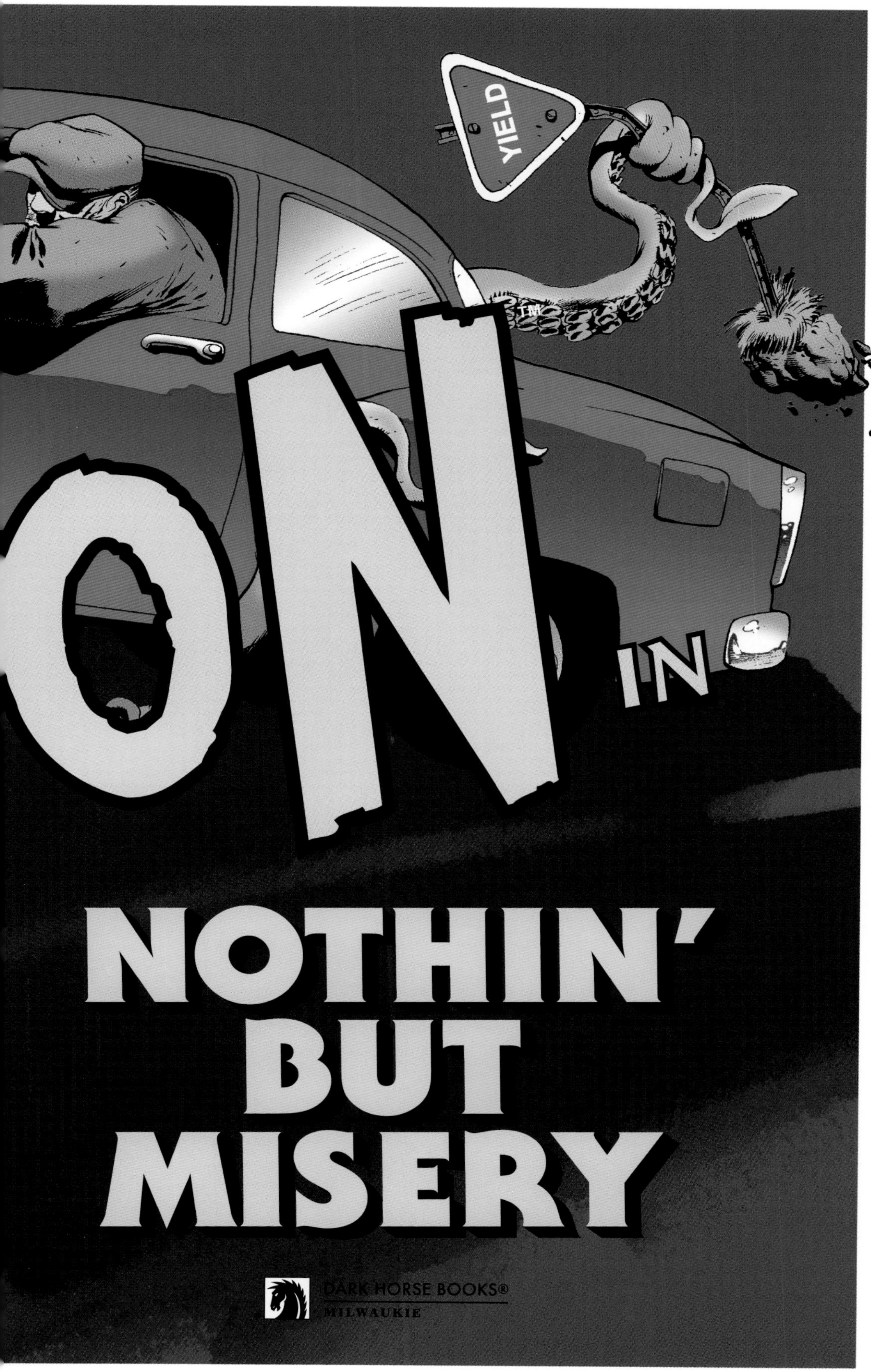
YIELD
ON™ IN

NOTHIN' BUT MISERY

DARK HORSE BOOKS®
MILWAUKIE

First edition:
editors SCOTT ALLIE & MATT DRYER

Second edition:
editor SCOTT ALLIE
assistant editor BRENDAN WRIGHT

designer AMY ARENDTS

president & publisher MIKE RICHARDSON

Neil Hankerson *executive vice president* • Tom Weddle *chief financial officer* • Randy Stradley *vice president of publishing* • Michael Martens *vice president of business development* • Anita Nelson *vice president of business affairs* • Micha Hershman *vice president of marketing* • David Scroggy *vice president of product development* • Dale LaFountain *vice president of information technology* • Darlene Vogel *director of purchasing* • Ken Lizzi *general counsel* • Davey Estrada *editorial director* • Scott Allie *senior managing editor* • Chris Warner *senior books editor* • Diana Schutz *executive editor* • Cary Grazzini *director of design and production* • Lia Ribacchi *art director* • Cara Niece *director of scheduling*

THE GOON™: NOTHIN' BUT MISERY

This volume collects issues #1–#4 of *The Goon* and *The Goon Color Special*, originally published by Albatross Exploding Funny Books, as well as the short story "Die, Fish, Die!" originally published in the final issue of *Dark Horse Presents*. Yes, after setting creative milestones with the likes of Chadwick and Miller, *DHP*, possibly the greatest anthology comic of all time, ran a *Goon* story by Eric Powell, and was subsequently canceled.

Published by
Dark Horse Books
A division of
Dark Horse Comics, Inc.
10956 SE Main Street
Milwaukie, OR 97222

DarkHorse.com

To find a comics shop in your area,
call the Comic Shop Locator Service toll-free at (888) 266-4226.

First edition: July 2003
Second edition: June 2011
ISBN 978-1-59582-624-4

10 9 8 7 6 5 4 3 2 1

Printed at Midas Printing International, Ltd., Huizhou, China

DOWN AT THE END OF LONELY STREET

by WILLIAM STOUT

I gotta admit it—I've got a thing for zombies. And hillbillies. That makes Eric Powell's comic, *The Goon*, just my cup of inbred tea.

I did some unsavory digging and uncovered how it all started. After a long day of guesting at Deliverance Con, Jack Kirby got all liquored up on some white lightnin' with Wally Wood and Graham Ingels late one full-moon night in a local fan's darkened Tennessee shack. One thing led to something unspeakable, which led to a very particular form of popular backwoods perversity, and before ya knew it, little Eric Powell was "born."

The feisty little runt needed shaving at birth and in many other ways was pretty much unstoppable. As an unwashed, cowlicked, pesky whelp he'd grab a meat fork and a chunk of hot charcoal from the smoke pit at the monthly Long Pig Barbecue celebration, and before anyone could stop him he'd have drawn close to thirty cut-and-smudge Laughing Demon tattoos on the rumps of both the conscious and unconscious lady folk attending the event.

Powell didn't improve with age; he only got more ambitious. His teen years were spent performing "experiments" that, if related here, would result in a permanent federal-government shutdown of Dark Horse Comics coupled with lengthy (and well-deserved) prison terms for publishers Richardson and Stradley.

Eventually, with the begrudging help of rehab at gunpoint, Eric saw the light. Or, more importantly (and more accurately), Eric convinced his parole officer that he'd seen the light. Working within Dark Horse's charitable Art for Dollars program, Eric began to release his demons in a much more positive form: comic books.

Promised his own book and mere house arrest instead of the chain gang if he produced a regular comic-book series, Eric went to work. *The Goon* is the result. A mini masterpiece of urban debris, Powell's nihilistic noir drops thirties and forties pop-cultural references (like dialogue from Frank Capra's nightmarish *It's a Wonderful Life*) amongst Texas chainsaw hillbilly hilarity (and old Monty Python reruns to boot) to devastating effect. Confused? Just think *Murder, He Says* (1945) with flesh-eating zombies.

Most of the *Goon* books were originally published in black and white, an appropriate choice considering the influence B and Z drive-in films have had on Powell's twisted psyche. Now that he's ventured into color, Powell's world is painted in somber umbers and grayed-down pigments that effectively convey both the psychological and tangible rubble of the Goon and his squalid environment. These ashen palettes are occasionally ruptured with a burst of red (usually—surprise!—blood) or potently spiced with a fetidly sweet, bilious green.

So, pour yourself a Mason jar full of yer grampa's best corn liquor, grab a pig-ear sandwich and a plateful of rib tips, kick up your feet in your La-Z-Boy, and strap yourself in for a series of lively thug-and-zombie stories where anything can happen.

'Cause it will.

William Stout
Pasadena, California

William Stout was the production designer for *The Return of the Living Dead* and worked with Tobe Hooper (*The Texas Chainsaw Massacre*) on *Invaders from Mars*, so he knows what the hell he's talking about.

PROLOGUE

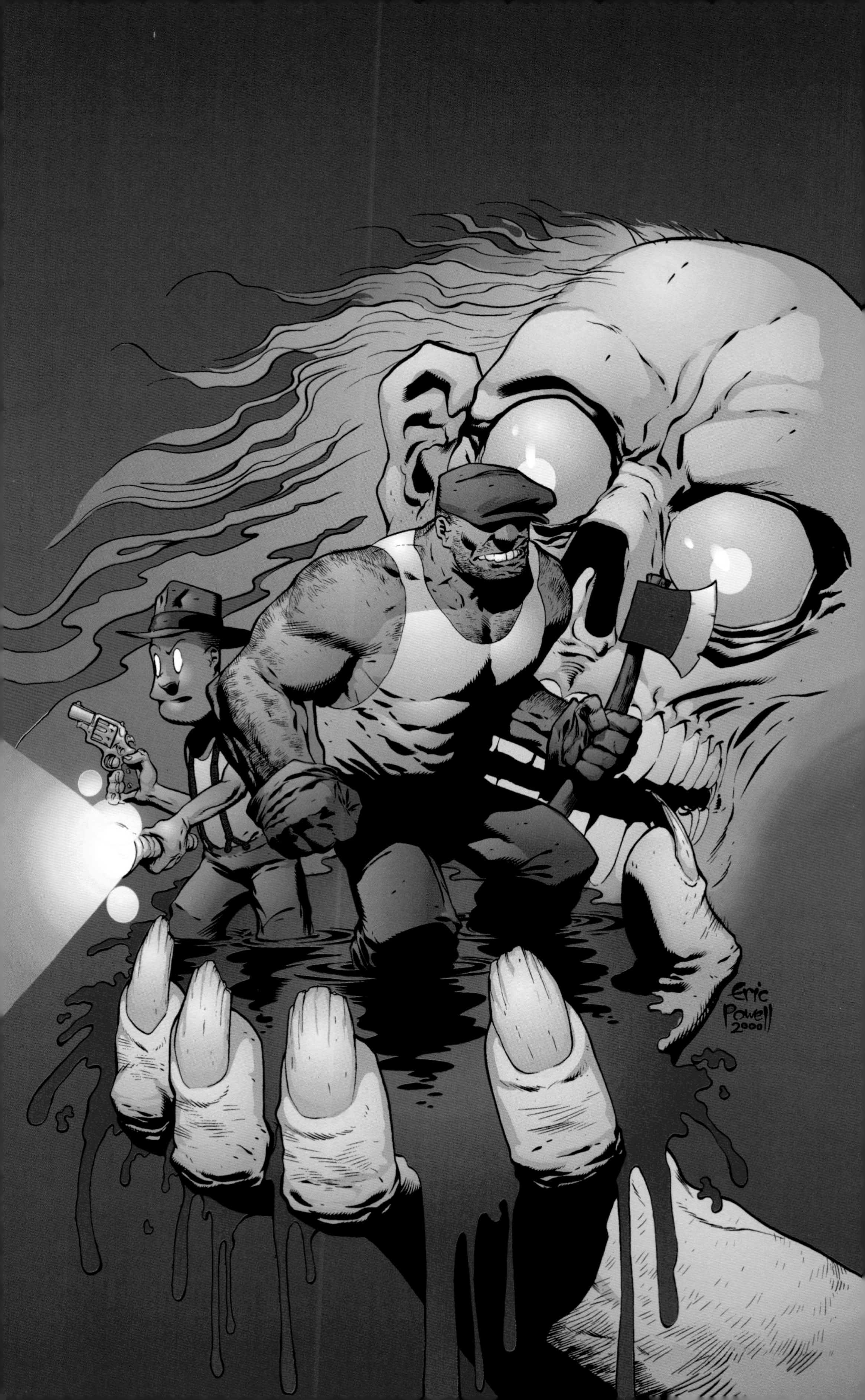
Eric Powell 2000

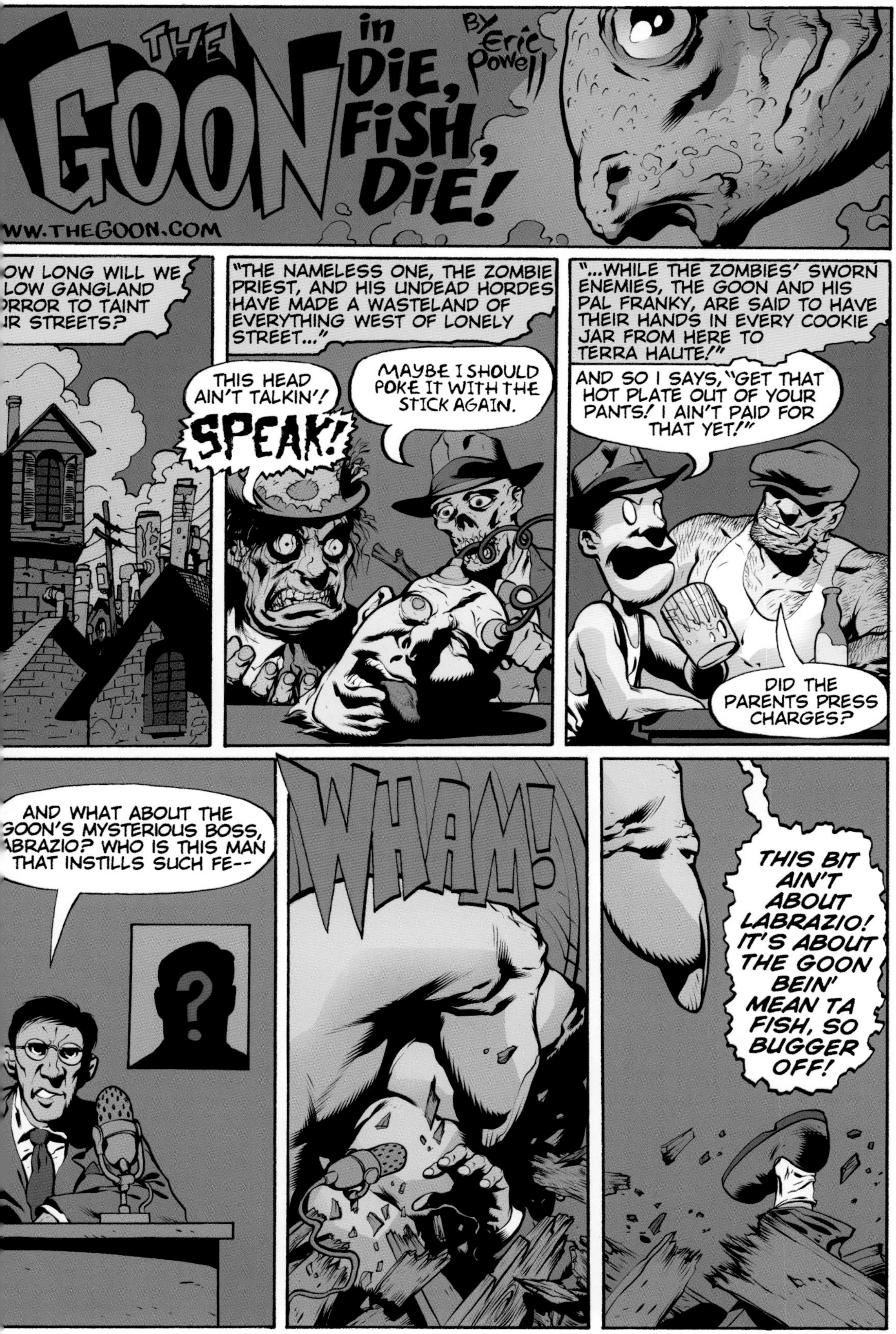
THE GOON
in
DIE, FISH, DIE!
BY Eric Powell
WWW.THEGOON.COM
OW LONG WILL WE LOW GANGLAND RROR TO TAINT IR STREETS?
"THE NAMELESS ONE, THE ZOMBIE PRIEST, AND HIS UNDEAD HORDES HAVE MADE A WASTELAND OF EVERYTHING WEST OF LONELY STREET..."
THIS HEAD AIN'T TALKIN'!
SPEAK!
MAYBE I SHOULD POKE IT WITH THE STICK AGAIN.
"...WHILE THE ZOMBIES' SWORN ENEMIES, THE GOON AND HIS PAL FRANKY, ARE SAID TO HAVE THEIR HANDS IN EVERY COOKIE JAR FROM HERE TO TERRA HAUTE!"
AND SO I SAYS, "GET THAT HOT PLATE OUT OF YOUR PANTS! I AIN'T PAID FOR THAT YET!"
DID THE PARENTS PRESS CHARGES?
AND WHAT ABOUT THE GOON'S MYSTERIOUS BOSS, ABRAZIO? WHO IS THIS MAN THAT INSTILLS SUCH FE--
WHAM!
THIS BIT AIN'T ABOUT LABRAZIO! IT'S ABOUT THE GOON BEIN' MEAN TA FISH, SO BUGGER OFF!

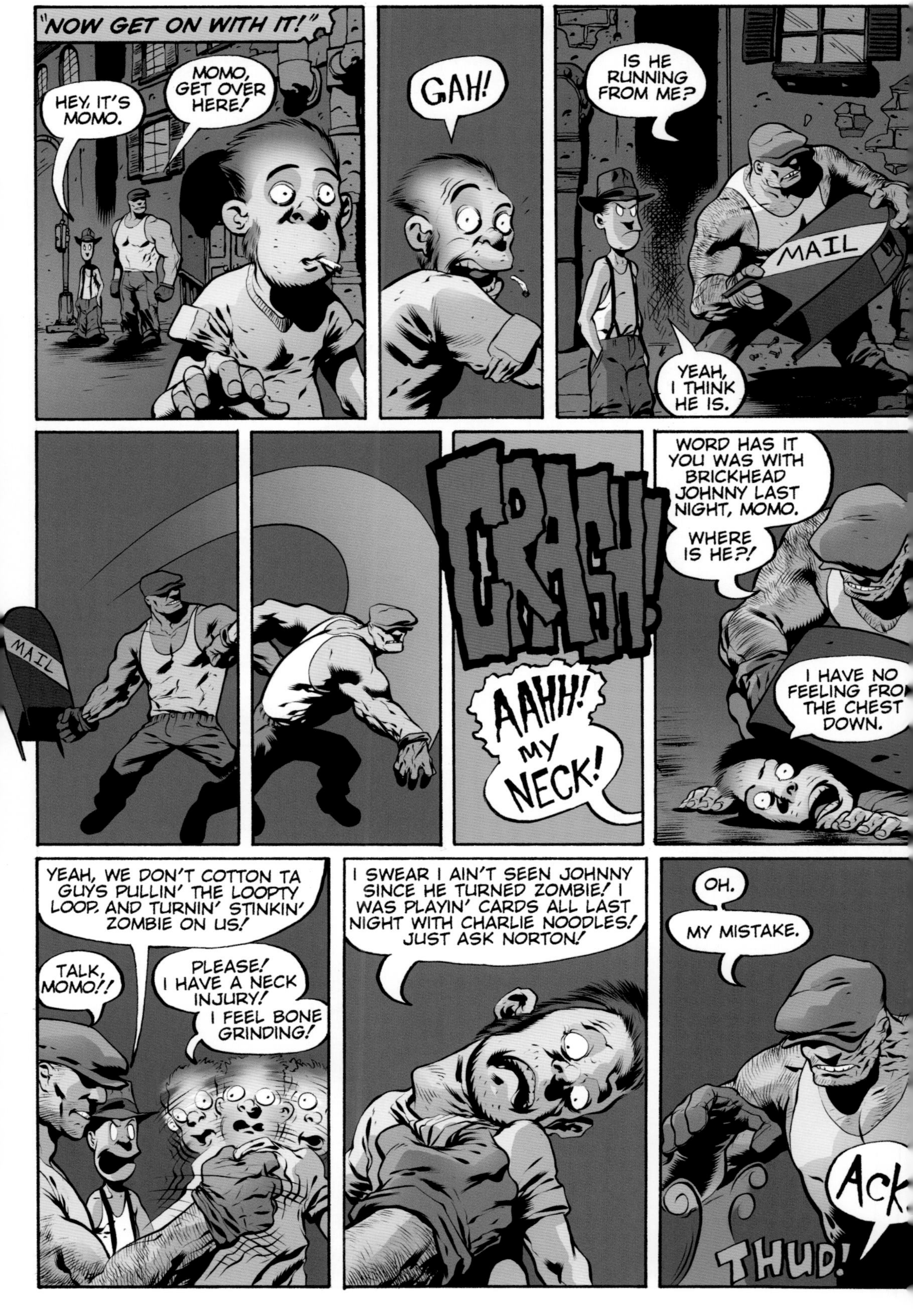
"NOW GET ON WITH IT!"
HEY, IT'S MOMO.
MOMO, GET OVER HERE!
GAH!
IS HE RUNNING FROM ME?
MAIL
YEAH, I THINK HE IS.
MAIL
CRASH!
AAHH! MY NECK!
WORD HAS IT YOU WAS WITH BRICKHEAD JOHNNY LAST NIGHT, MOMO.
WHERE IS HE?!
I HAVE NO FEELING FROM THE CHEST DOWN.
YEAH, WE DON'T COTTON TA GUYS PULLIN' THE LOOPTY LOOP, AND TURNIN' STINKIN' ZOMBIE ON US!
TALK, MOMO!!
PLEASE! I HAVE A NECK INJURY!
I FEEL BONE GRINDING!
I SWEAR I AIN'T SEEN JOHNNY SINCE HE TURNED ZOMBIE! I WAS PLAYIN' CARDS ALL LAST NIGHT WITH CHARLIE NOODLES! JUST ASK NORTON!
OH.
MY MISTAKE.
ACK
THUD!

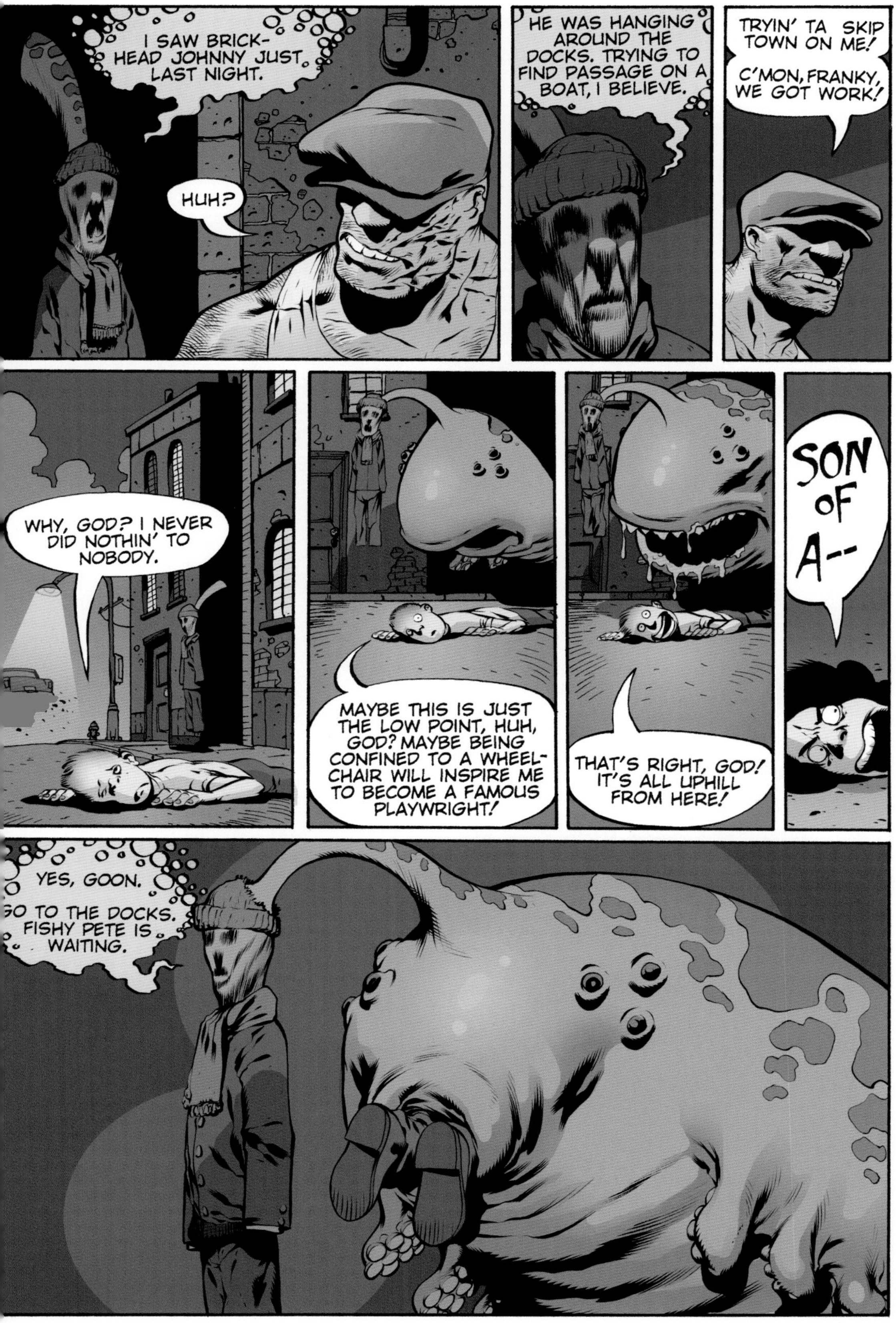
I SAW BRICK-HEAD JOHNNY JUST LAST NIGHT.
HUH?
HE WAS HANGING AROUND THE DOCKS. TRYING TO FIND PASSAGE ON A BOAT, I BELIEVE.
TRYIN' TA SKIP TOWN ON ME!
C'MON, FRANKY, WE GOT WORK!
WHY, GOD? I NEVER DID NOTHIN' TO NOBODY.
MAYBE THIS IS JUST THE LOW POINT, HUH, GOD? MAYBE BEING CONFINED TO A WHEEL-CHAIR WILL INSPIRE ME TO BECOME A FAMOUS PLAYWRIGHT!
THAT'S RIGHT, GOD! IT'S ALL UPHILL FROM HERE!
SON OF A--
YES, GOON.
GO TO THE DOCKS. FISHY PETE IS WAITING.

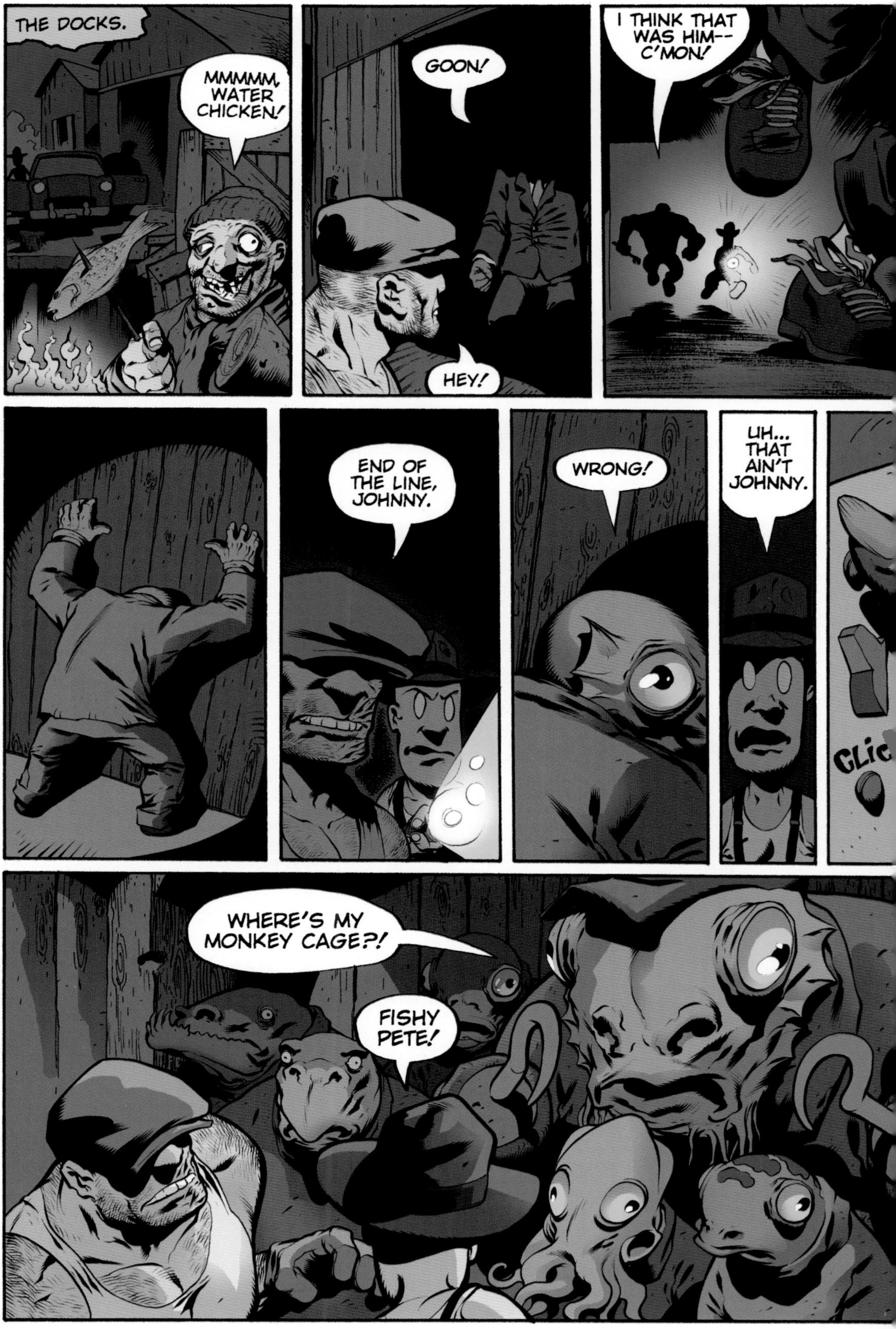
THE DOCKS.
MMMMM, WATER CHICKEN!
GOON!
HEY!
I THINK THAT WAS HIM-- C'MON!
END OF THE LINE, JOHNNY.
WRONG!
UH... THAT AIN'T JOHNNY.
WHERE'S MY MONKEY CAGE?!
FISHY PETE!

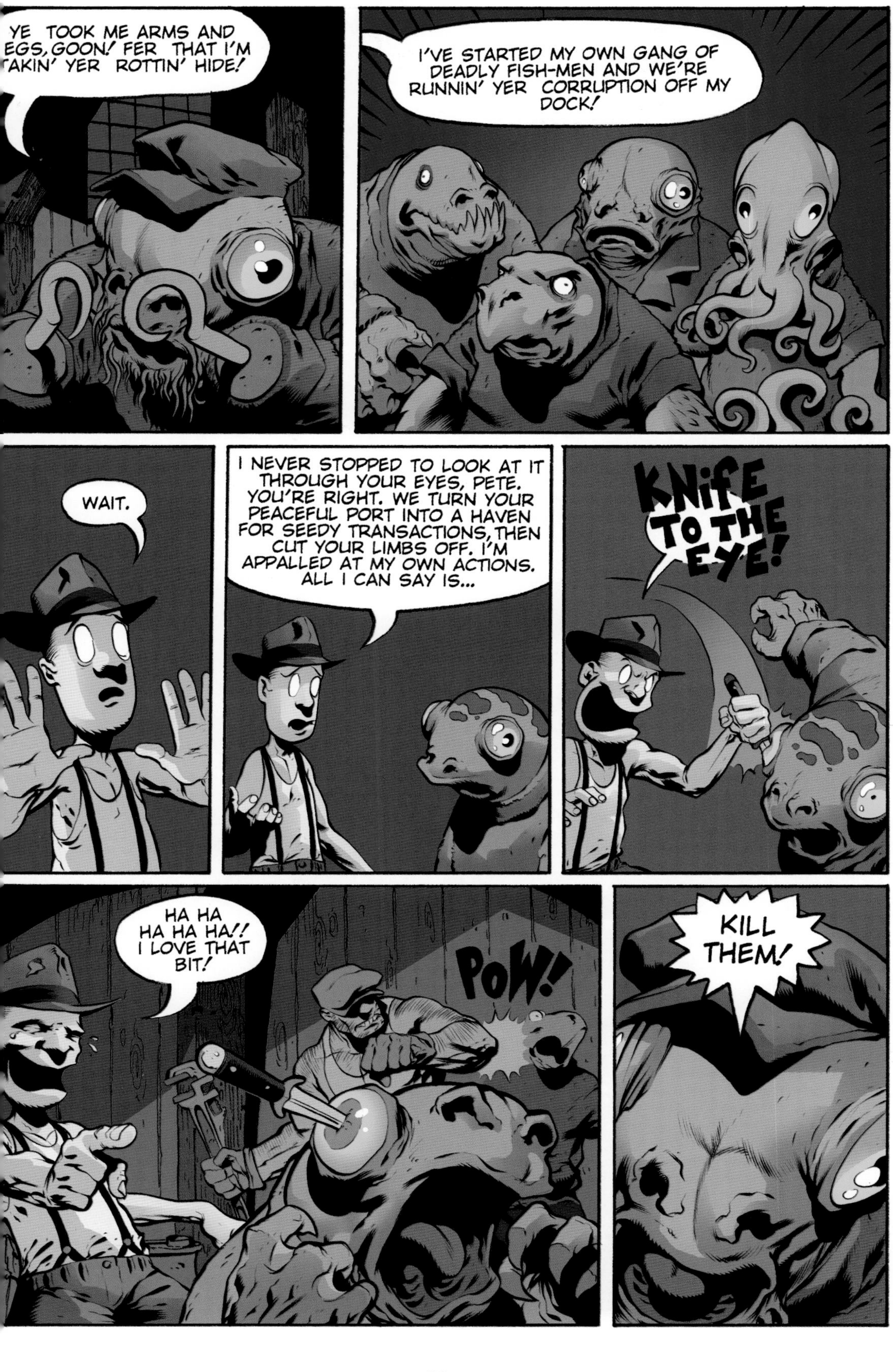
YE TOOK ME ARMS AND
EGS, GOON! FER THAT I'M
TAKIN' YER ROTTIN' HIDE!
I'VE STARTED MY OWN GANG OF DEADLY FISH-MEN AND WE'RE RUNNIN' YER CORRUPTION OFF MY DOCK!
WAIT.
I NEVER STOPPED TO LOOK AT IT THROUGH YOUR EYES, PETE. YOU'RE RIGHT. WE TURN YOUR PEACEFUL PORT INTO A HAVEN FOR SEEDY TRANSACTIONS, THEN CUT YOUR LIMBS OFF. I'M APPALLED AT MY OWN ACTIONS. ALL I CAN SAY IS...
KNIFE TO THE EYE!
HA HA HA HA HA!! I LOVE THAT BIT!
POW!
KILL THEM!

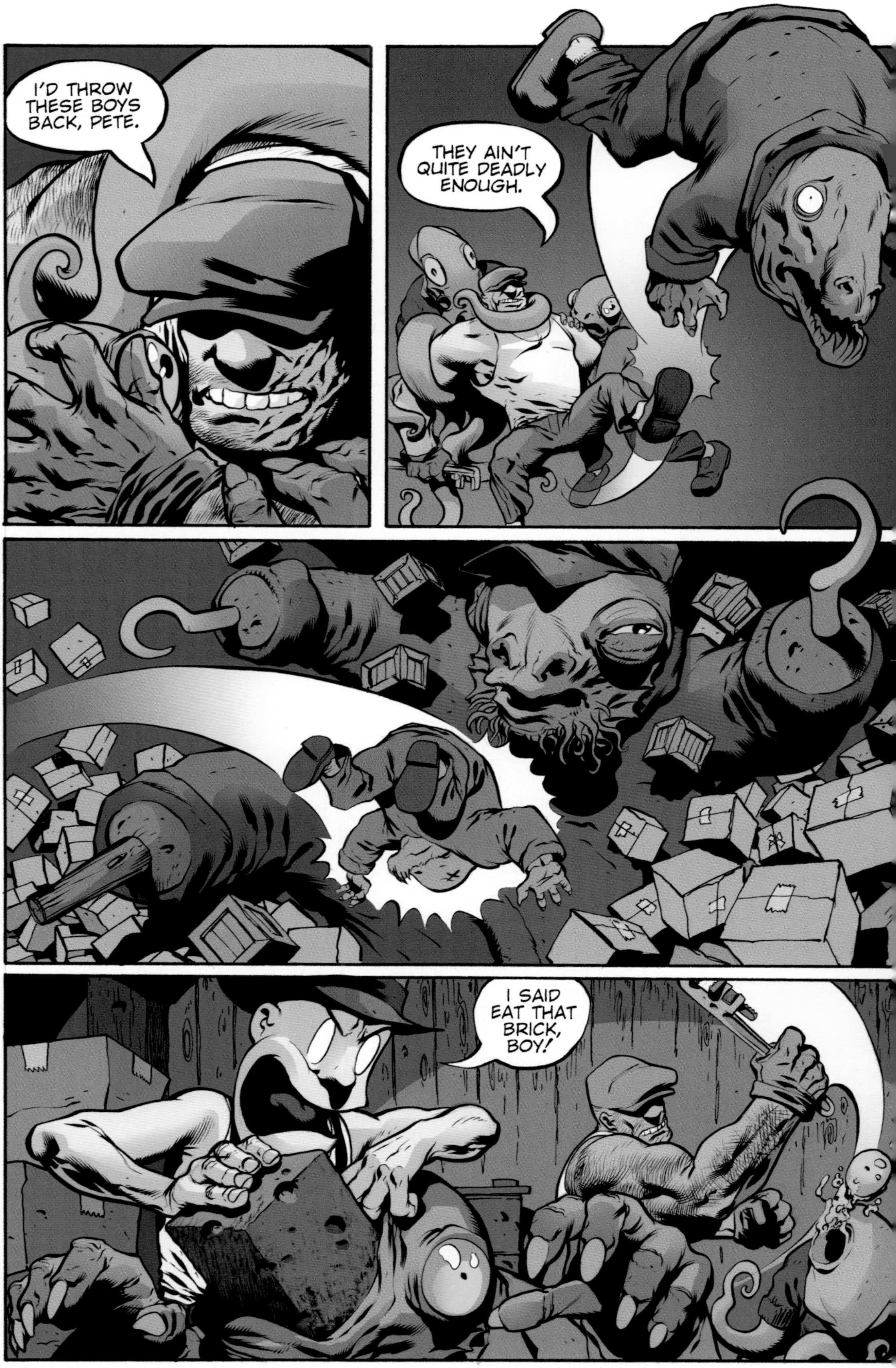
I'D THROW THESE BOYS BACK, PETE.
THEY AIN'T QUITE DEADLY ENOUGH.
I SAID EAT THAT BRICK, BOY!

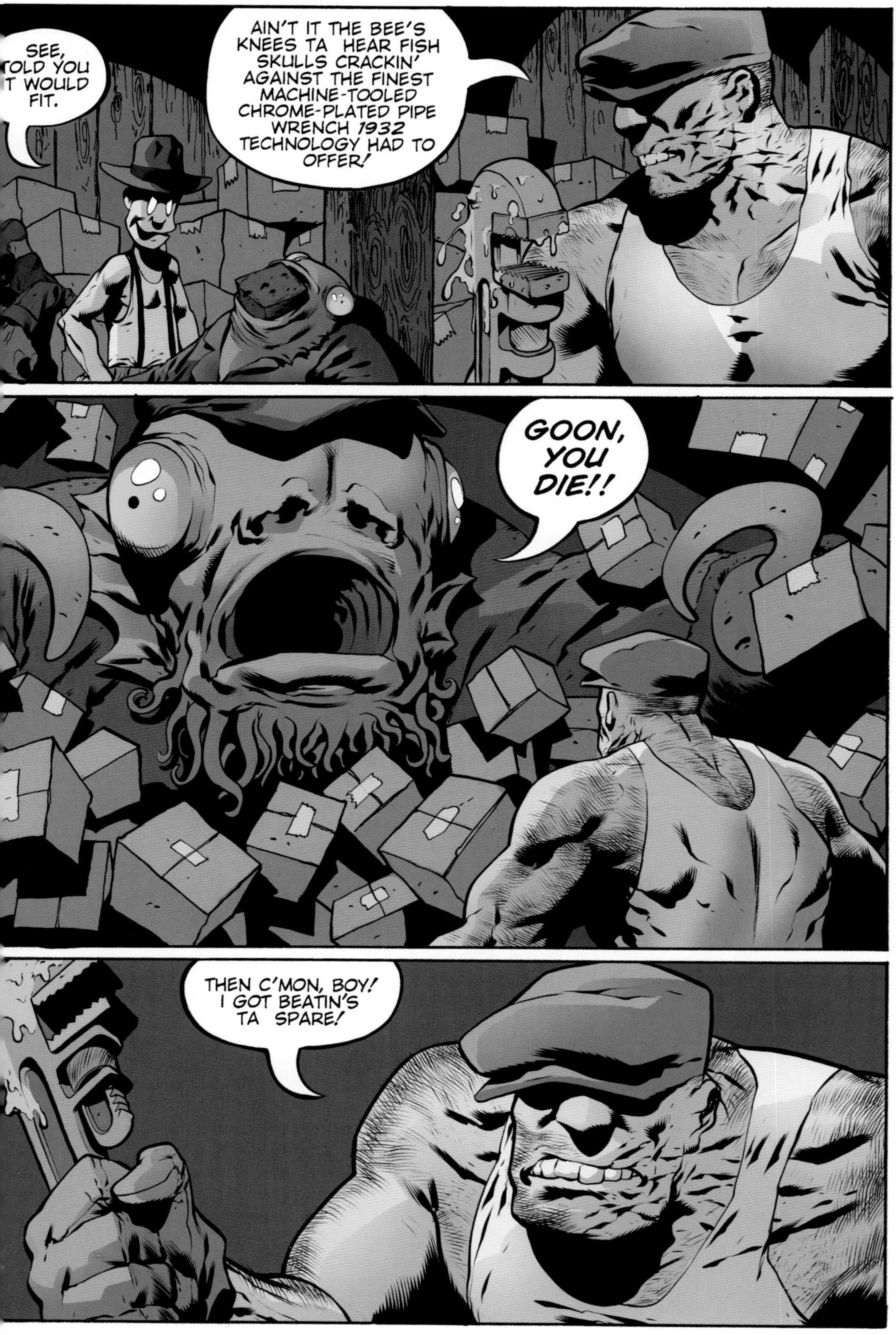
SEE, TOLD YOU T WOULD FIT.
AIN'T IT THE BEE'S KNEES TA HEAR FISH SKULLS CRACKIN' AGAINST THE FINEST MACHINE-TOOLED CHROME-PLATED PIPE WRENCH 1932 TECHNOLOGY HAD TO OFFER!
GOON, YOU DIE!!
THEN C'MON, BOY! I GOT BEATIN'S TA SPARE!

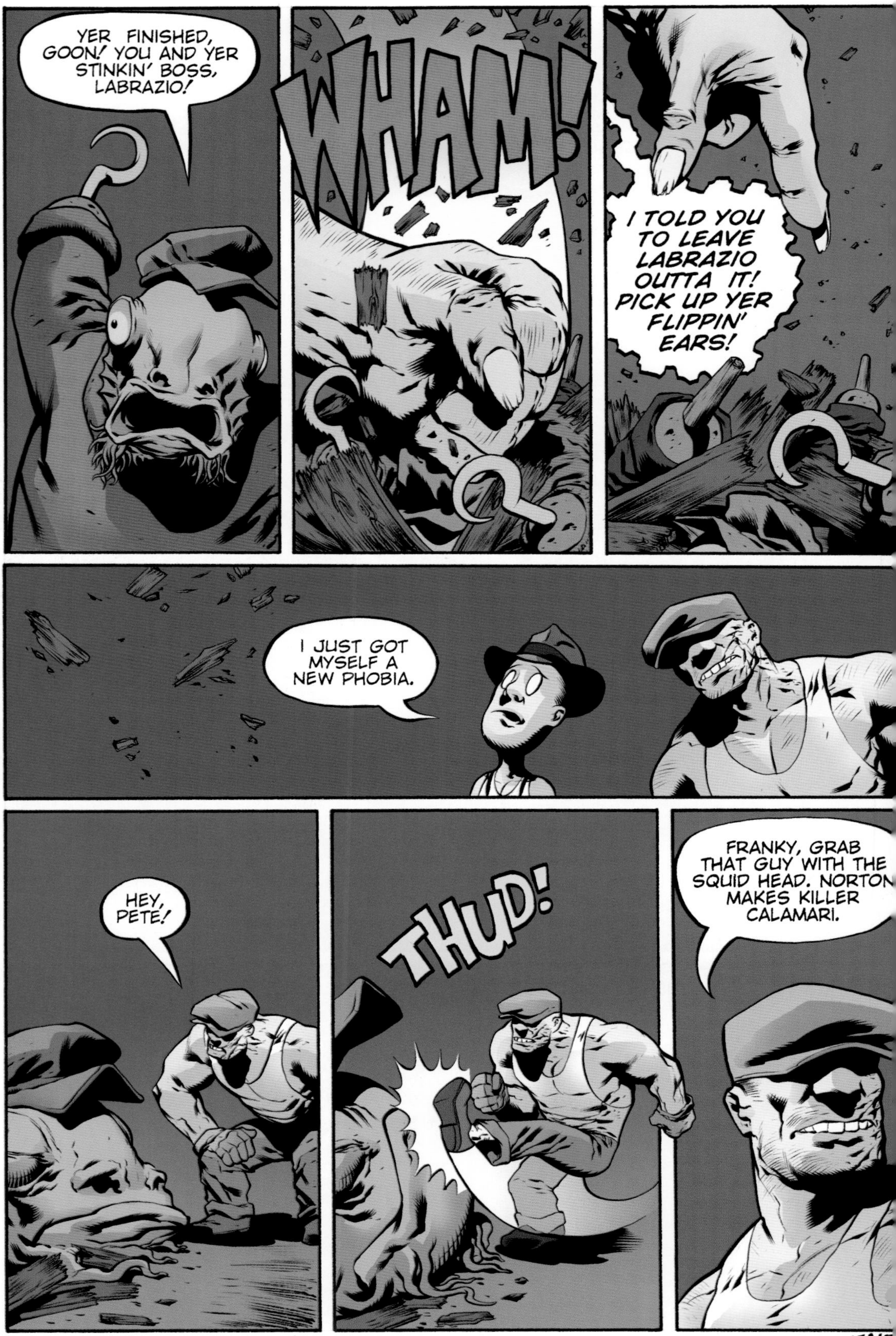
YER FINISHED, GOON! YOU AND YER STINKIN' BOSS, LABRAZIO!
WHAM!
I TOLD YOU TO LEAVE LABRAZIO OUTTA IT! PICK UP YER FLIPPIN' EARS!
I JUST GOT MYSELF A NEW PHOBIA.
HEY, PETE!
THUD!
FRANKY, GRAB THAT GUY WITH THE SQUID HEAD. NORTON MAKES KILLER CALAMARI.
END

CHAPTER 1

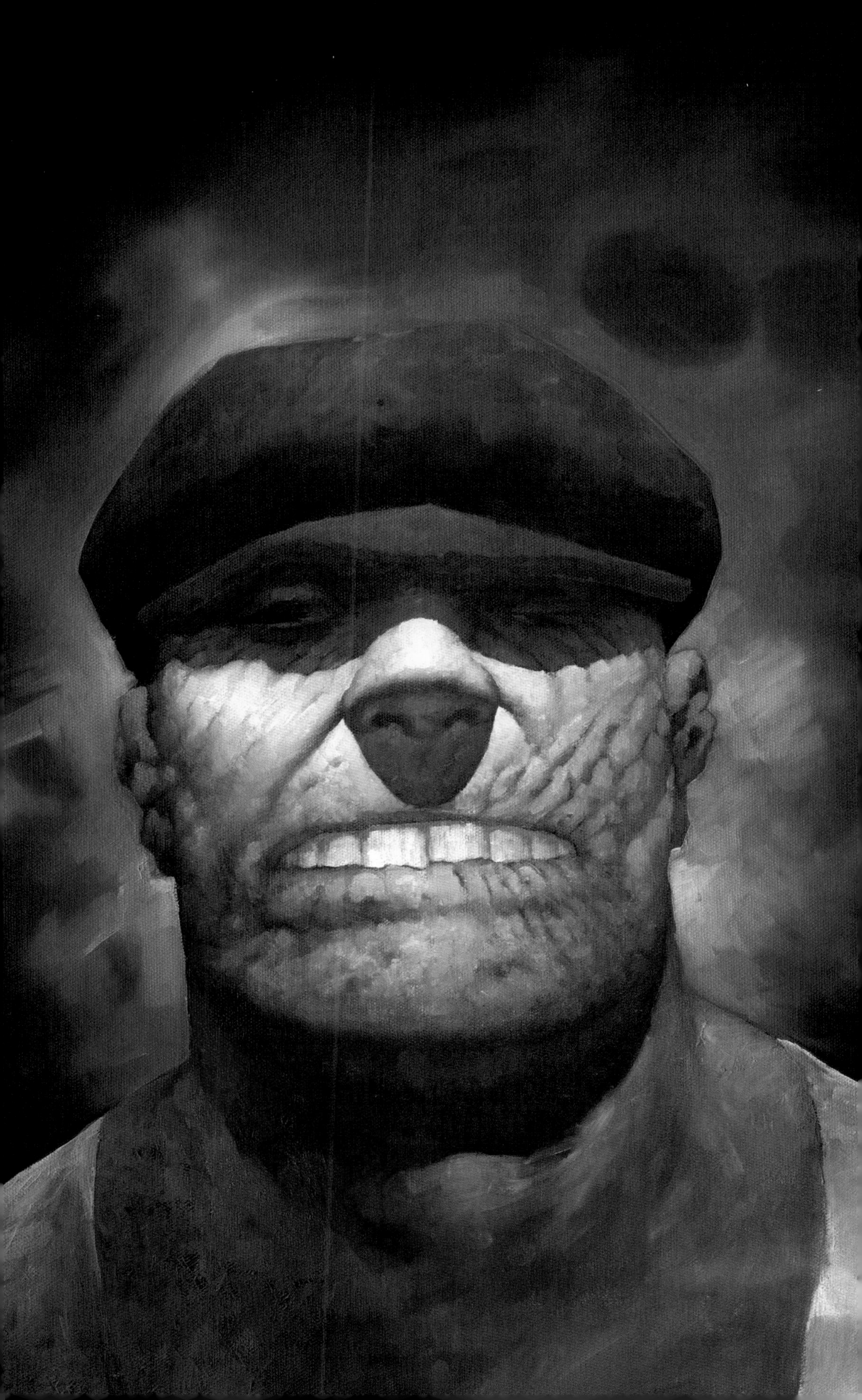

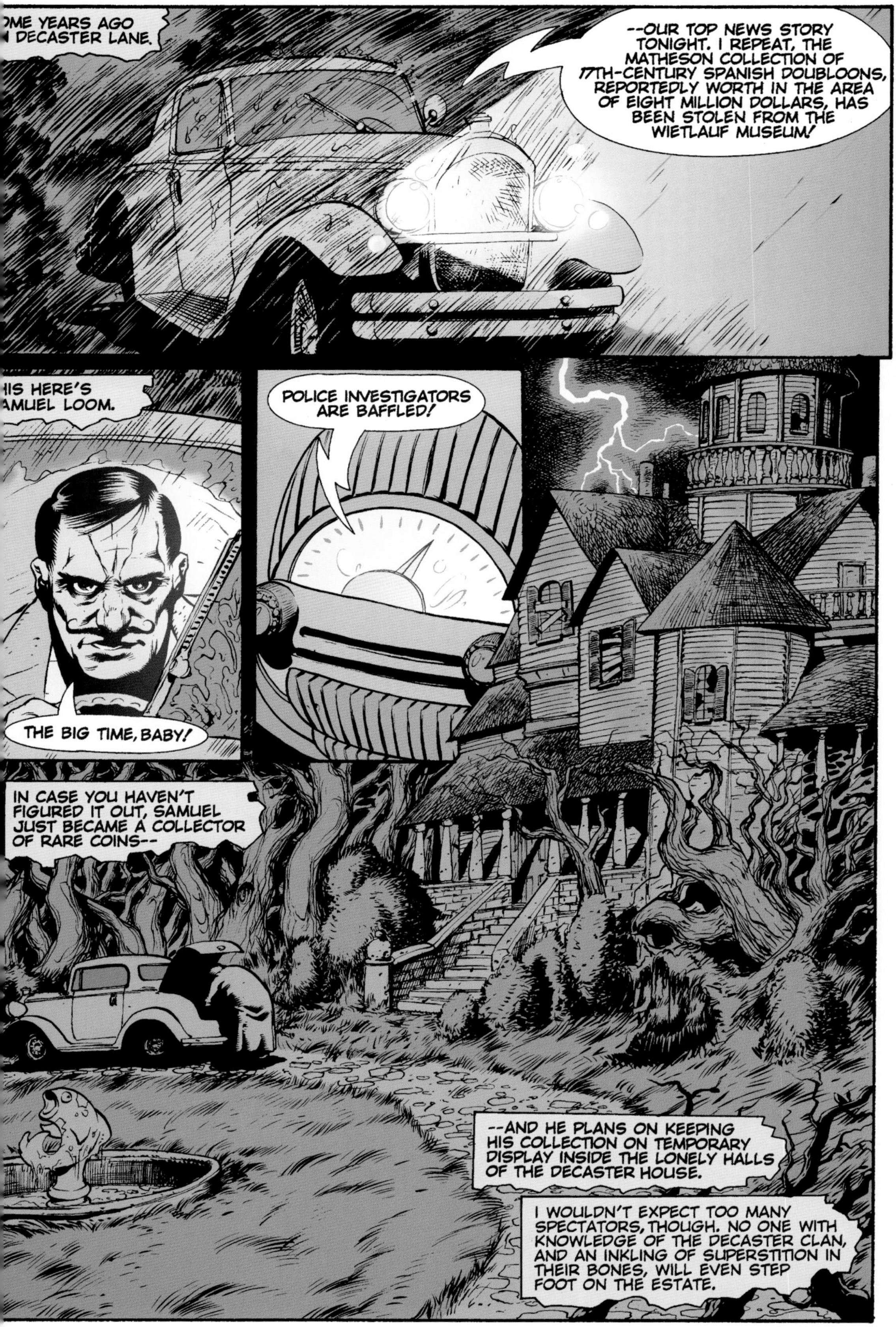
OME YEARS AGO
I DECASTER LANE.
--OUR TOP NEWS STORY TONIGHT. I REPEAT, THE MATHESON COLLECTION OF 17TH-CENTURY SPANISH DOUBLOONS, REPORTEDLY WORTH IN THE AREA OF EIGHT MILLION DOLLARS, HAS BEEN STOLEN FROM THE WIETLAUF MUSEUM!
HIS HERE'S
AMUEL LOOM.
THE BIG TIME, BABY!
POLICE INVESTIGATORS ARE BAFFLED!
IN CASE YOU HAVEN'T FIGURED IT OUT, SAMUEL JUST BECAME A COLLECTOR OF RARE COINS--
--AND HE PLANS ON KEEPING HIS COLLECTION ON TEMPORARY DISPLAY INSIDE THE LONELY HALLS OF THE DECASTER HOUSE.
I WOULDN'T EXPECT TOO MANY SPECTATORS, THOUGH. NO ONE WITH KNOWLEDGE OF THE DECASTER CLAN, AND AN INKLING OF SUPERSTITION IN THEIR BONES, WILL EVEN STEP FOOT ON THE ESTATE.

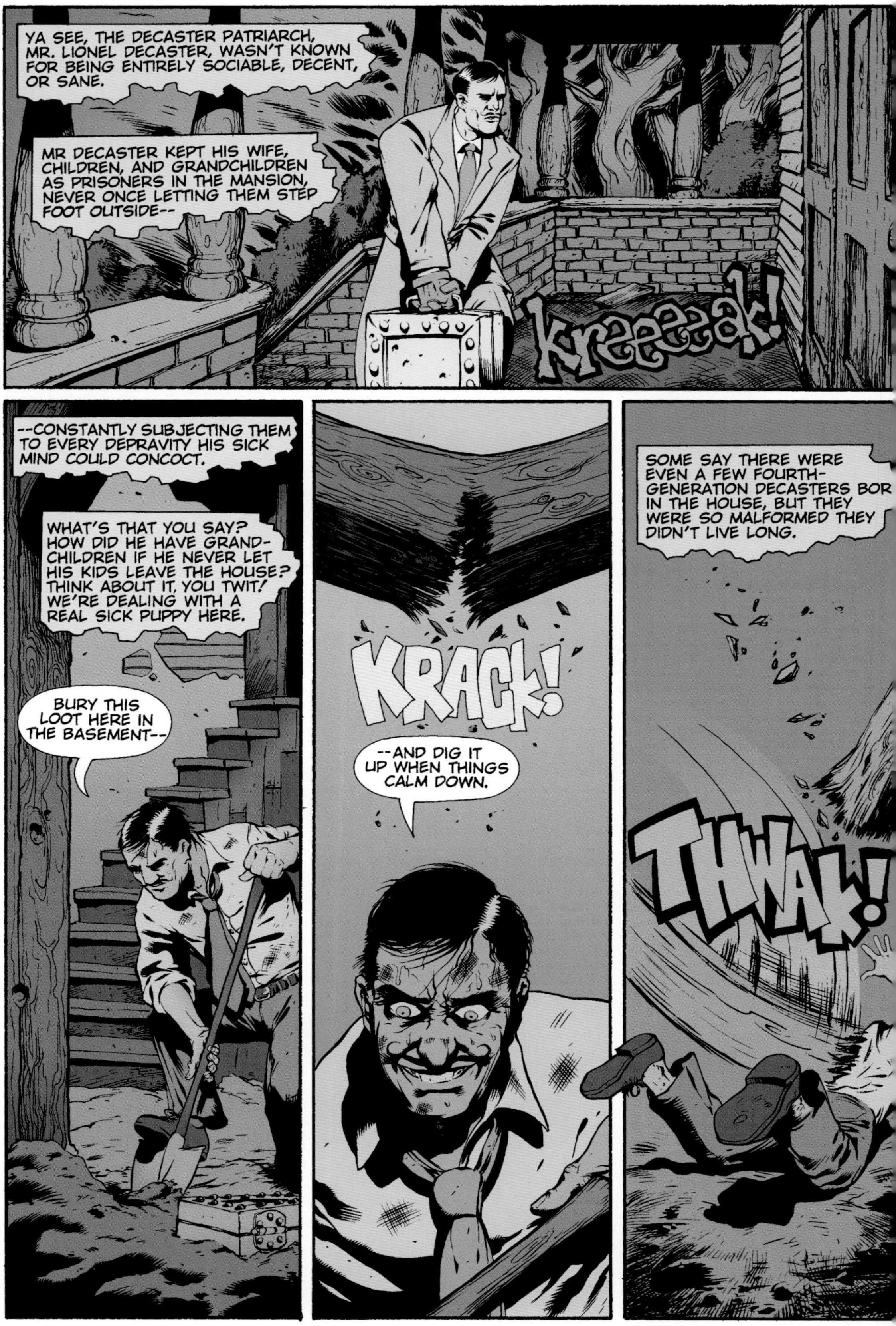
YA SEE, THE DECASTER PATRIARCH, MR. LIONEL DECASTER, WASN'T KNOWN FOR BEING ENTIRELY SOCIABLE, DECENT, OR SANE.
MR DECASTER KEPT HIS WIFE, CHILDREN, AND GRANDCHILDREN AS PRISONERS IN THE MANSION, NEVER ONCE LETTING THEM STEP FOOT OUTSIDE--
KREEEEAK!
--CONSTANTLY SUBJECTING THEM TO EVERY DEPRAVITY HIS SICK MIND COULD CONCOCT.
WHAT'S THAT YOU SAY? HOW DID HE HAVE GRAND-CHILDREN IF HE NEVER LET HIS KIDS LEAVE THE HOUSE? THINK ABOUT IT, YOU TWIT! WE'RE DEALING WITH A REAL SICK PUPPY HERE.
BURY THIS LOOT HERE IN THE BASEMENT--
KRACK!
--AND DIG IT UP WHEN THINGS CALM DOWN.
SOME SAY THERE WERE EVEN A FEW FOURTH-GENERATION DECASTERS BOR IN THE HOUSE, BUT THEY WERE SO MALFORMED THEY DIDN'T LIVE LONG.
THWAK!

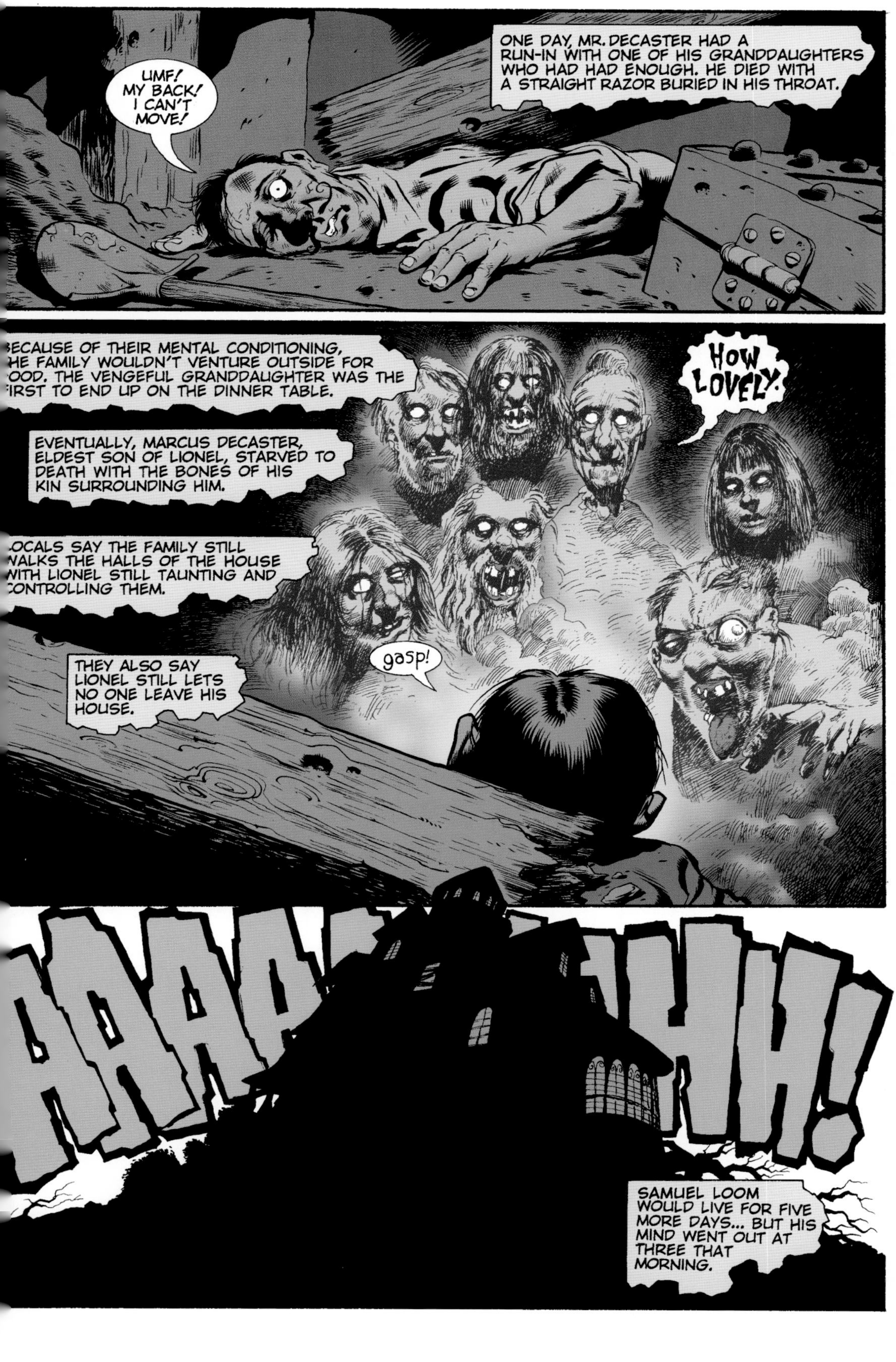

ONE DAY, MR. DECASTER HAD A RUN-IN WITH ONE OF HIS GRANDDAUGHTERS WHO HAD HAD ENOUGH. HE DIED WITH A STRAIGHT RAZOR BURIED IN HIS THROAT.
UMF! MY BACK! I CAN'T MOVE!
BECAUSE OF THEIR MENTAL CONDITIONING, THE FAMILY WOULDN'T VENTURE OUTSIDE FOR FOOD. THE VENGEFUL GRANDDAUGHTER WAS THE FIRST TO END UP ON THE DINNER TABLE.
HOW LOVELY.
EVENTUALLY, MARCUS DECASTER, ELDEST SON OF LIONEL, STARVED TO DEATH WITH THE BONES OF HIS KIN SURROUNDING HIM.
LOCALS SAY THE FAMILY STILL WALKS THE HALLS OF THE HOUSE WITH LIONEL STILL TAUNTING AND CONTROLLING THEM.
THEY ALSO SAY LIONEL STILL LETS NO ONE LEAVE HIS HOUSE.
gasp!
AAAAHH!
SAMUEL LOOM WOULD LIVE FOR FIVE MORE DAYS... BUT HIS MIND WENT OUT AT THREE THAT MORNING.

BLAM! BLAM!
NOW LET'S MOVE FORWARD IN TIME TO SOME HAPPIER SURROUNDINGS.
AH, THERE'S THE GOON... PUMPING THIRTY-EIGHT CALIBER SLUGS INTO A GIANT SQUID.
MUCH BETTER!
SPLAT!
SERVES YA RIGHT, YA SLIMY BUGGER!
C'MERE, GOON. I GOT SOMETHIN FOR YA.
SPLASH! SPLASH!

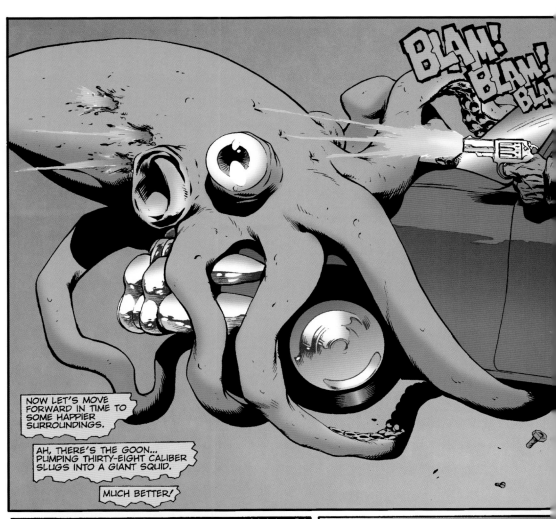

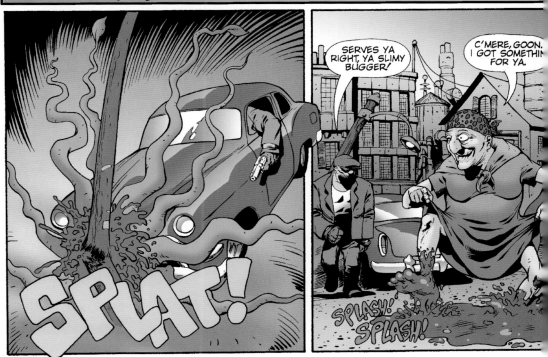

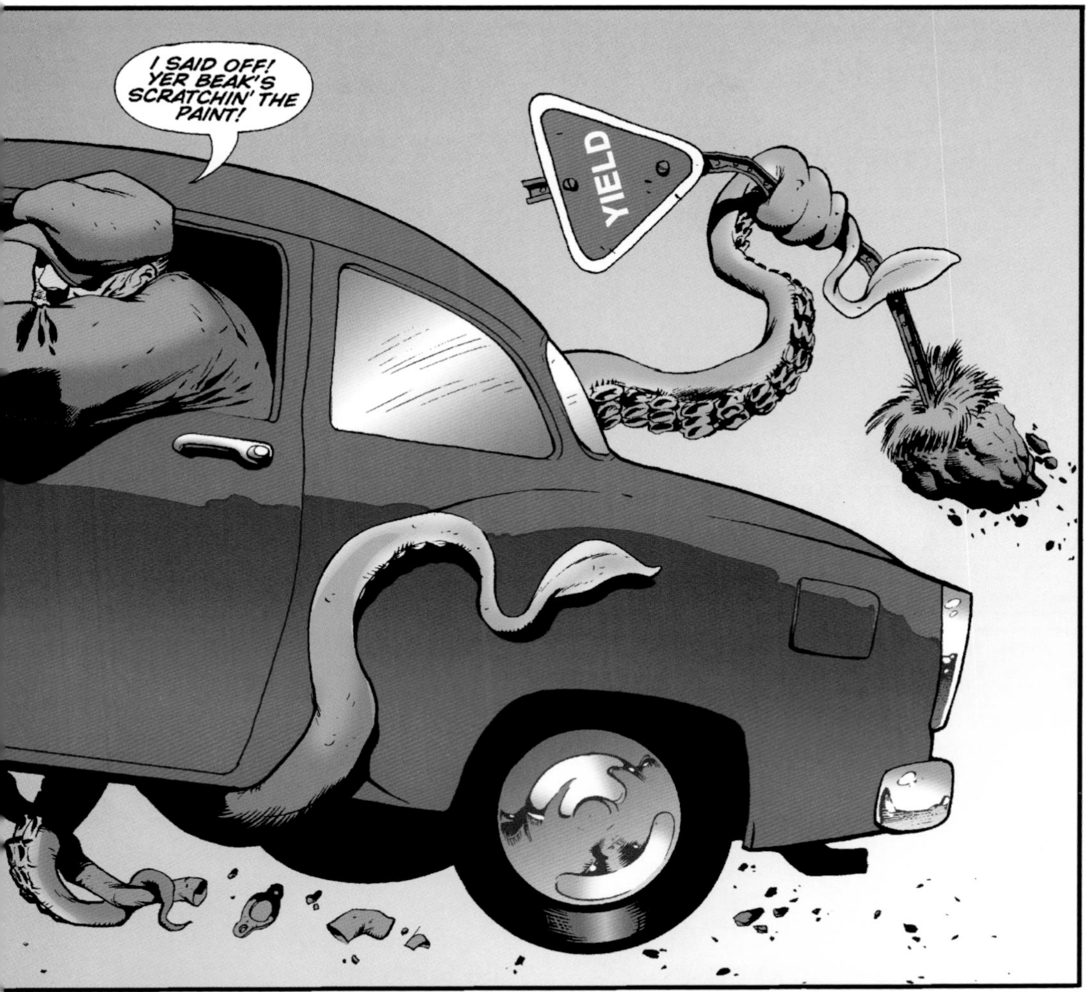
I SAID OFF! YER BEAK'S SCRATCHIN' THE PAINT!
YIELD

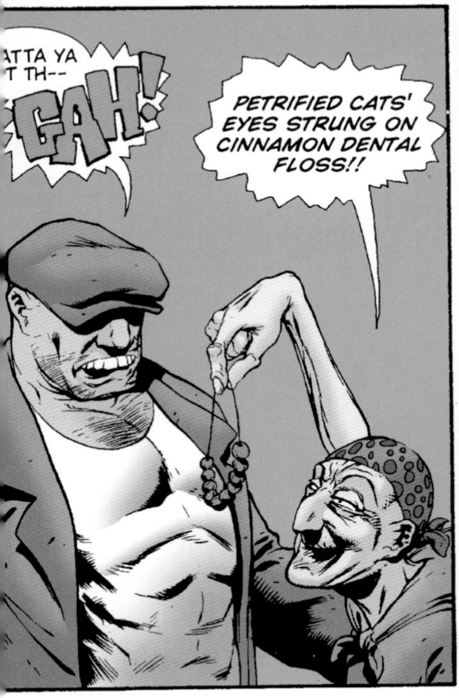
ATTA YA
T TH--
GAH!
PETRIFIED CATS' EYES STRUNG ON CINNAMON DENTAL FLOSS!!

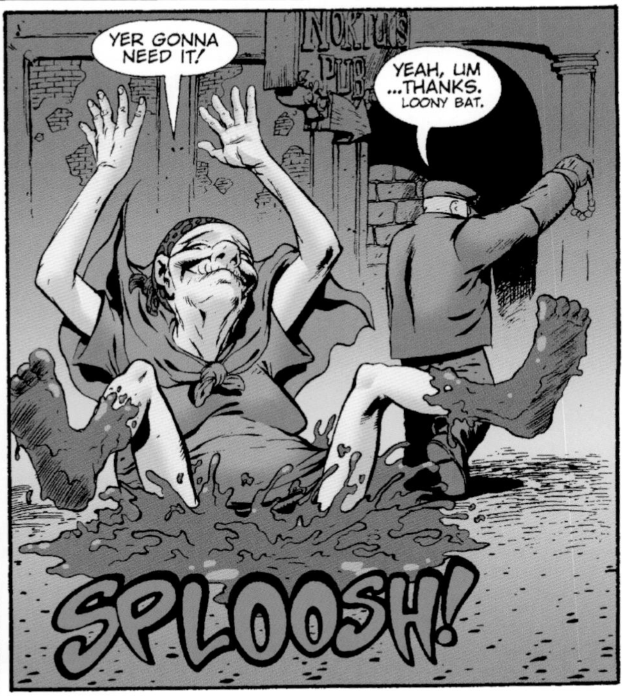
YER GONNA NEED IT!
YEAH, UM ...THANKS. LOONY BAT.
SPLOOSH!

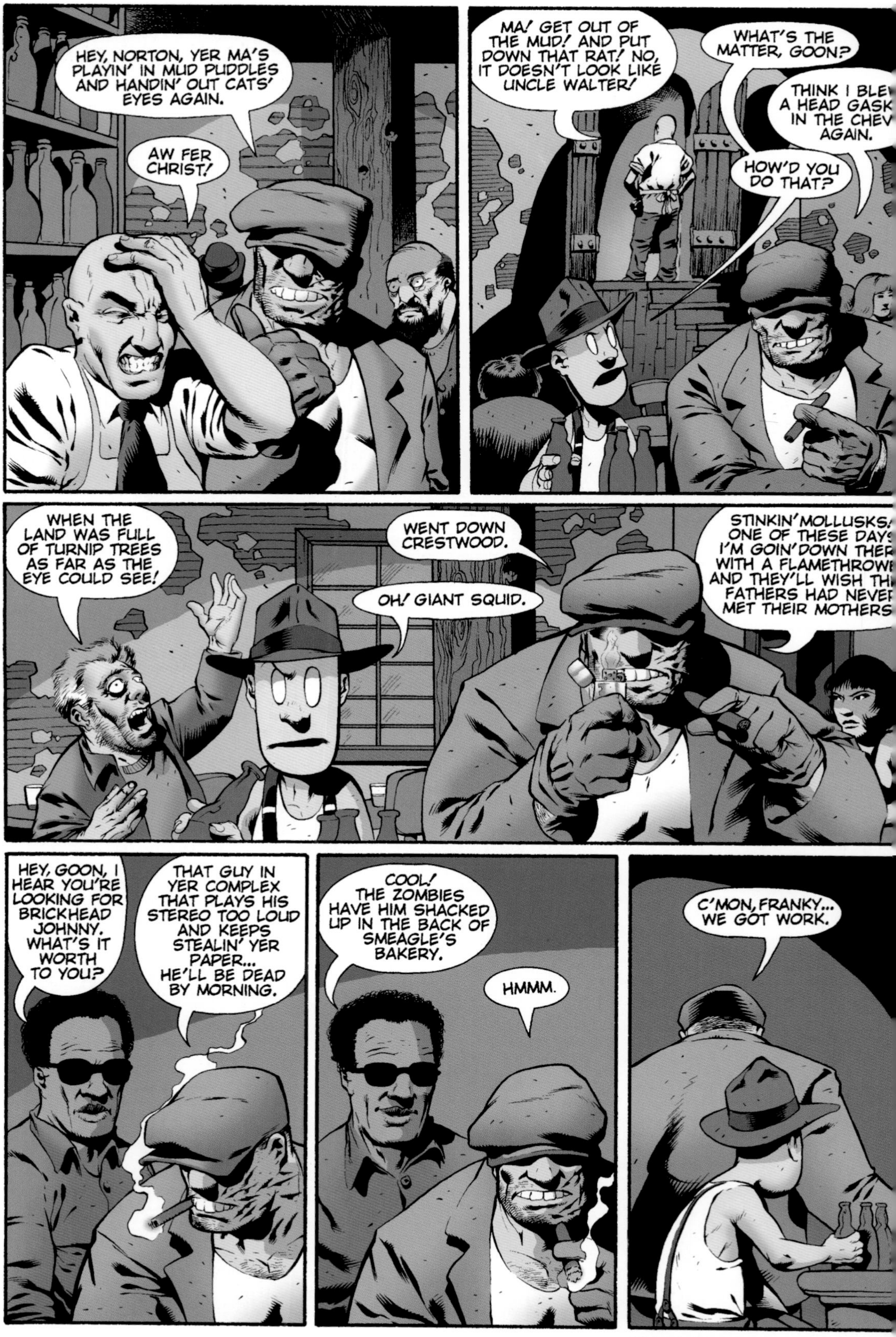
HEY, NORTON, YER MA'S PLAYIN' IN MUD PUDDLES AND HANDIN' OUT CATS' EYES AGAIN.
AW FER CHRIST!
MA! GET OUT OF THE MUD! AND PUT DOWN THAT RAT! NO, IT DOESN'T LOOK LIKE UNCLE WALTER!
WHAT'S THE MATTER, GOON?
HOW'D YOU DO THAT?
WHEN THE LAND WAS FULL OF TURNIP TREES AS FAR AS THE EYE COULD SEE!
WENT DOWN CRESTWOOD.
OH! GIANT SQUID.
HEY, GOON, I HEAR YOU'RE LOOKING FOR BRICKHEAD JOHNNY. WHAT'S IT WORTH TO YOU?
THAT GUY IN YER COMPLEX THAT PLAYS HIS STEREO TOO LOUD AND KEEPS STEALIN' YER PAPER... HE'LL BE DEAD BY MORNING.
COOL! THE ZOMBIES HAVE HIM SHACKED UP IN THE BACK OF SMEAGLE'S BAKERY.
HMMM.
C'MON, FRANKY... WE GOT WORK.

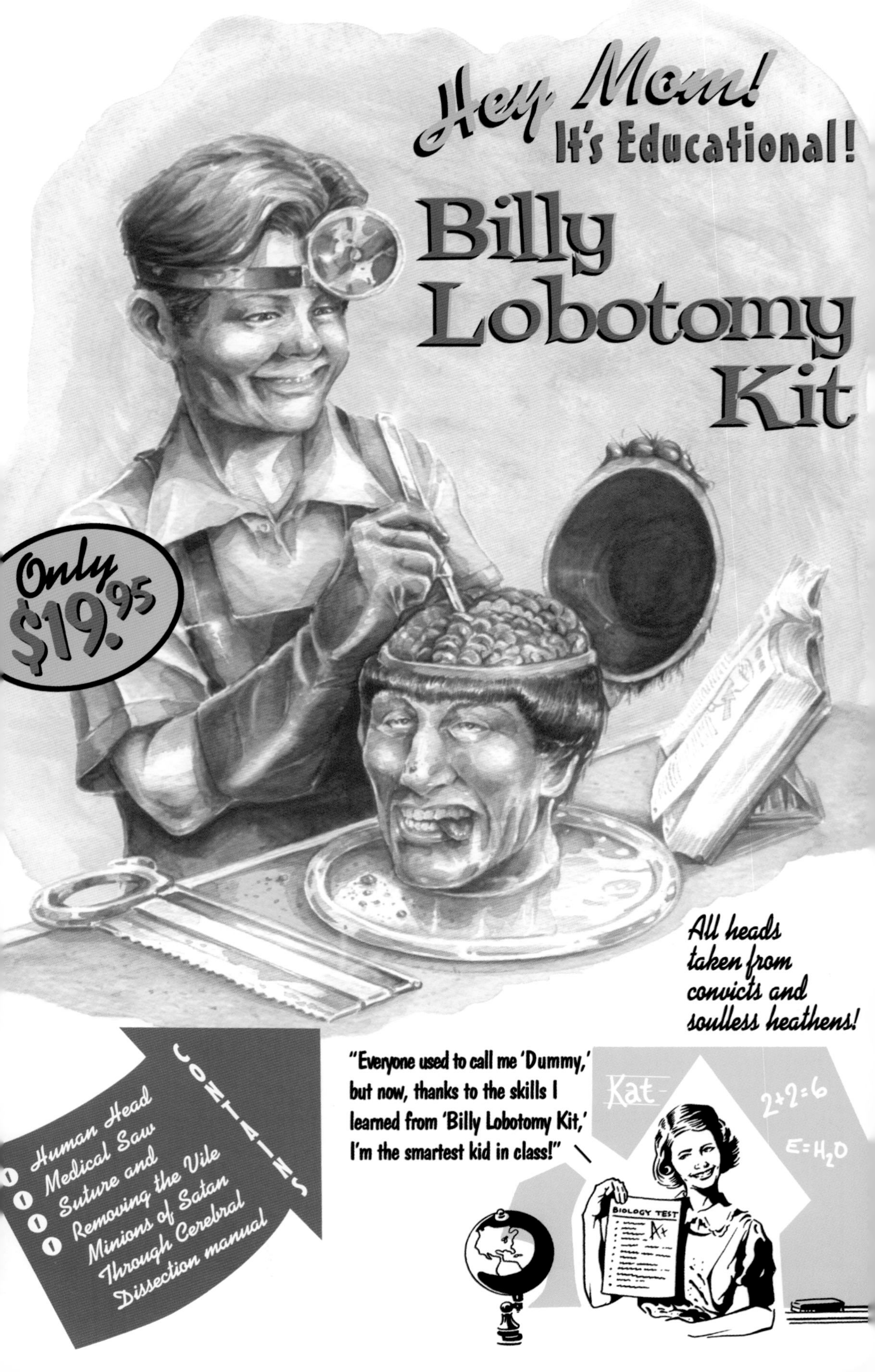

Hey Mom!
It's Educational!
Billy Lobotomy Kit
Only $19.95
All heads taken from convicts and soulless heathens!
CONTAINS
Human Head
Medical Saw
Suture and
Removing the Vile Minions of Satan Through Cerebral Dissection manual
"Everyone used to call me 'Dummy,' but now, thanks to the skills I learned from 'Billy Lobotomy Kit,' I'm the smartest kid in class!"
Kat
2+2=6
E=H2O
BIOLOGY TEST
A+

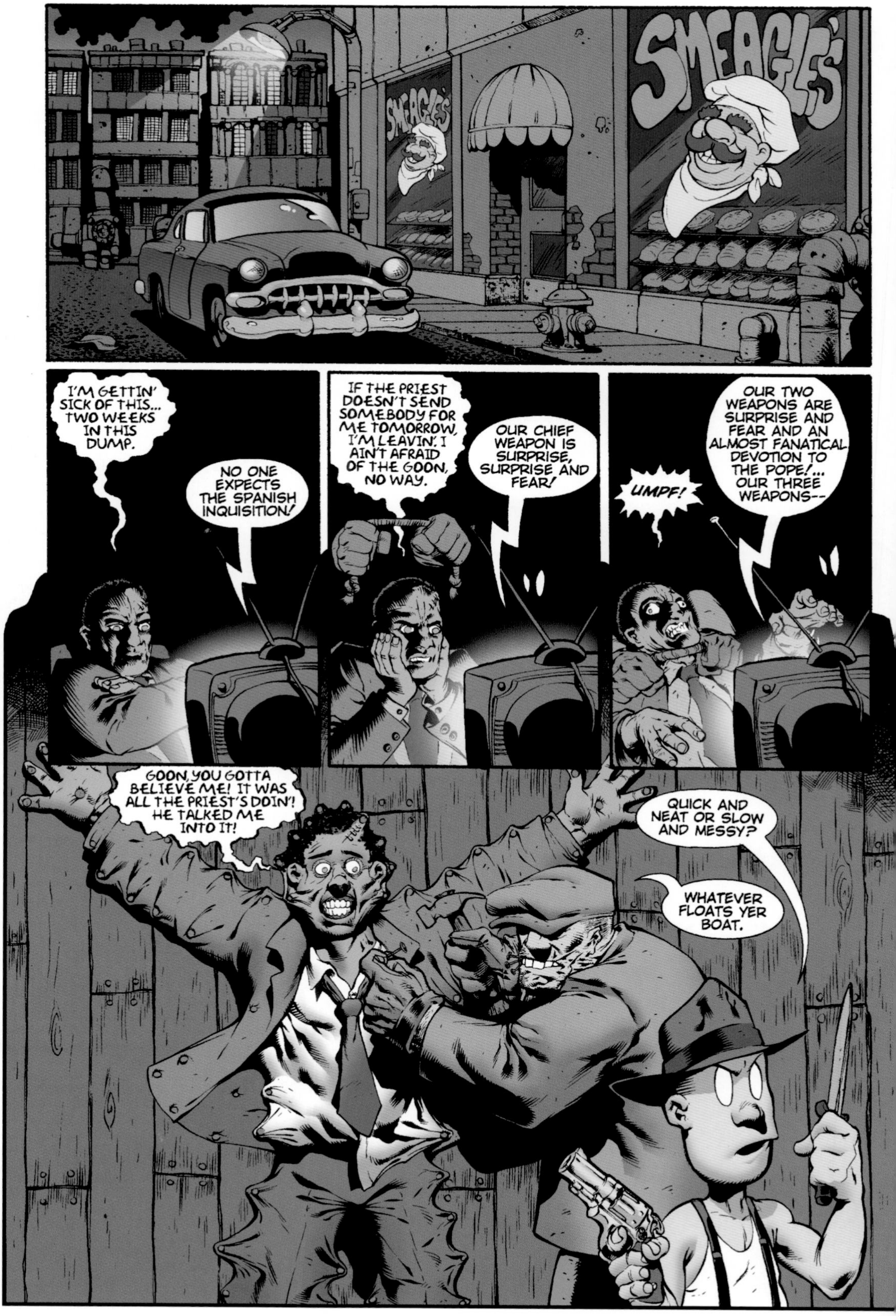
SMEAGLE'S
SMEAGLE'S
I'M GETTIN' SICK OF THIS... TWO WEEKS IN THIS DUMP.
NO ONE EXPECTS THE SPANISH INQUISITION!
IF THE PRIEST DOESN'T SEND SOMEBODY FOR ME TOMORROW, I'M LEAVIN'. I AIN'T AFRAID OF THE GOON, NO WAY.
OUR CHIEF WEAPON IS SURPRISE, SURPRISE AND FEAR!
UMPF!
OUR TWO WEAPONS ARE SURPRISE AND FEAR AND AN ALMOST FANATICAL DEVOTION TO THE POPE!... OUR THREE WEAPONS--
GOON, YOU GOTTA BELIEVE ME! IT WAS ALL THE PRIEST'S DOIN'! HE TALKED ME INTO IT!
QUICK AND NEAT OR SLOW AND MESSY?
WHATEVER FLOATS YER BOAT.

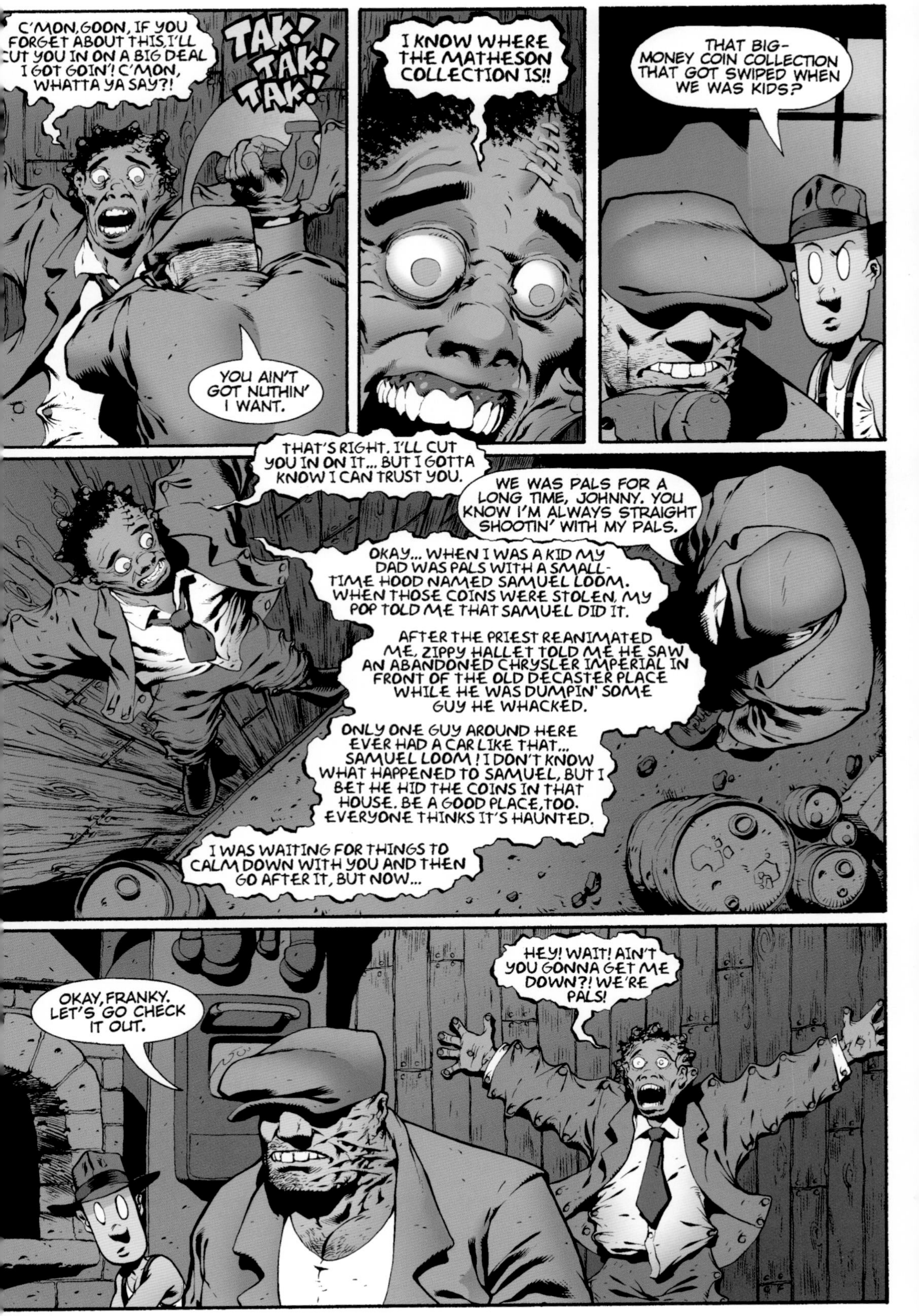
C'MON, GOON, IF YOU FORGET ABOUT THIS, I'LL CUT YOU IN ON A BIG DEAL I GOT GOIN'! C'MON, WHATTA YA SAY?!
TAK! TAK! TAK!
YOU AIN'T GOT NUTHIN' I WANT.
I KNOW WHERE THE MATHESON COLLECTION IS!!
THAT BIG-MONEY COIN COLLECTION THAT GOT SWIPED WHEN WE WAS KIDS?
THAT'S RIGHT. I'LL CUT YOU IN ON IT... BUT I GOTTA KNOW I CAN TRUST YOU.
WE WAS PALS FOR A LONG TIME, JOHNNY. YOU KNOW I'M ALWAYS STRAIGHT SHOOTIN' WITH MY PALS.
OKAY... WHEN I WAS A KID MY DAD WAS PALS WITH A SMALL-TIME HOOD NAMED SAMUEL LOOM. WHEN THOSE COINS WERE STOLEN, MY POP TOLD ME THAT SAMUEL DID IT.
AFTER THE PRIEST REANIMATED ME, ZIPPY HALLET TOLD ME HE SAW AN ABANDONED CHRYSLER IMPERIAL IN FRONT OF THE OLD DECASTER PLACE WHILE HE WAS DUMPIN' SOME GUY HE WHACKED.
ONLY ONE GUY AROUND HERE EVER HAD A CAR LIKE THAT... SAMUEL LOOM! I DON'T KNOW WHAT HAPPENED TO SAMUEL, BUT I BET HE HID THE COINS IN THAT HOUSE. BE A GOOD PLACE, TOO. EVERYONE THINKS IT'S HAUNTED.
I WAS WAITING FOR THINGS TO CALM DOWN WITH YOU AND THEN GO AFTER IT, BUT NOW...
OKAY, FRANKY. LET'S GO CHECK IT OUT.
HEY! WAIT! AIN'T YOU GONNA GET ME DOWN?! WE'RE PALS!

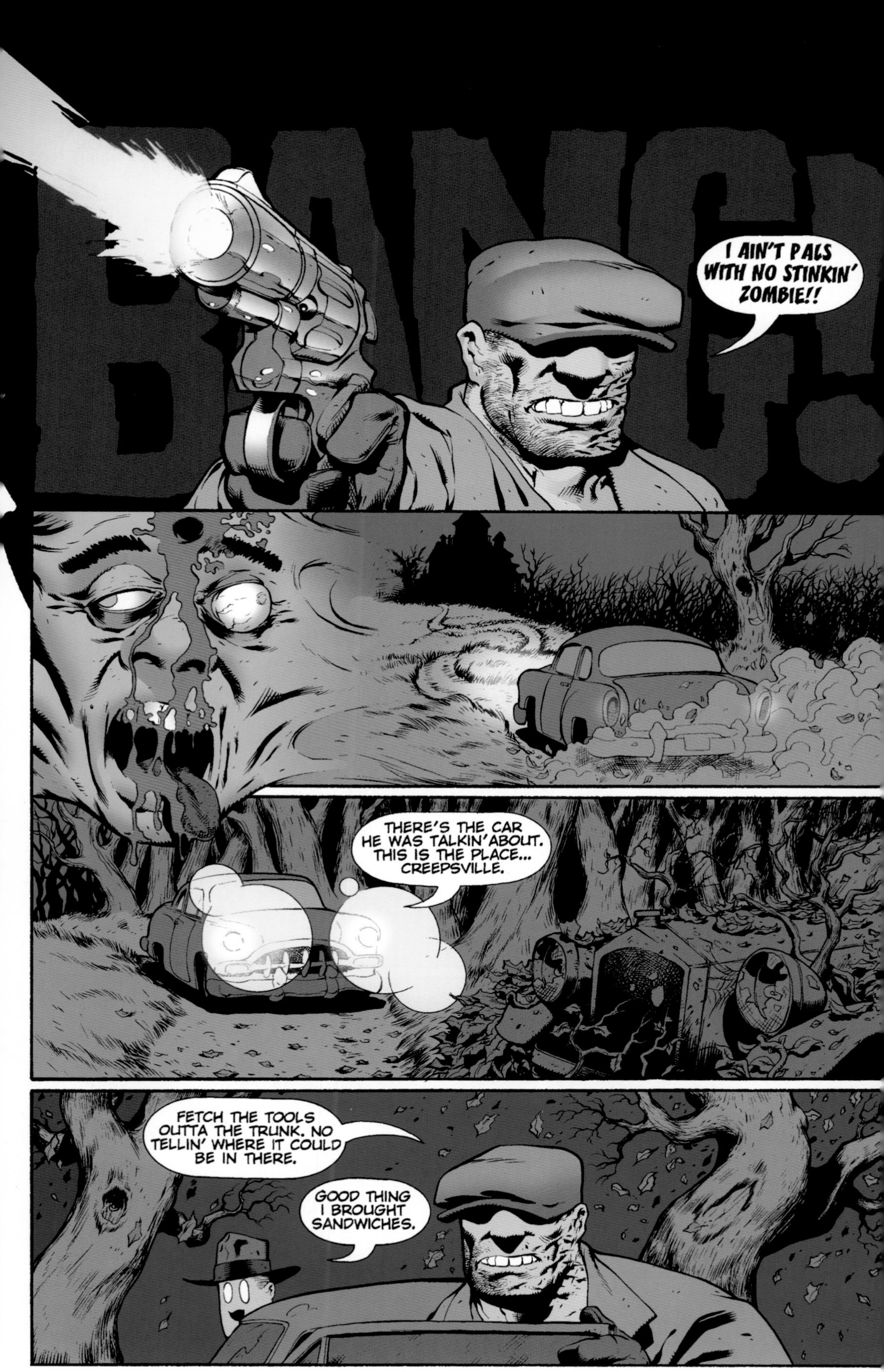
BANG!
I AIN'T PALS WITH NO STINKIN' ZOMBIE!!
THERE'S THE CAR HE WAS TALKIN' ABOUT. THIS IS THE PLACE... CREEPSVILLE.
FETCH THE TOOLS OUTTA THE TRUNK. NO TELLIN' WHERE IT COULD BE IN THERE.
GOOD THING I BROUGHT SANDWICHES.

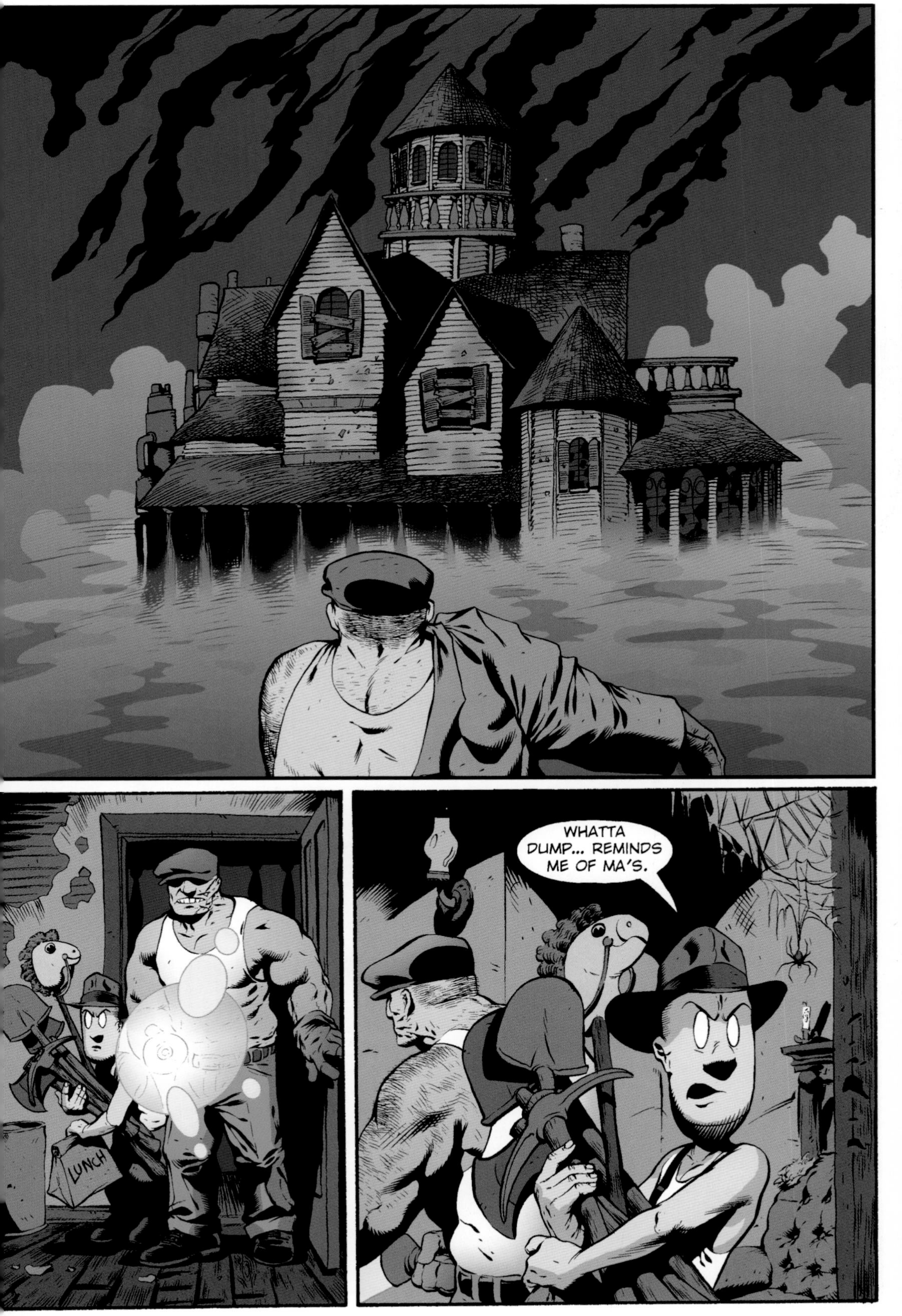
LUNCH
WHATTA DUMP... REMINDS ME OF MA'S.

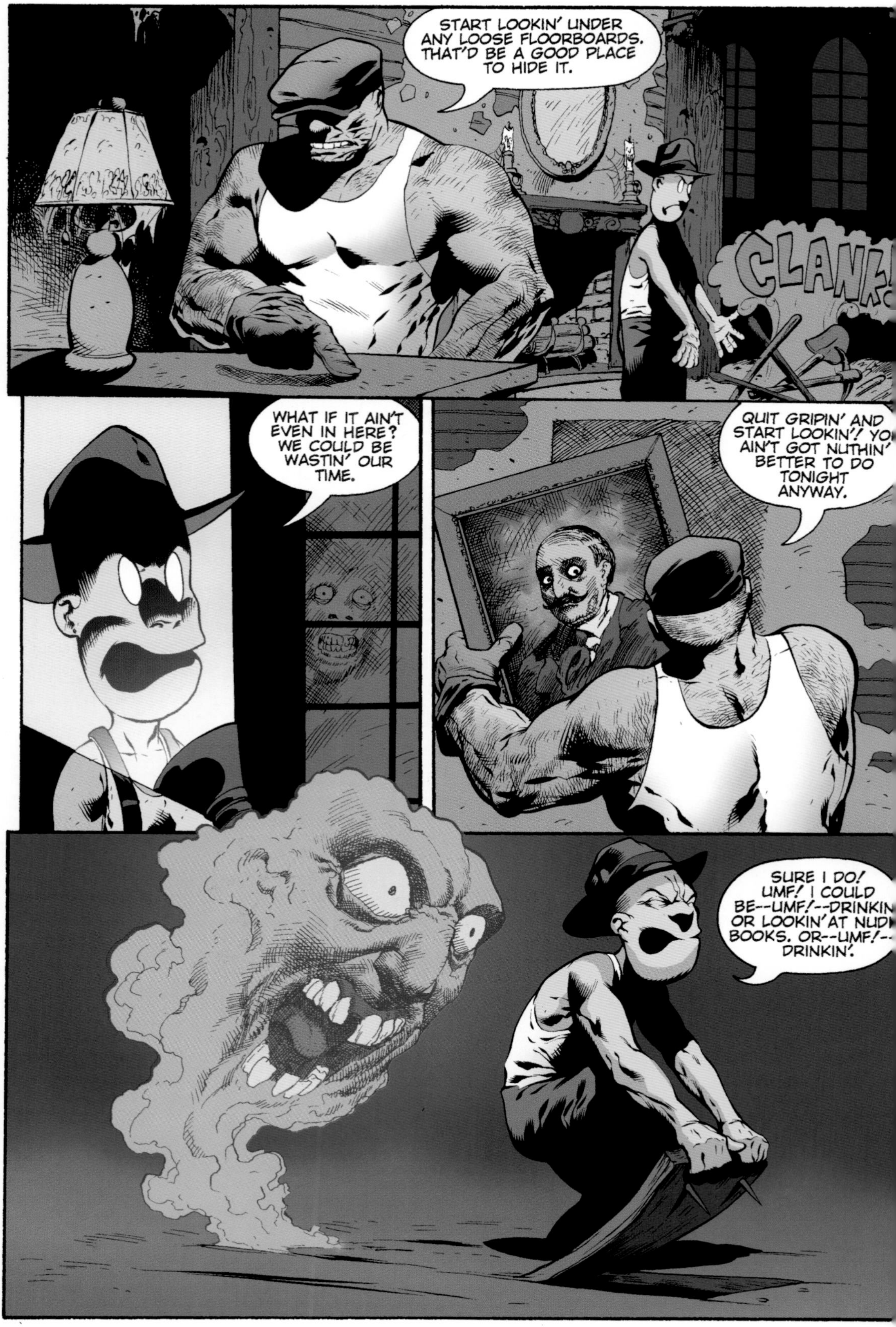
START LOOKIN' UNDER ANY LOOSE FLOORBOARDS. THAT'D BE A GOOD PLACE TO HIDE IT.
CLANK
WHAT IF IT AIN'T EVEN IN HERE? WE COULD BE WASTIN' OUR TIME.
QUIT GRIPIN' AND START LOOKIN'! YO AIN'T GOT NUTHIN' BETTER TO DO TONIGHT ANYWAY.
SURE I DO! UMF! I COULD BE--UMF!--DRINKIN OR LOOKIN' AT NUD BOOKS. OR--UMF!-- DRINKIN'.

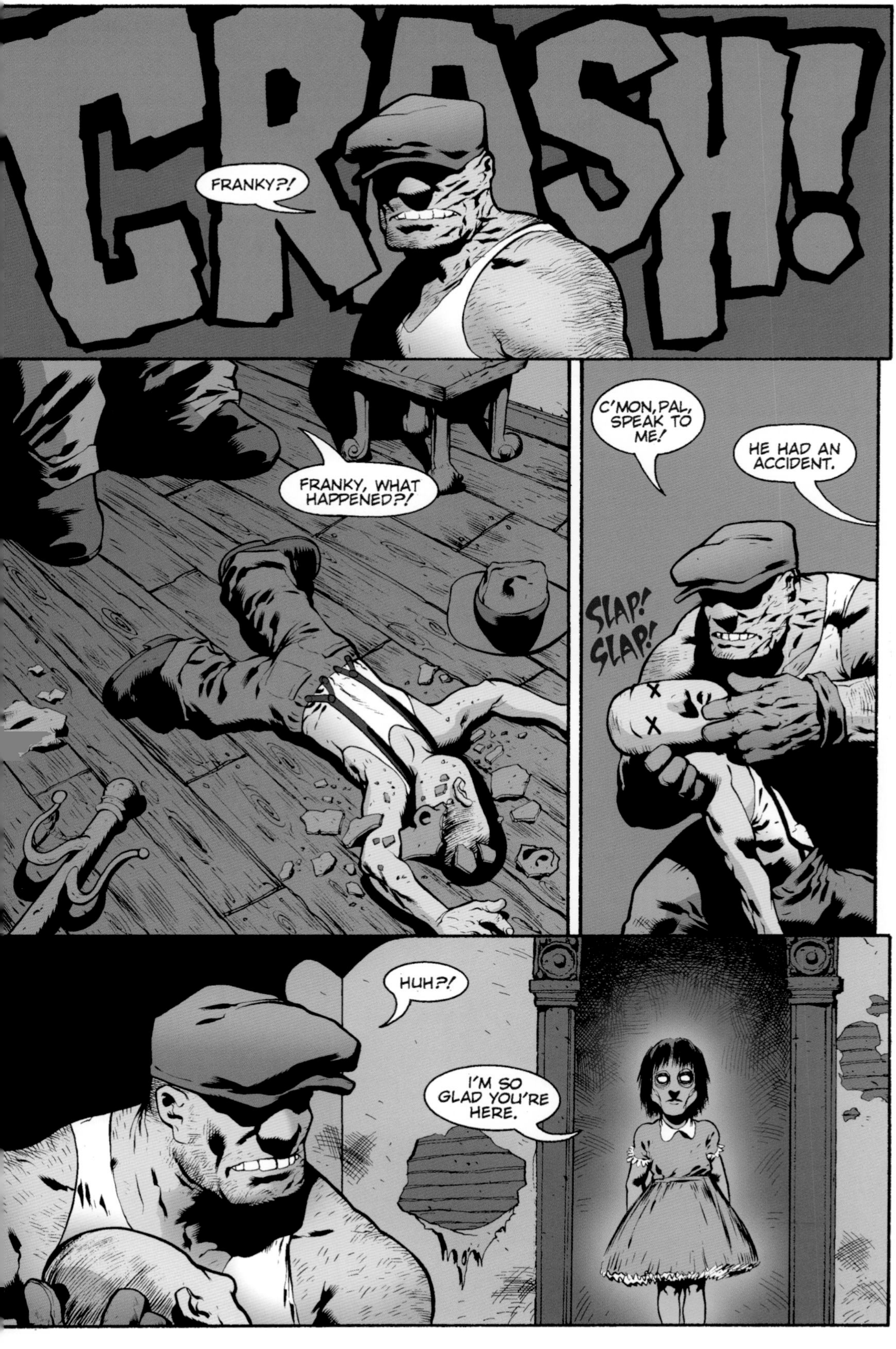
CRASH!
FRANKY?!
FRANKY, WHAT HAPPENED?!
C'MON, PAL, SPEAK TO ME!
HE HAD AN ACCIDENT.
SLAP! SLAP!
HUH?!
I'M SO GLAD YOU'RE HERE.

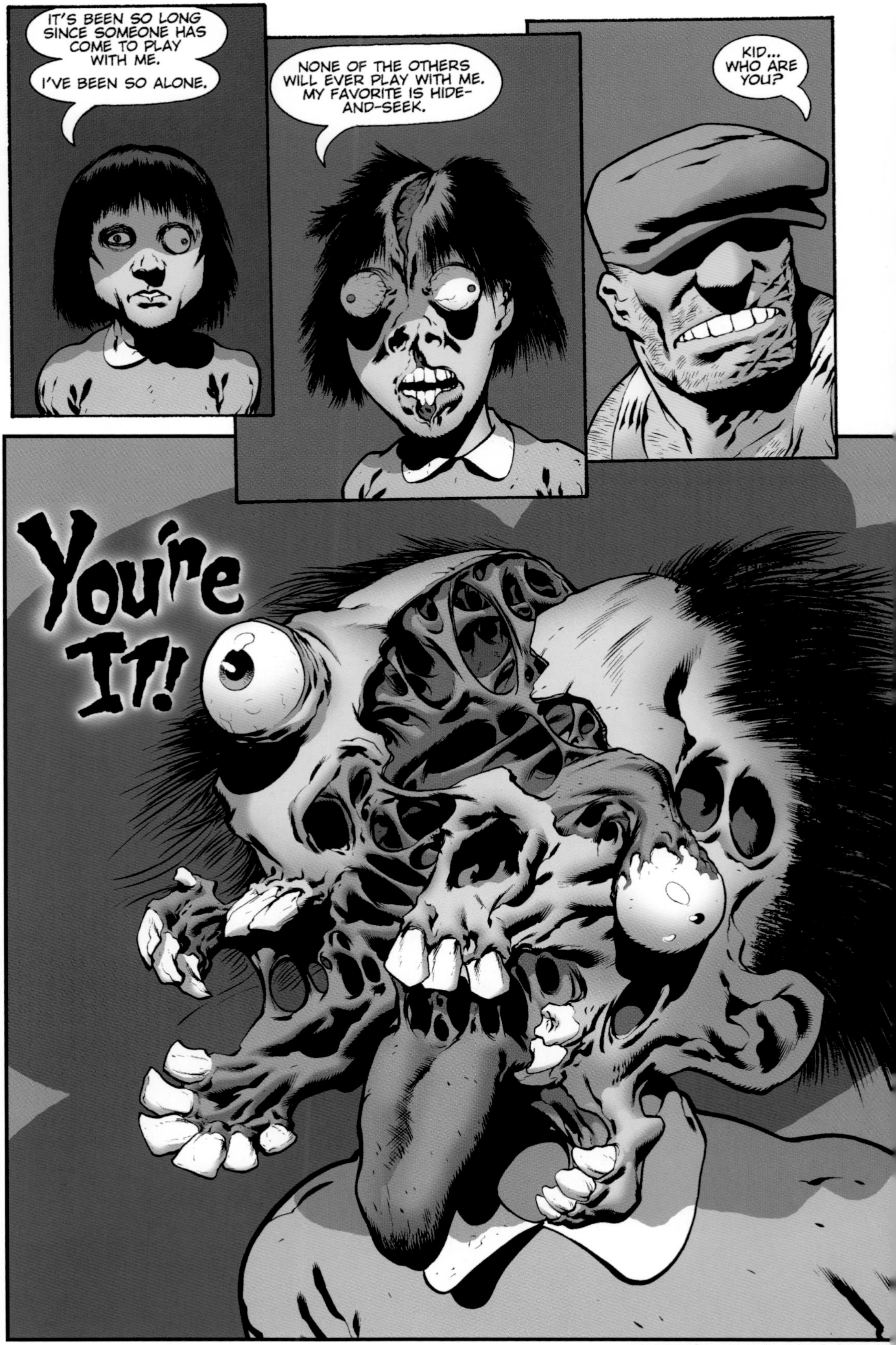
IT'S BEEN SO LONG SINCE SOMEONE HAS COME TO PLAY WITH ME.
I'VE BEEN SO ALONE.
NONE OF THE OTHERS WILL EVER PLAY WITH ME. MY FAVORITE IS HIDE-AND-SEEK.
KID... WHO ARE YOU?
You're It!

CONTINUED ON 2ND PAGE FOLLOW

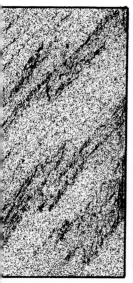

PLEASE STAND BY

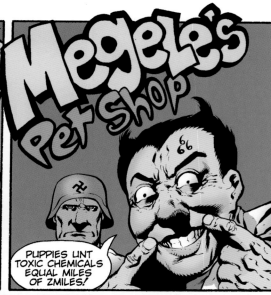

PUPPIES UNT TOXIC CHEMICALS EQUAL MILES OF ZMILES!

UNT HERE VE HAVE ZMALL DOG WITH DA HEAD OF A BADGER IN DA EYE ZOCKET!

UNT ALSO TRANSPLANTED PRIVATES OF ZA LARGE HIPPOPOTAMUS!

I VANT DA VITE GERBILS HERE, UNT DA BROWN GERBILS HERE! VE VILL HAVE NO MIXING OF DA GERBILS!!

GERBILS

GOEBBELS?! GOEBBELS?! VHERE?!

I ZED GERBILS! GERBILS!

UNT MOOKS! AAHHHHH!!

WHACK!

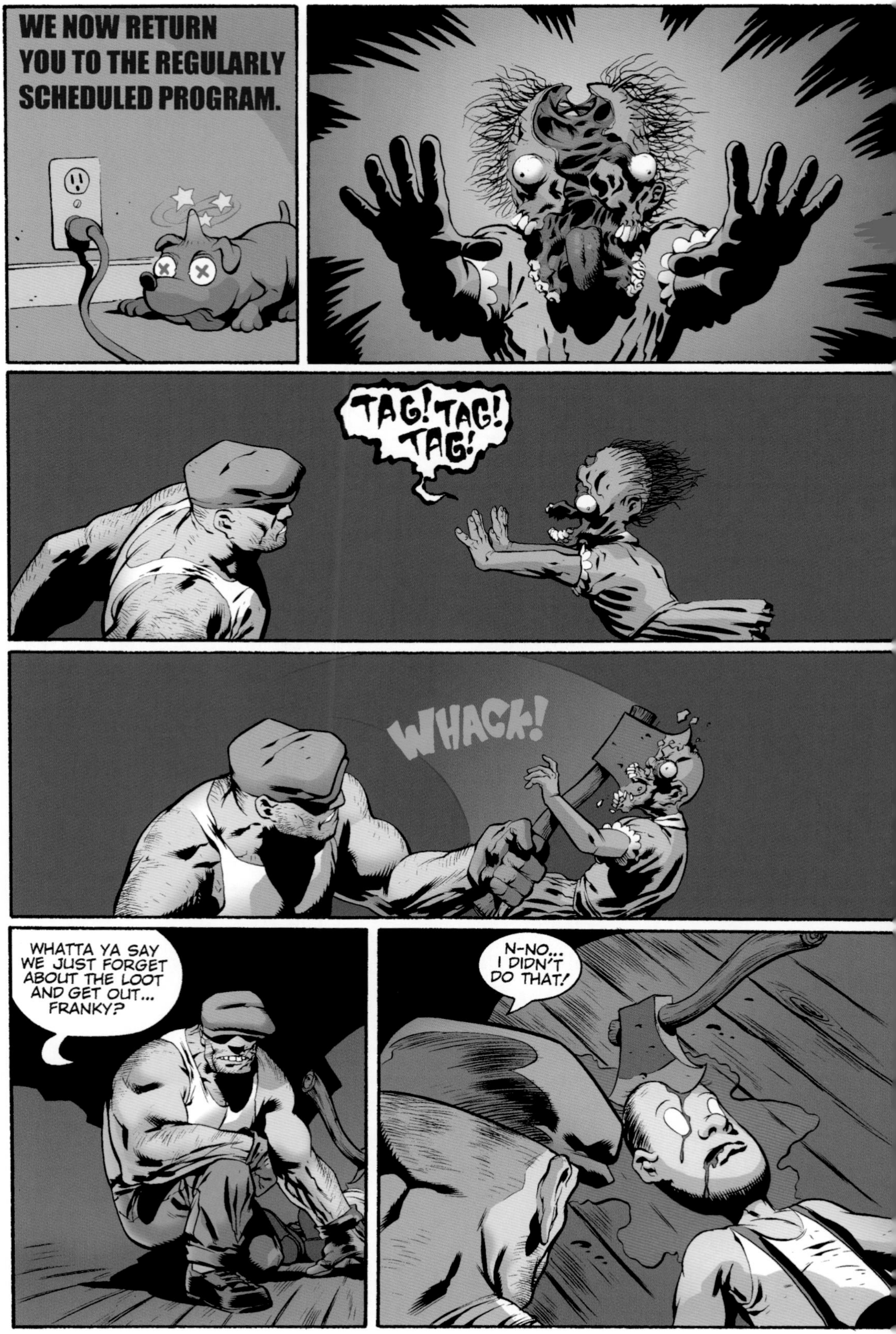
WE NOW RETURN YOU TO THE REGULARLY SCHEDULED PROGRAM.
TAG! TAG! TAG!
WHACK!
WHATTA YA SAY WE JUST FORGET ABOUT THE LOOT AND GET OUT... FRANKY?
N-NO... I DIDN'T DO THAT!

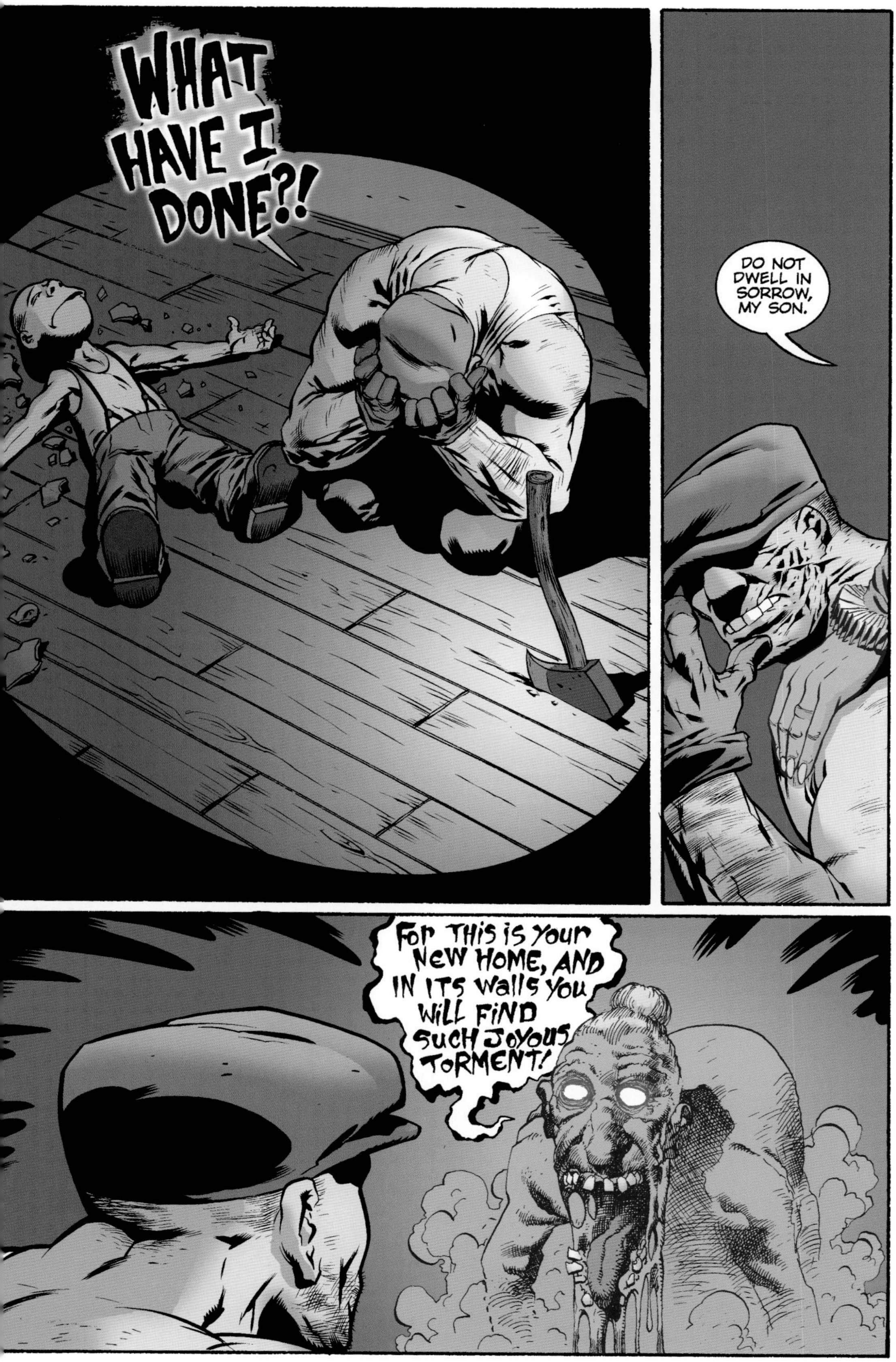
WHAT HAVE I DONE?!
DO NOT DWELL IN SORROW, MY SON.
FOR THIS IS YOUR NEW HOME, AND IN ITS WALLS YOU WILL FIND SUCH JOYOUS TORMENT!

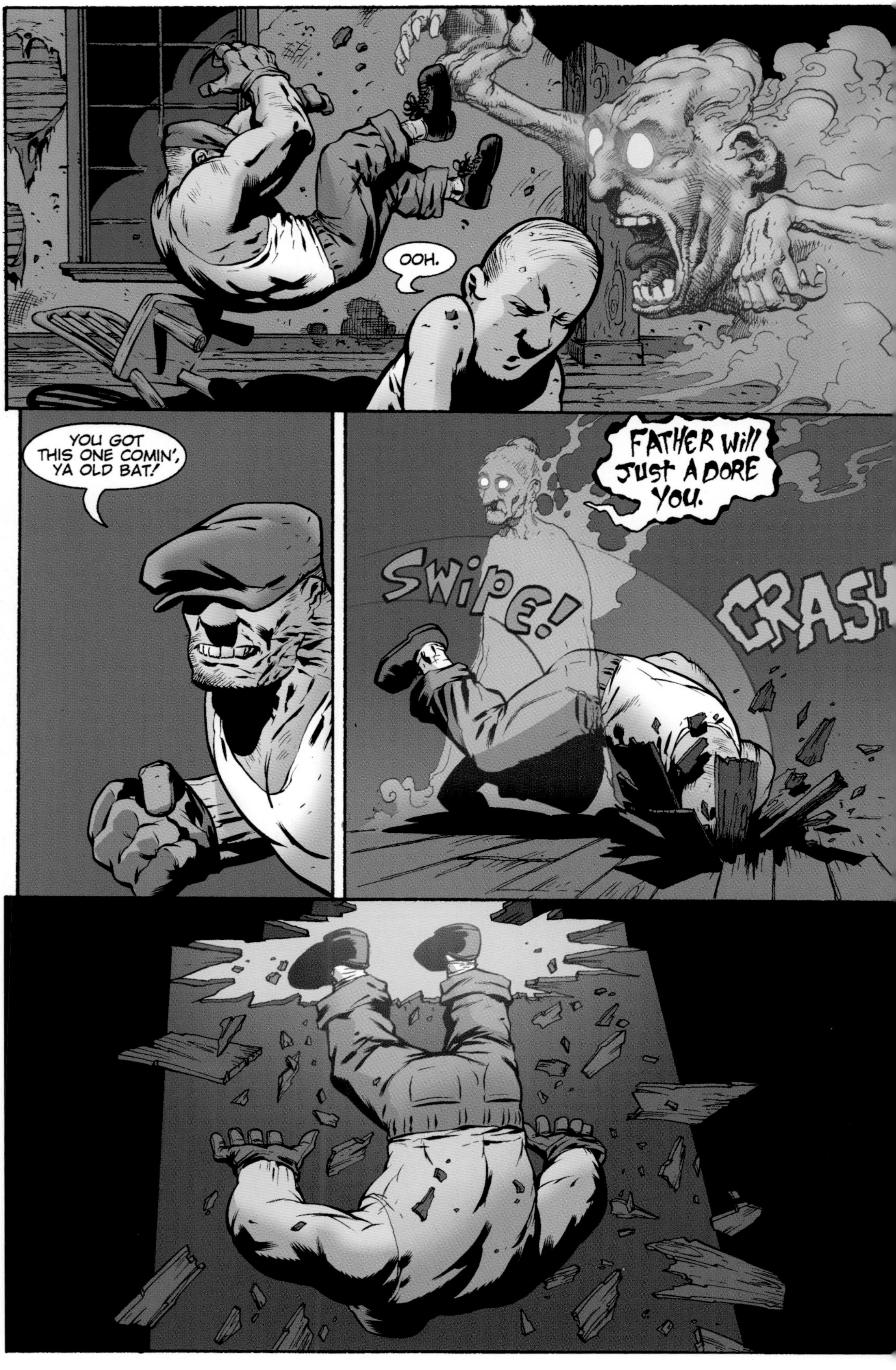
OOH.
YOU GOT THIS ONE COMIN', YA OLD BAT!
FATHER will JUST ADORE YOU.
SWIPE!
CRASH

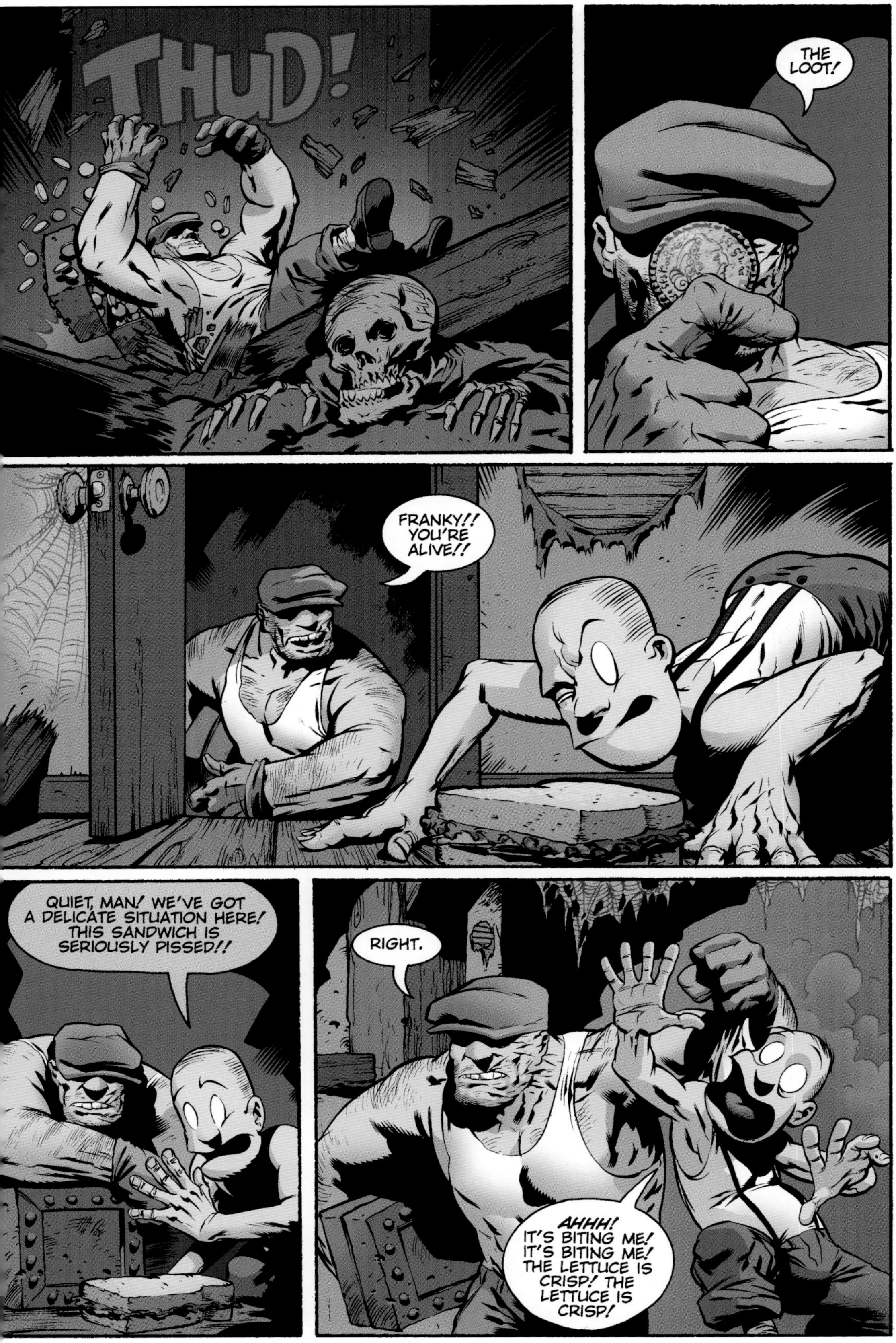
THUD!
THE LOOT!
FRANKY!! YOU'RE ALIVE!!
QUIET, MAN! WE'VE GOT A DELICATE SITUATION HERE! THIS SANDWICH IS SERIOUSLY PISSED!!
RIGHT.
AHHH! IT'S BITING ME! IT'S BITING ME! THE LETTUCE IS CRISP! THE LETTUCE IS CRISP!

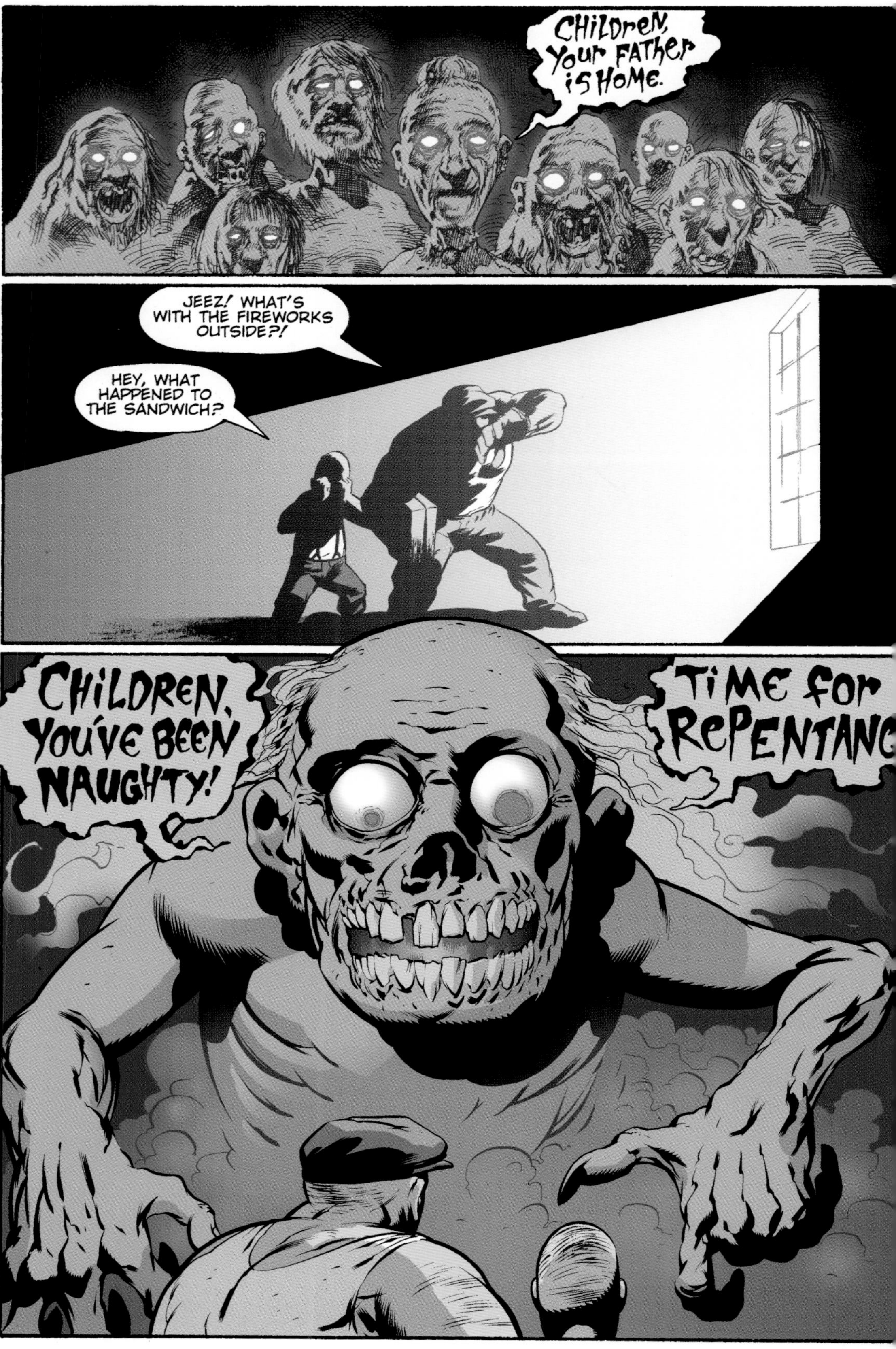
CHILDREN, YOUR FATHER IS HOME.
JEEZ! WHAT'S WITH THE FIREWORKS OUTSIDE?!
HEY, WHAT HAPPENED TO THE SANDWICH?
CHILDREN, YOU'VE BEEN NAUGHTY!
TIME FOR REPENTANC

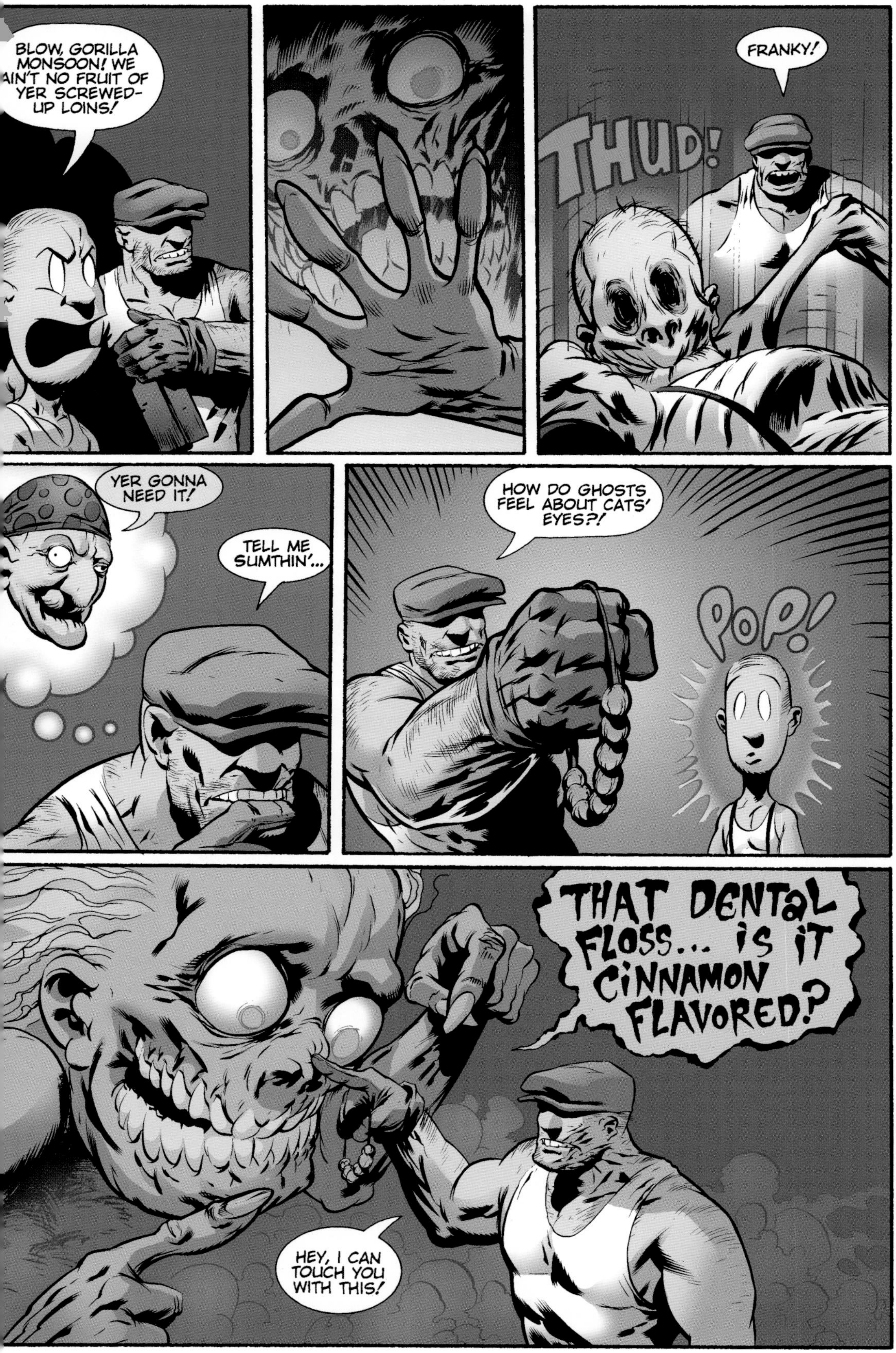
BLOW, GORILLA MONSOON! WE AIN'T NO FRUIT OF YER SCREWED-UP LOINS!
FRANKY!
THUD!
YER GONNA NEED IT!
TELL ME SUMTHIN'...
HOW DO GHOSTS FEEL ABOUT CATS' EYES?!
POP!
THAT DENTAL FLOSS... IS IT CINNAMON FLAVORED?
HEY, I CAN TOUCH YOU WITH THIS!

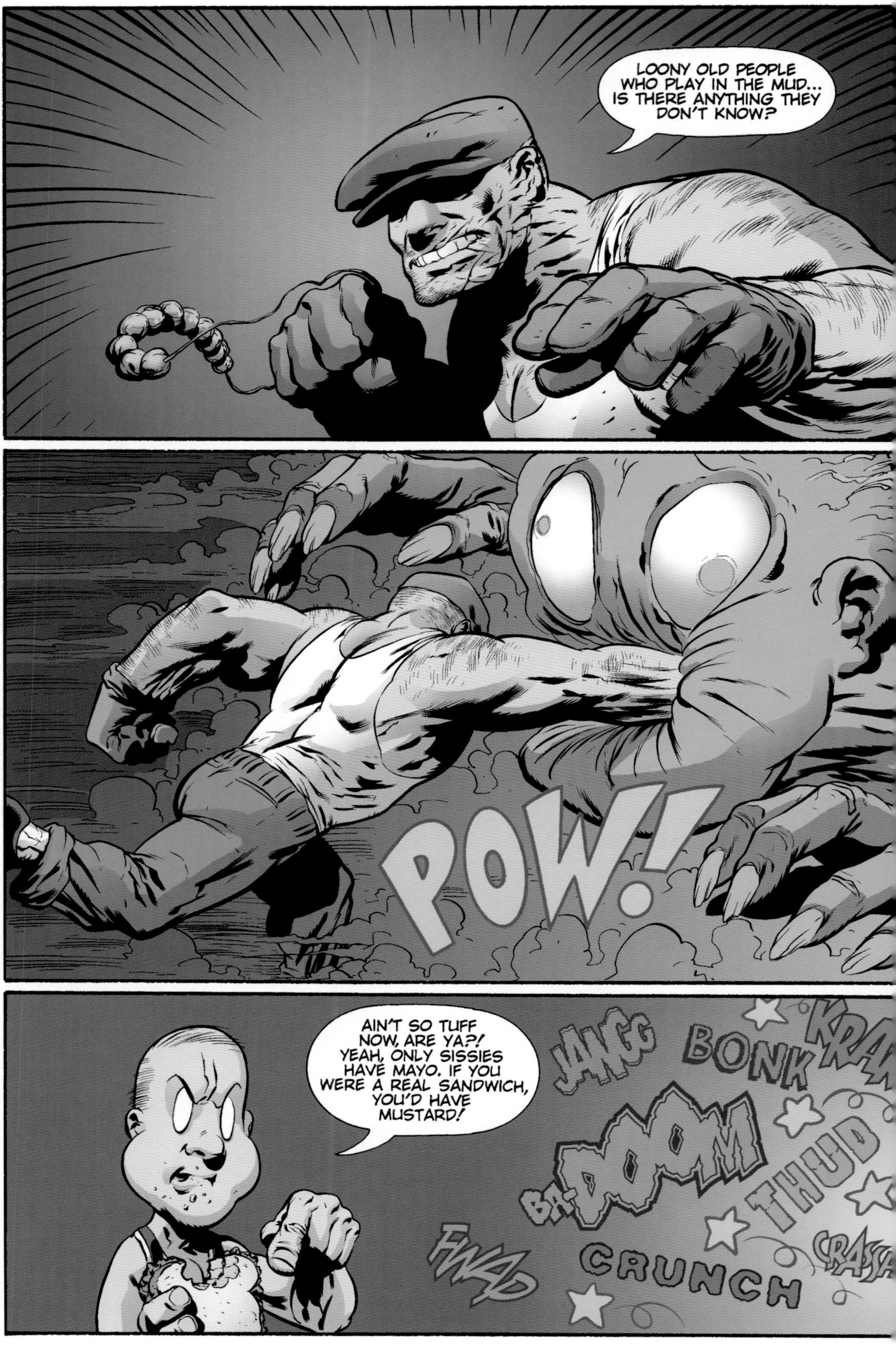
LOONY OLD PEOPLE WHO PLAY IN THE MUD... IS THERE ANYTHING THEY DON'T KNOW?
POW!
AIN'T SO TUFF NOW, ARE YA?! YEAH, ONLY SISSIES HAVE MAYO. IF YOU WERE A REAL SANDWICH, YOU'D HAVE MUSTARD!
JANGG
BONK
BA-DOOM
THUD
CRUNCH

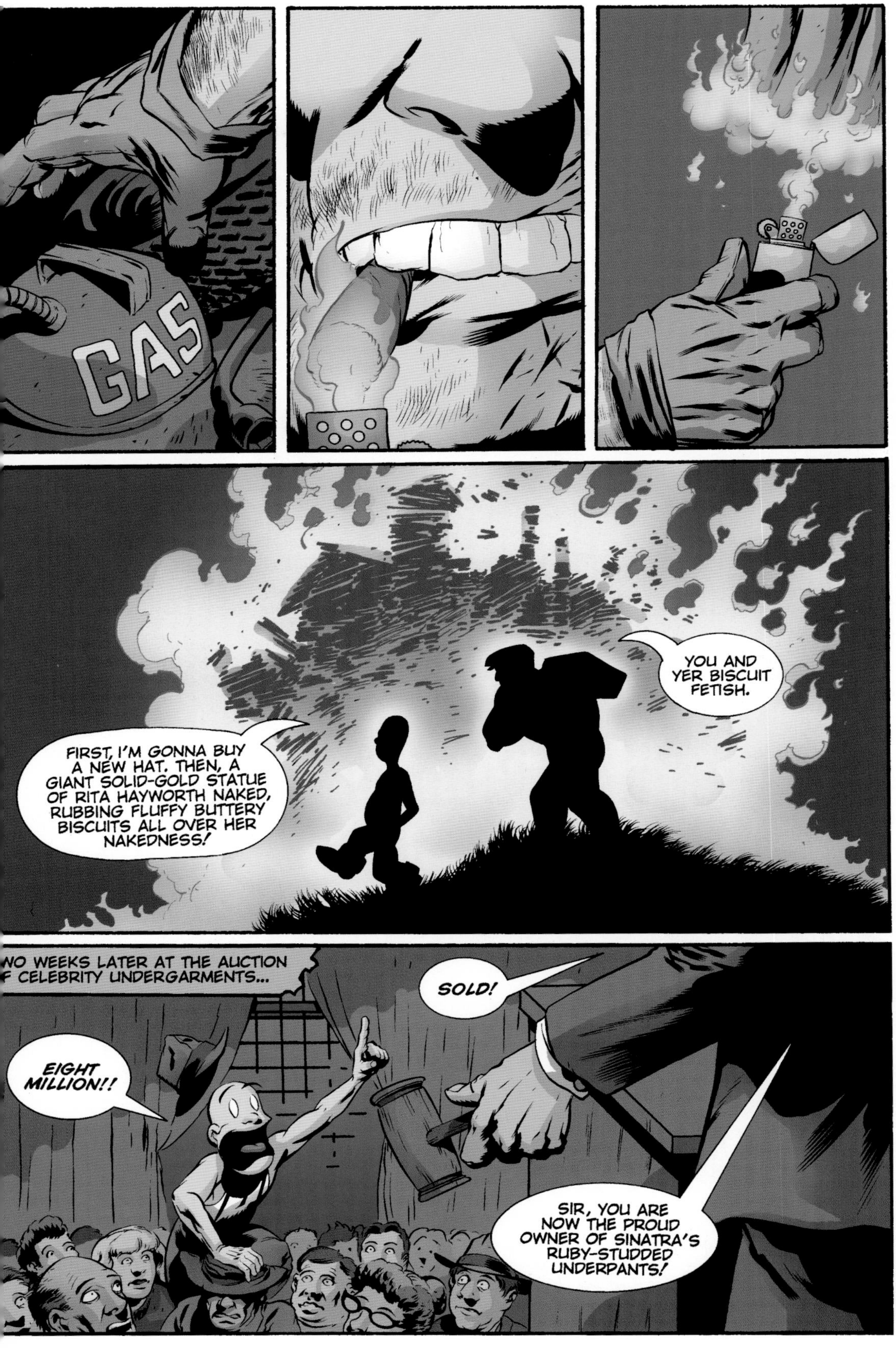
GAS
FIRST, I'M GONNA BUY A NEW HAT. THEN, A GIANT SOLID-GOLD STATUE OF RITA HAYWORTH NAKED, RUBBING FLUFFY BUTTERY BISCUITS ALL OVER HER NAKEDNESS!
YOU AND YER BISCUIT FETISH.
WO WEEKS LATER AT THE AUCTION
F CELEBRITY UNDERGARMENTS...
EIGHT MILLION!!
SOLD!
SIR, YOU ARE NOW THE PROUD OWNER OF SINATRA'S RUBY-STUDDED UNDERPANTS!

CHAPTER 2

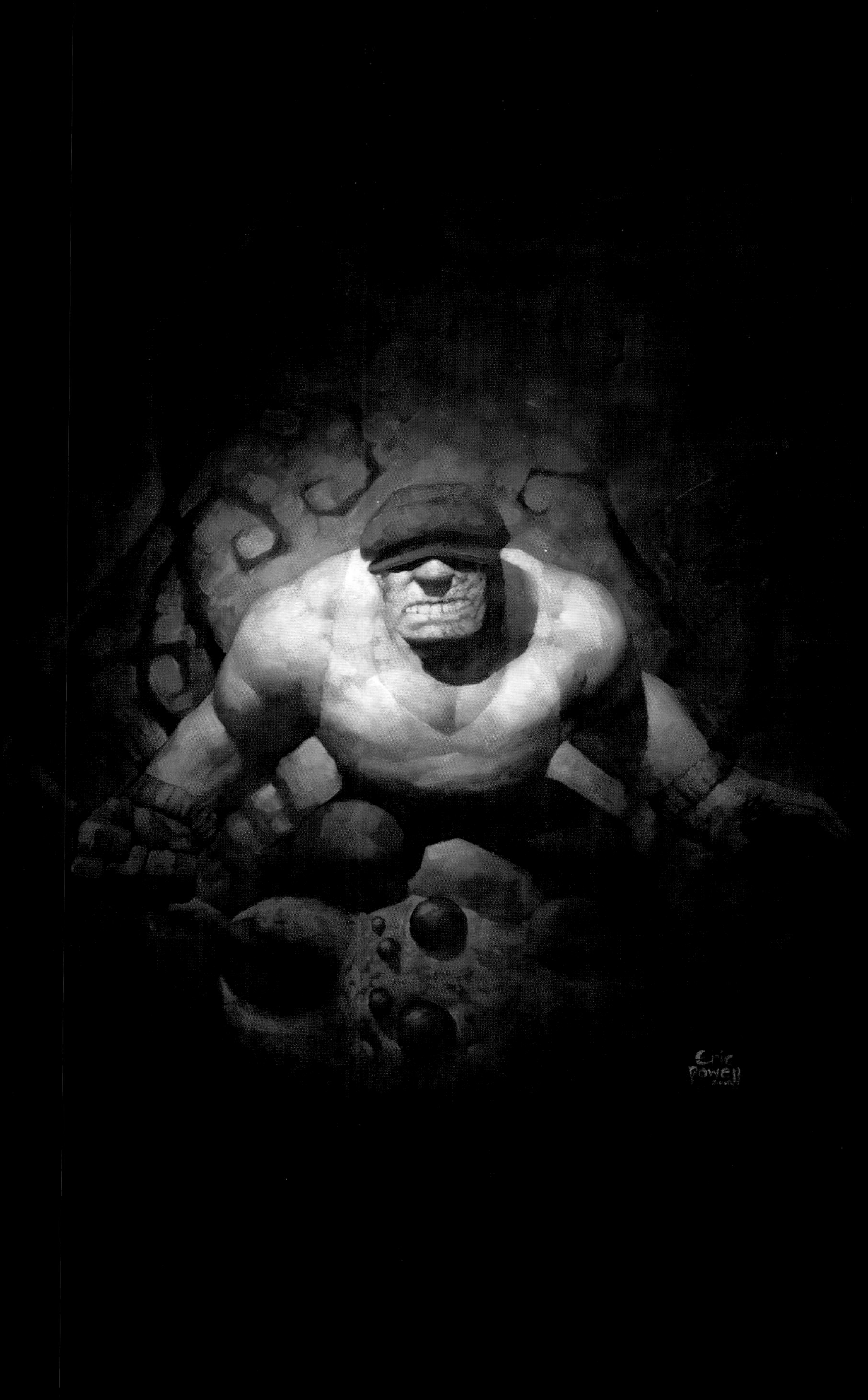
Eric
Powell

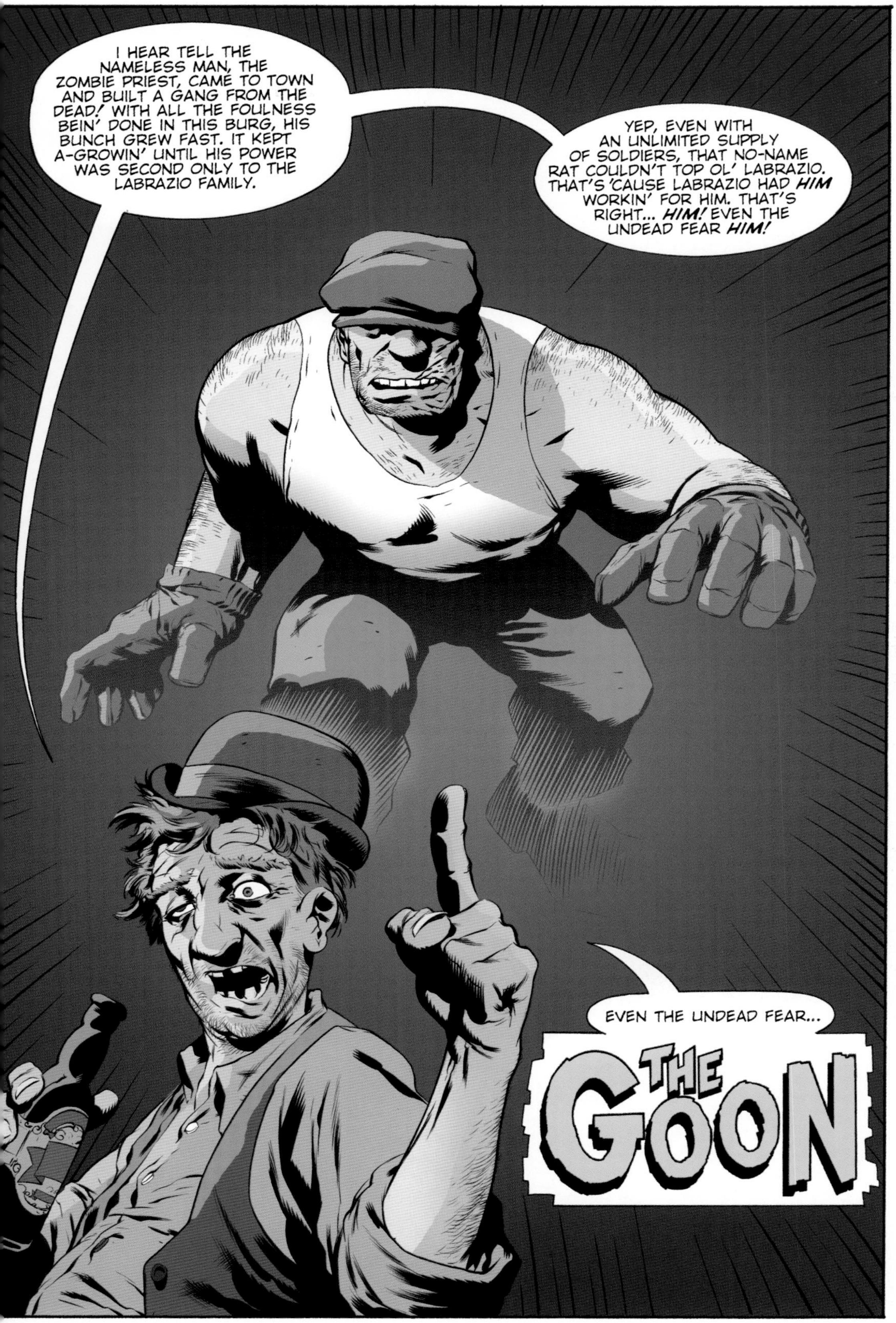
I HEAR TELL THE NAMELESS MAN, THE ZOMBIE PRIEST, CAME TO TOWN AND BUILT A GANG FROM THE DEAD! WITH ALL THE FOULNESS BEIN' DONE IN THIS BURG, HIS BUNCH GREW FAST. IT KEPT A-GROWIN' UNTIL HIS POWER WAS SECOND ONLY TO THE LABRAZIO FAMILY.
YEP, EVEN WITH AN UNLIMITED SUPPLY OF SOLDIERS, THAT NO-NAME RAT COULDN'T TOP OL' LABRAZIO. THAT'S 'CAUSE LABRAZIO HAD *HIM* WORKIN' FOR HIM. THAT'S RIGHT... *HIM!* EVEN THE UNDEAD FEAR *HIM!*
EVEN THE UNDEAD FEAR...
THE GOON

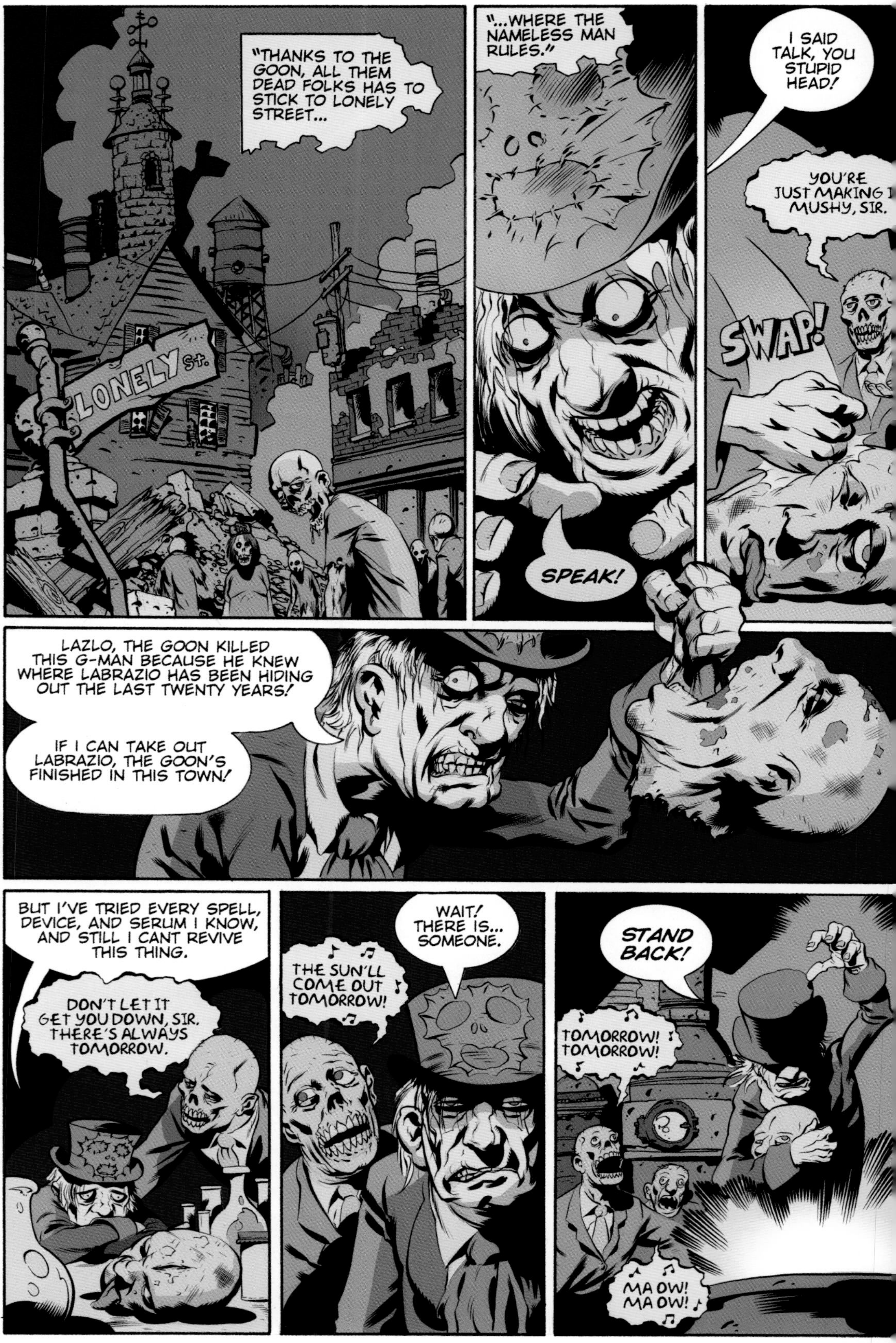
"THANKS TO THE GOON, ALL THEM DEAD FOLKS HAS TO STICK TO LONELY STREET...
LONELY St.
"...WHERE THE NAMELESS MAN RULES."
SPEAK!
I SAID TALK, YOU STUPID HEAD!
SWAP!
YOU'RE JUST MAKING I MUSHY, SIR.
LAZLO, THE GOON KILLED THIS G-MAN BECAUSE HE KNEW WHERE LABRAZIO HAS BEEN HIDING OUT THE LAST TWENTY YEARS!
IF I CAN TAKE OUT LABRAZIO, THE GOON'S FINISHED IN THIS TOWN!
BUT I'VE TRIED EVERY SPELL, DEVICE, AND SERUM I KNOW, AND STILL I CANT REVIVE THIS THING.
DON'T LET IT GET YOU DOWN, SIR. THERE'S ALWAYS TOMORROW.
WAIT! THERE IS... SOMEONE.
THE SUN'LL COME OUT TOMORROW!
STAND BACK!
TOMORROW! TOMORROW!
MA OW! MA OW!

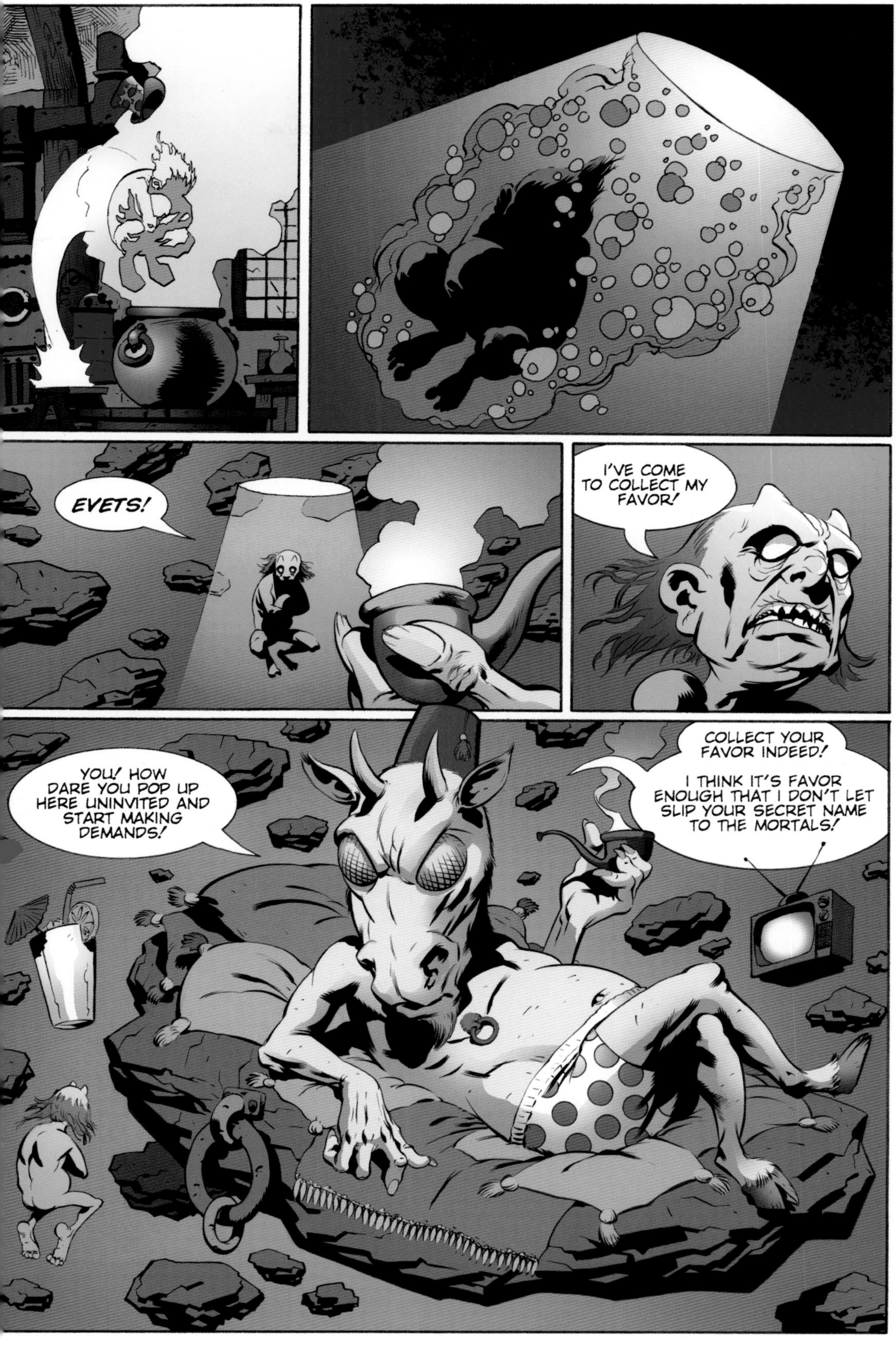
EVETS!
I'VE COME TO COLLECT MY FAVOR!
YOU! HOW DARE YOU POP UP HERE UNINVITED AND START MAKING DEMANDS!
COLLECT YOUR FAVOR INDEED!
I THINK IT'S FAVOR ENOUGH THAT I DON'T LET SLIP YOUR SECRET NAME TO THE MORTALS!

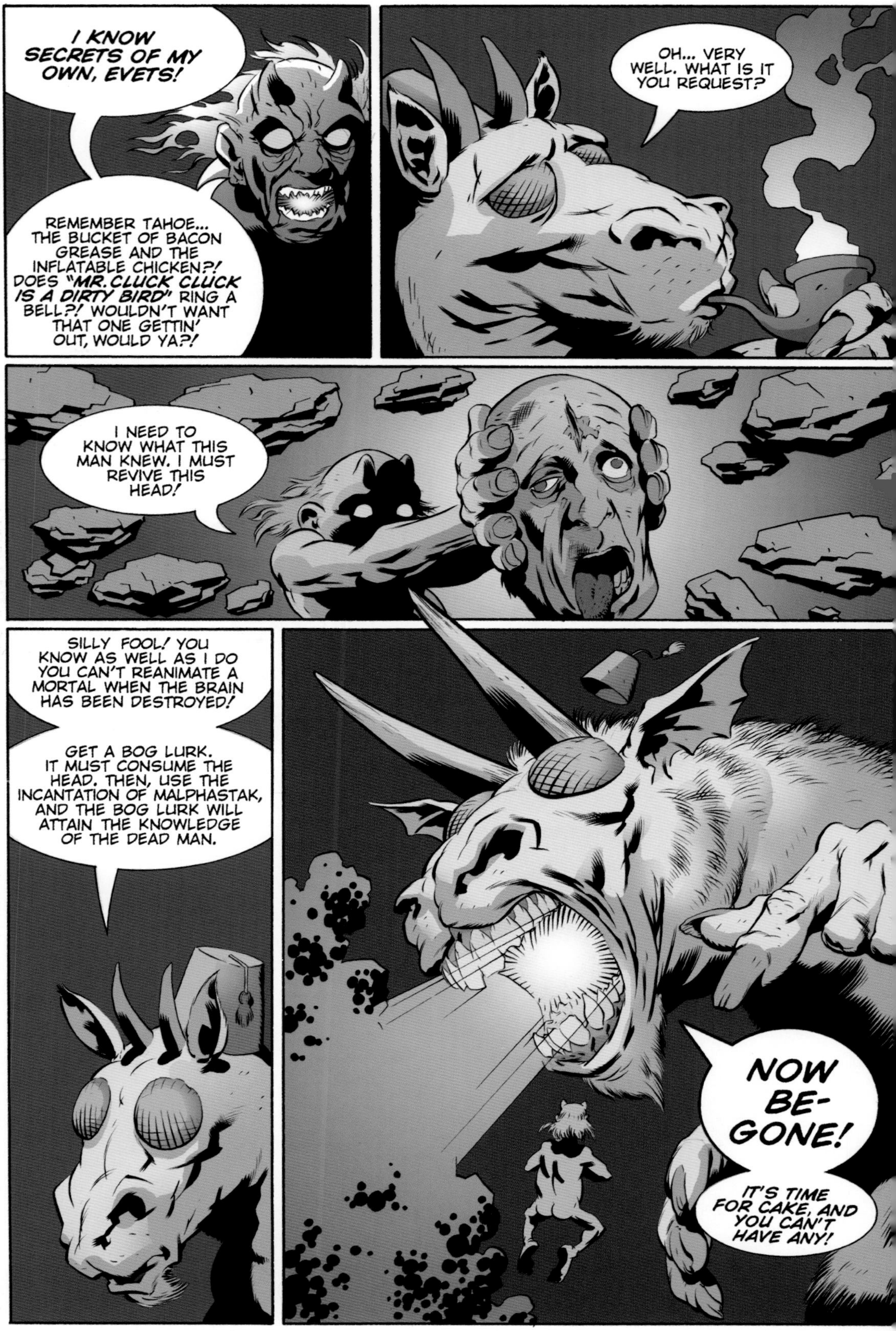
I KNOW SECRETS OF MY OWN, EVETS!
REMEMBER TAHOE... THE BUCKET OF BACON GREASE AND THE INFLATABLE CHICKEN?! DOES "MR.CLUCK CLUCK IS A DIRTY BIRD" RING A BELL?! WOULDN'T WANT THAT ONE GETTIN' OUT, WOULD YA?!
OH... VERY WELL. WHAT IS IT YOU REQUEST?
I NEED TO KNOW WHAT THIS MAN KNEW. I MUST REVIVE THIS HEAD!
SILLY FOOL! YOU KNOW AS WELL AS I DO YOU CAN'T REANIMATE A MORTAL WHEN THE BRAIN HAS BEEN DESTROYED!
GET A BOG LURK. IT MUST CONSUME THE HEAD. THEN, USE THE INCANTATION OF MALPHASTAK, AND THE BOG LURK WILL ATTAIN THE KNOWLEDGE OF THE DEAD MAN.
NOW BE-GONE!
IT'S TIME FOR CAKE, AND YOU CAN'T HAVE ANY!

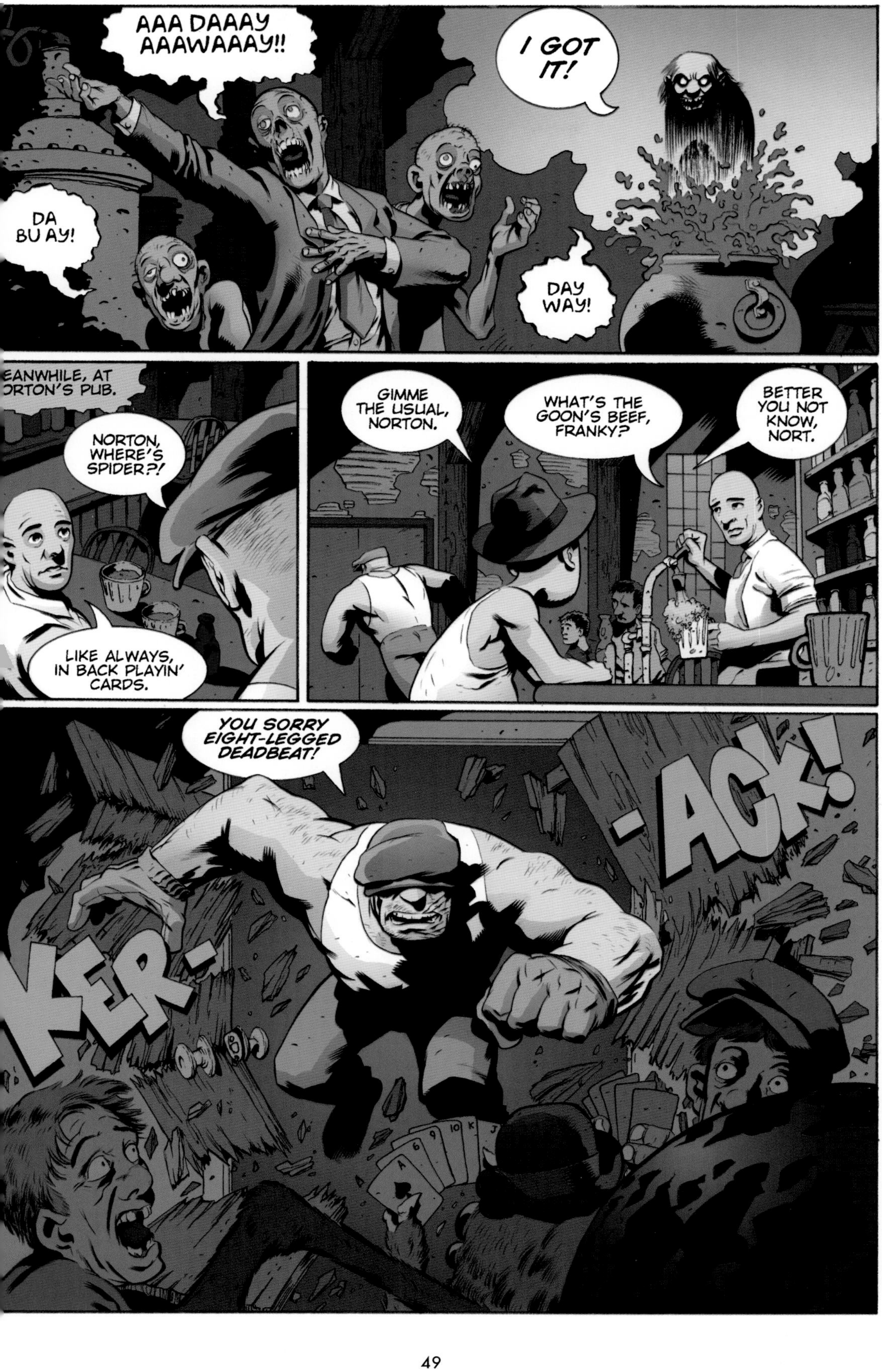
AAA DAAAY AAAWAAAY!!
I GOT IT!
DA BU AY!
DAY WAY!
EANWHILE, AT ORTON'S PUB.
NORTON, WHERE'S SPIDER?!
LIKE ALWAYS, IN BACK PLAYIN' CARDS.
GIMME THE USUAL, NORTON.
WHAT'S THE GOON'S BEEF, FRANKY?
BETTER YOU NOT KNOW, NORT.
YOU SORRY EIGHT-LEGGED DEADBEAT!
KER-
-ACK!

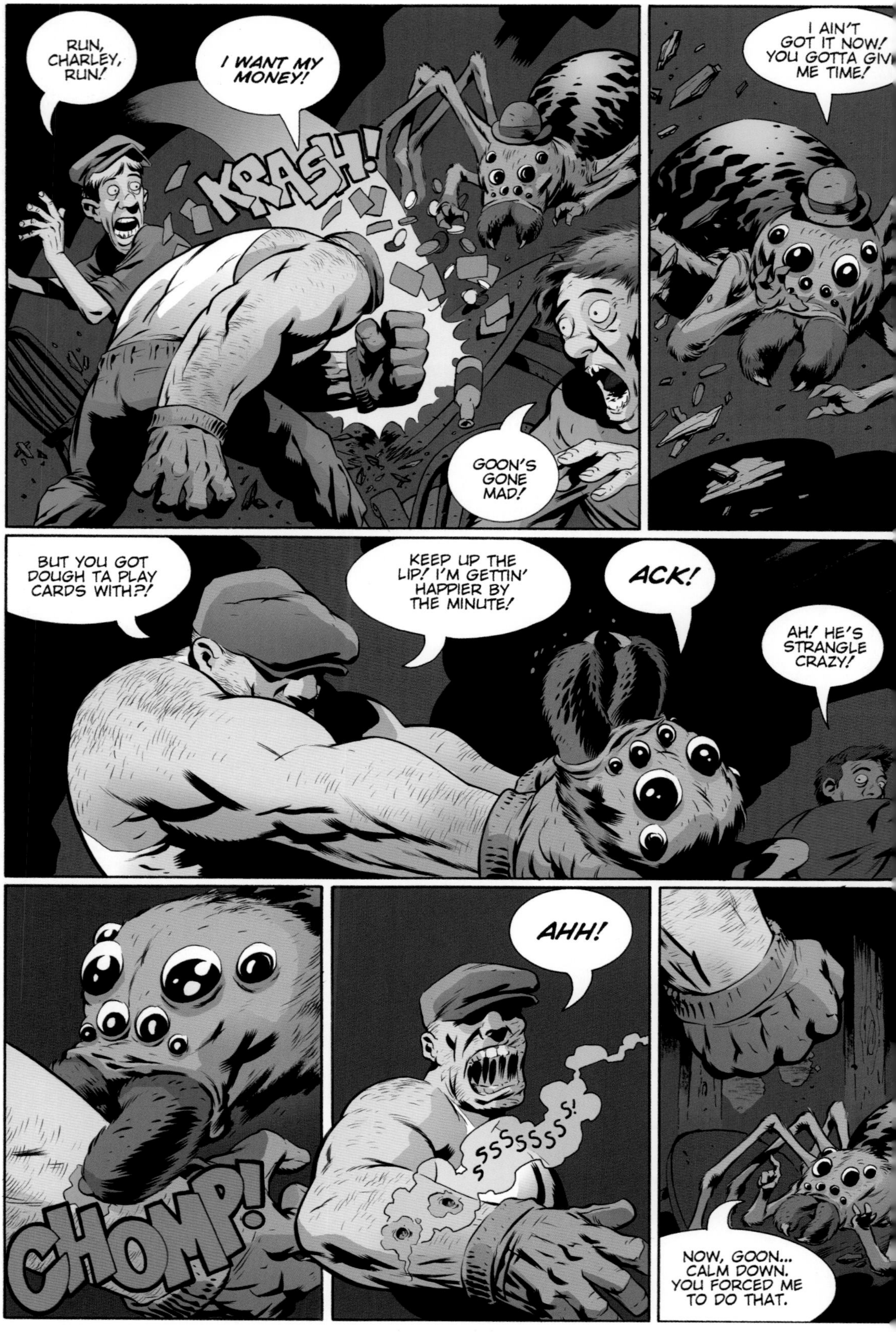
RUN, CHARLEY, RUN!
I WANT MY MONEY!
KRASH!
GOON'S GONE MAD!
I AIN'T GOT IT NOW! YOU GOTTA GIV ME TIME!
BUT YOU GOT DOUGH TA PLAY CARDS WITH?!
KEEP UP THE LIP! I'M GETTIN' HAPPIER BY THE MINUTE!
ACK!
AH! HE'S STRANGLE CRAZY!
CHOMP!
AHH!
SSSSSSSS!
NOW, GOON... CALM DOWN. YOU FORCED ME TO DO THAT.

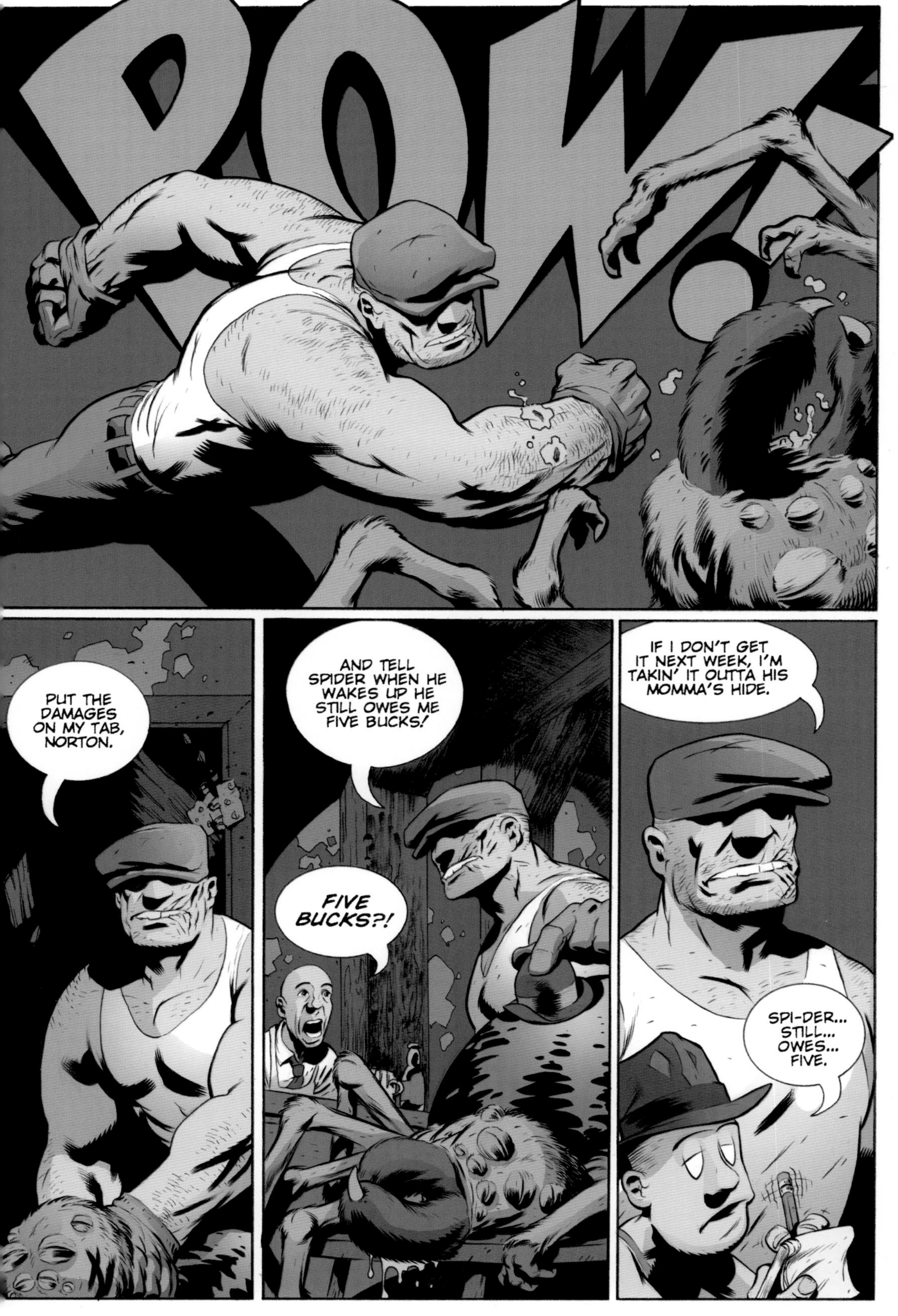
POW
PUT THE DAMAGES ON MY TAB, NORTON.
AND TELL SPIDER WHEN HE WAKES UP HE STILL OWES ME FIVE BUCKS!
FIVE BUCKS?!
IF I DON'T GET IT NEXT WEEK, I'M TAKIN' IT OUTTA HIS MOMMA'S HIDE.
SPI-DER... STILL... OWES... FIVE.

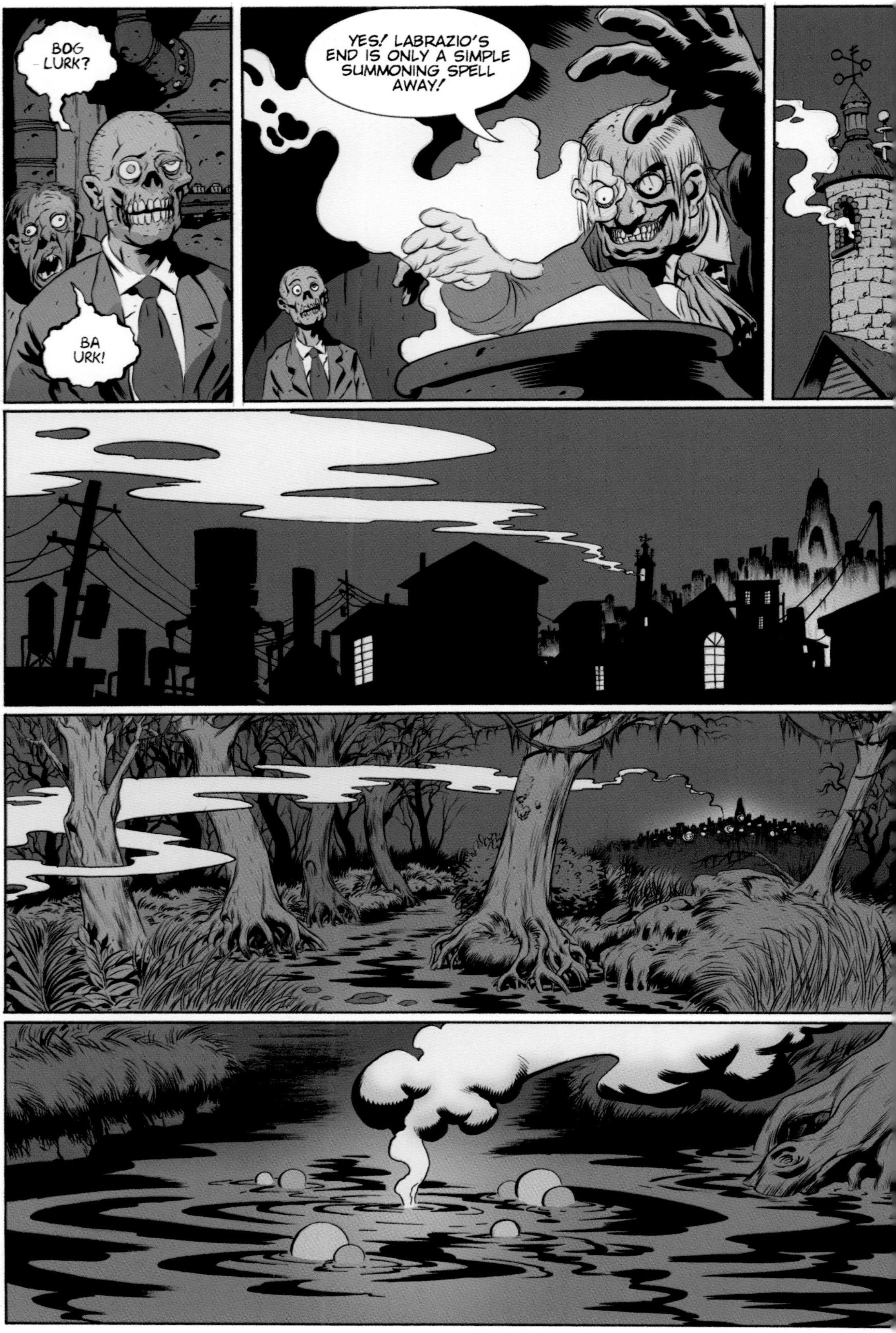
BOG LURK?
BA URK!
YES! LABRAZIO'S END IS ONLY A SIMPLE SUMMONING SPELL AWAY!

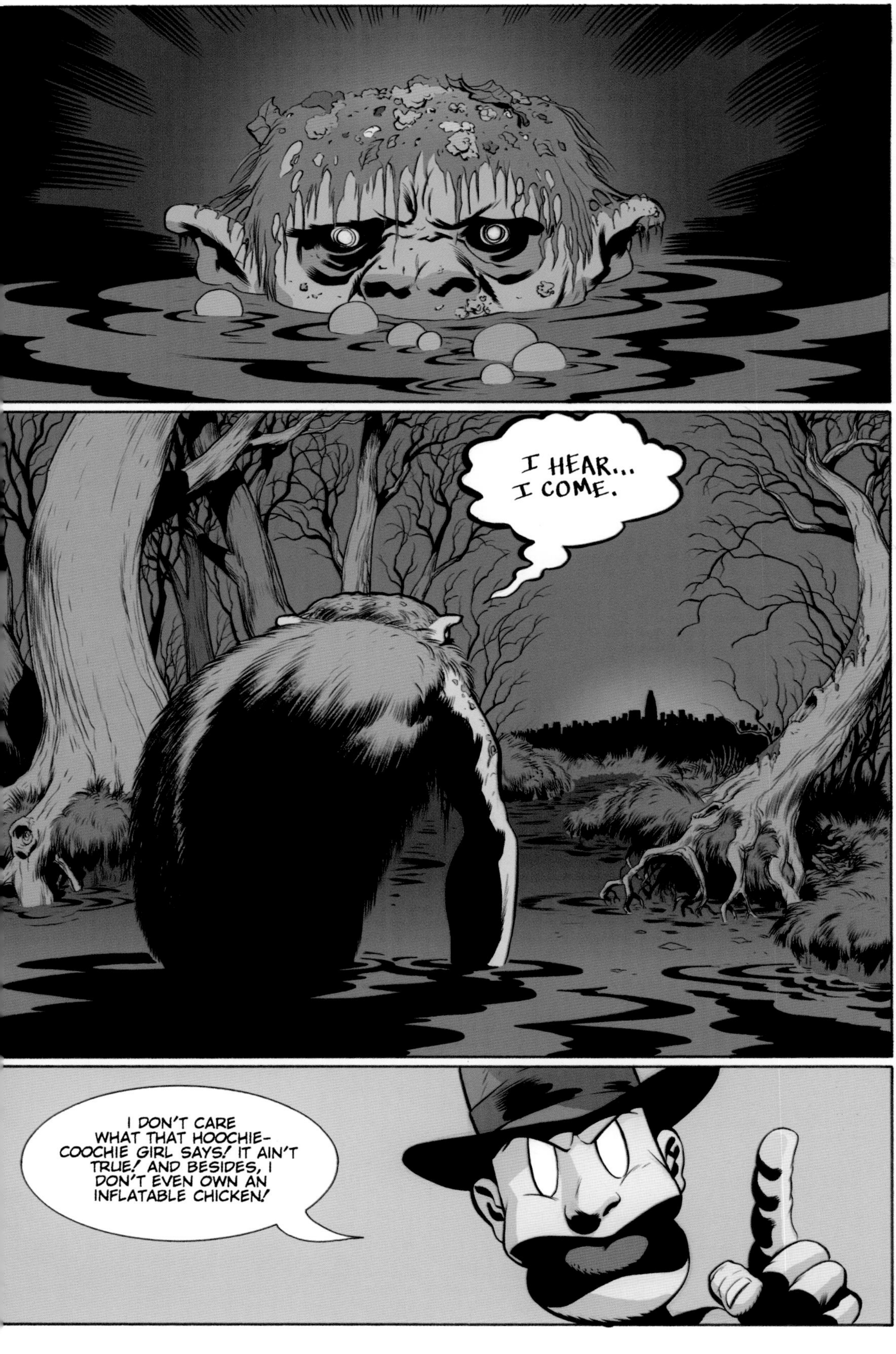
I HEAR...
I COME.
I DON'T CARE WHAT THAT HOOCHIE-COOCHIE GIRL SAYS! IT AIN'T TRUE! AND BESIDES, I DON'T EVEN OWN AN INFLATABLE CHICKEN!

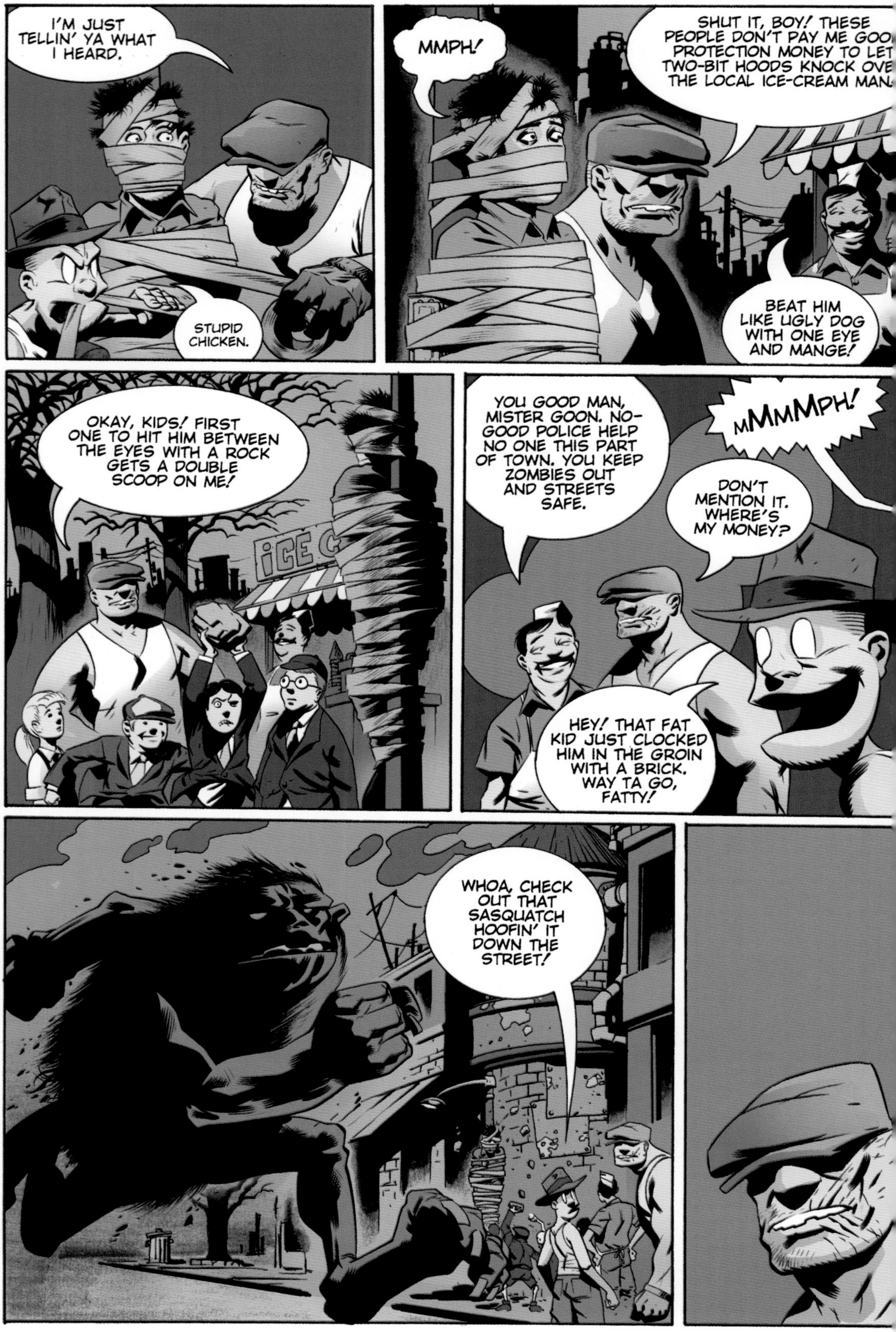
I'M JUST TELLIN' YA WHAT I HEARD.
STUPID CHICKEN.
MMPH!
SHUT IT, BOY! THESE PEOPLE DON'T PAY ME GOO PROTECTION MONEY TO LET TWO-BIT HOODS KNOCK OVE THE LOCAL ICE-CREAM MAN.
BEAT HIM LIKE UGLY DOG WITH ONE EYE AND MANGE!
OKAY, KIDS! FIRST ONE TO HIT HIM BETWEEN THE EYES WITH A ROCK GETS A DOUBLE SCOOP ON ME!
ICE C
YOU GOOD MAN, MISTER GOON. NO-GOOD POLICE HELP NO ONE THIS PART OF TOWN. YOU KEEP ZOMBIES OUT AND STREETS SAFE.
MMMMPH!
DON'T MENTION IT. WHERE'S MY MONEY?
HEY! THAT FAT KID JUST CLOCKED HIM IN THE GROIN WITH A BRICK. WAY TA GO, FATTY!
WHOA, CHECK OUT THAT SASQUATCH HOOFIN' IT DOWN THE STREET!

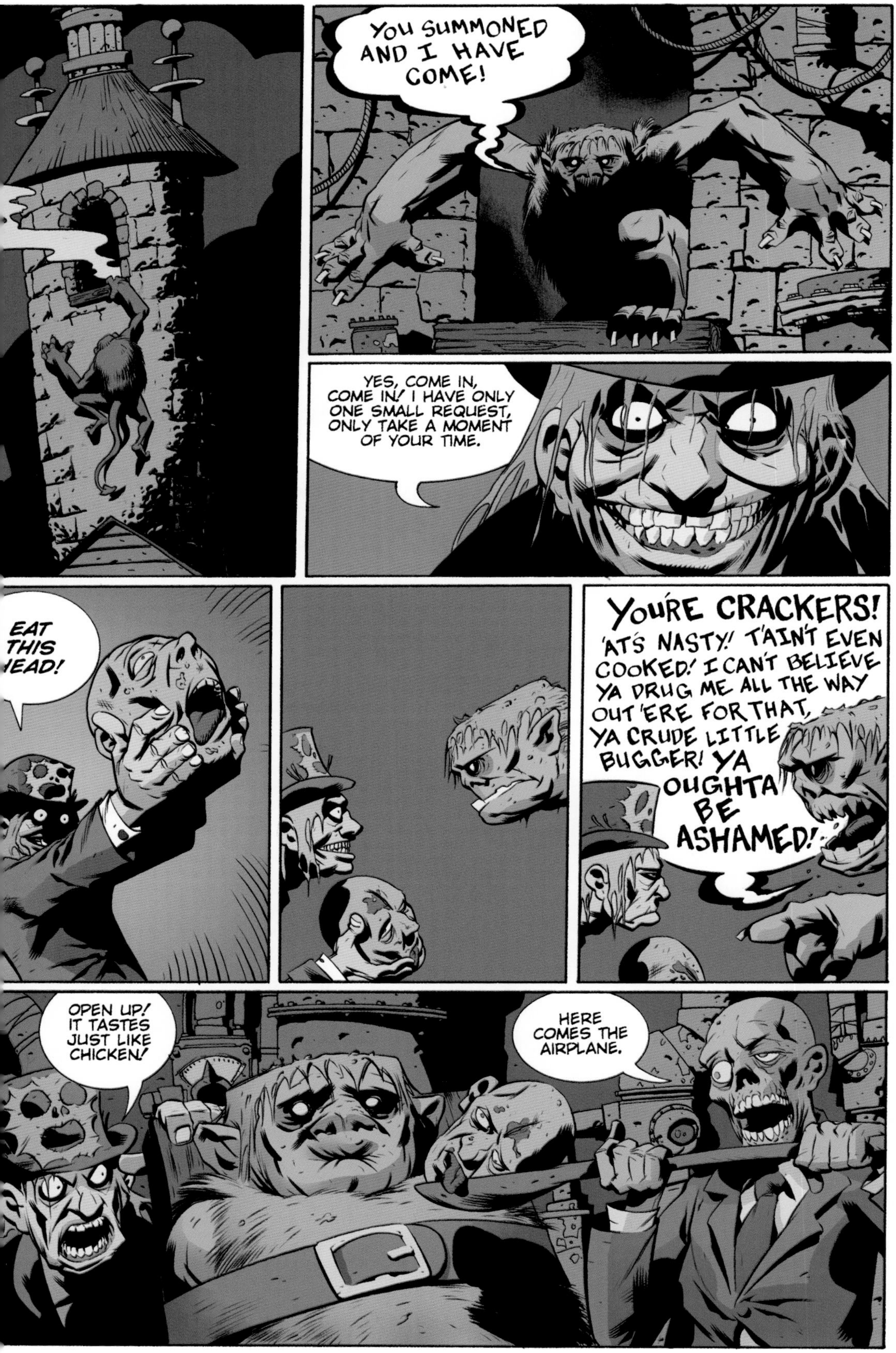
YOU SUMMONED AND I HAVE COME!
YES, COME IN, COME IN! I HAVE ONLY ONE SMALL REQUEST, ONLY TAKE A MOMENT OF YOUR TIME.
EAT THIS HEAD!
YOU'RE CRACKERS! 'AT'S NASTY! T'AIN'T EVEN COOKED! I CAN'T BELIEVE YA DRUG ME ALL THE WAY OUT 'ERE FOR THAT, YA CRUDE LITTLE BUGGER! YA OUGHTA BE ASHAMED!
OPEN UP! IT TASTES JUST LIKE CHICKEN!
HERE COMES THE AIRPLANE.

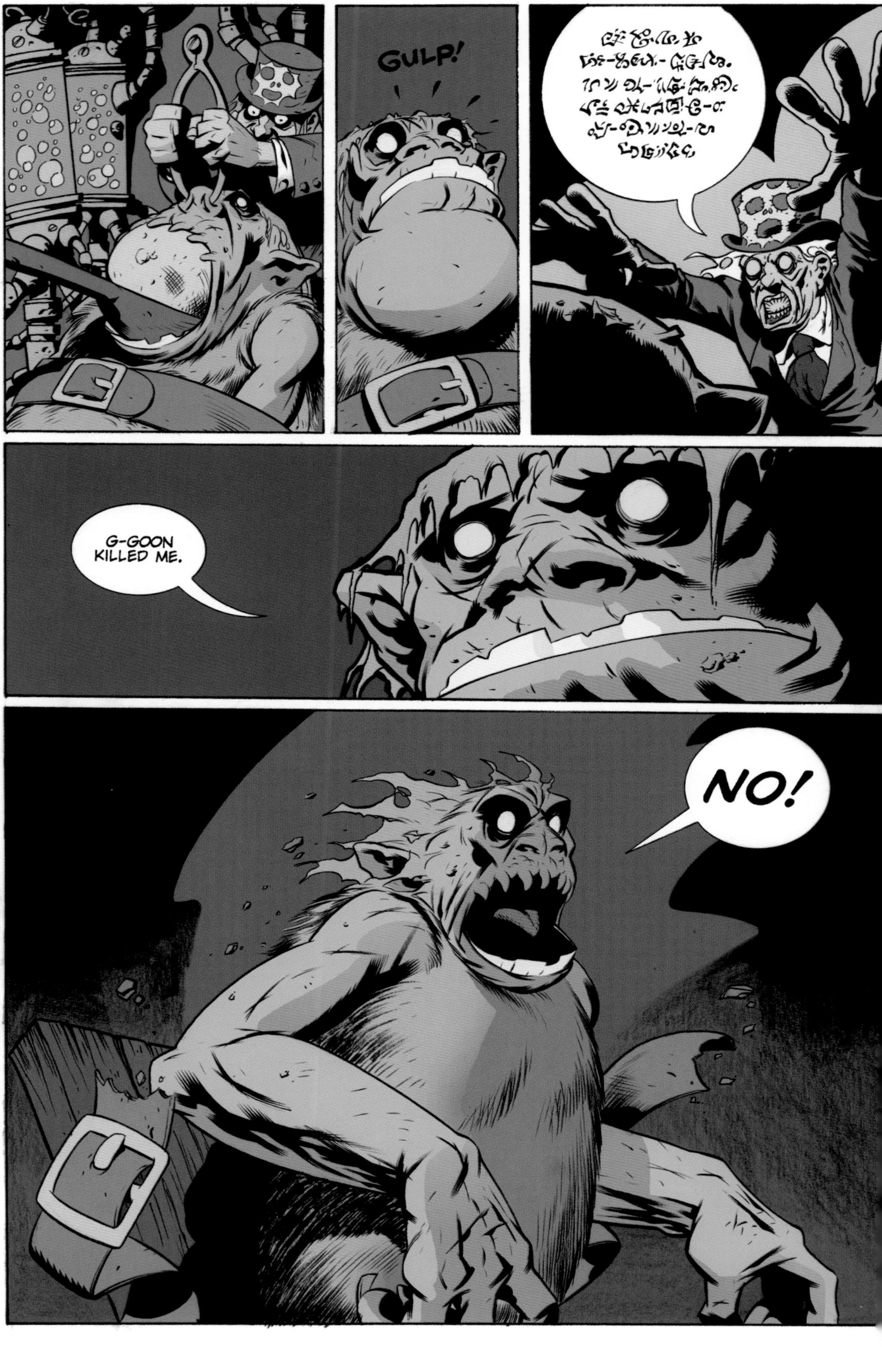
GULP!
G-GOON KILLED ME.
NO!

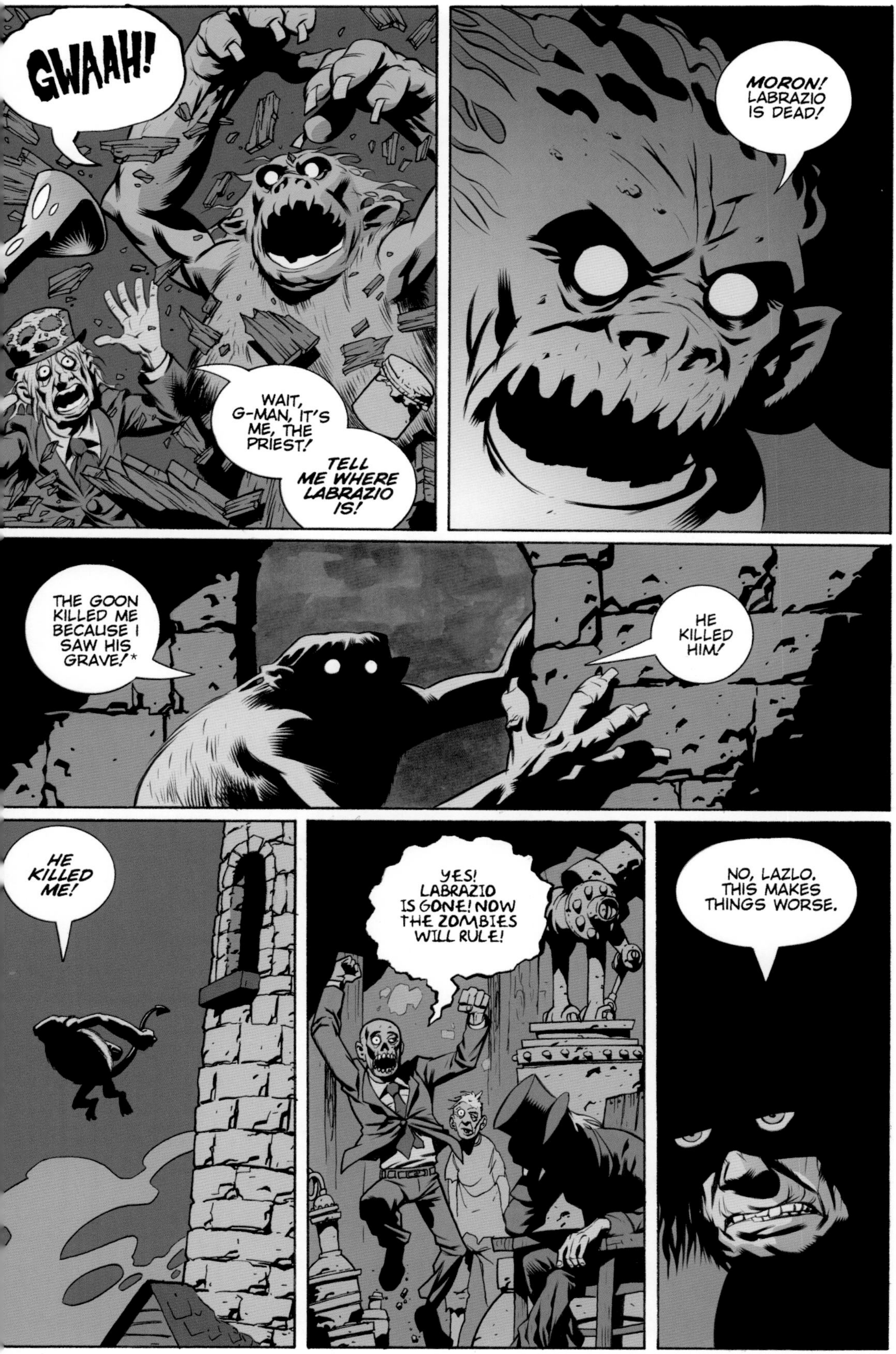
GWAAH!
WAIT, G-MAN, IT'S ME, THE PRIEST!
TELL ME WHERE LABRAZIO IS!
MORON! LABRAZIO IS DEAD!
THE GOON KILLED ME BECAUSE I SAW HIS GRAVE!*
HE KILLED HIM!
HE KILLED ME!
YES! LABRAZIO IS GONE! NOW THE ZOMBIES WILL RULE!
NO, LAZLO. THIS MAKES THINGS WORSE.

*THE GOON VOLUME 0: ROUGH STUFF

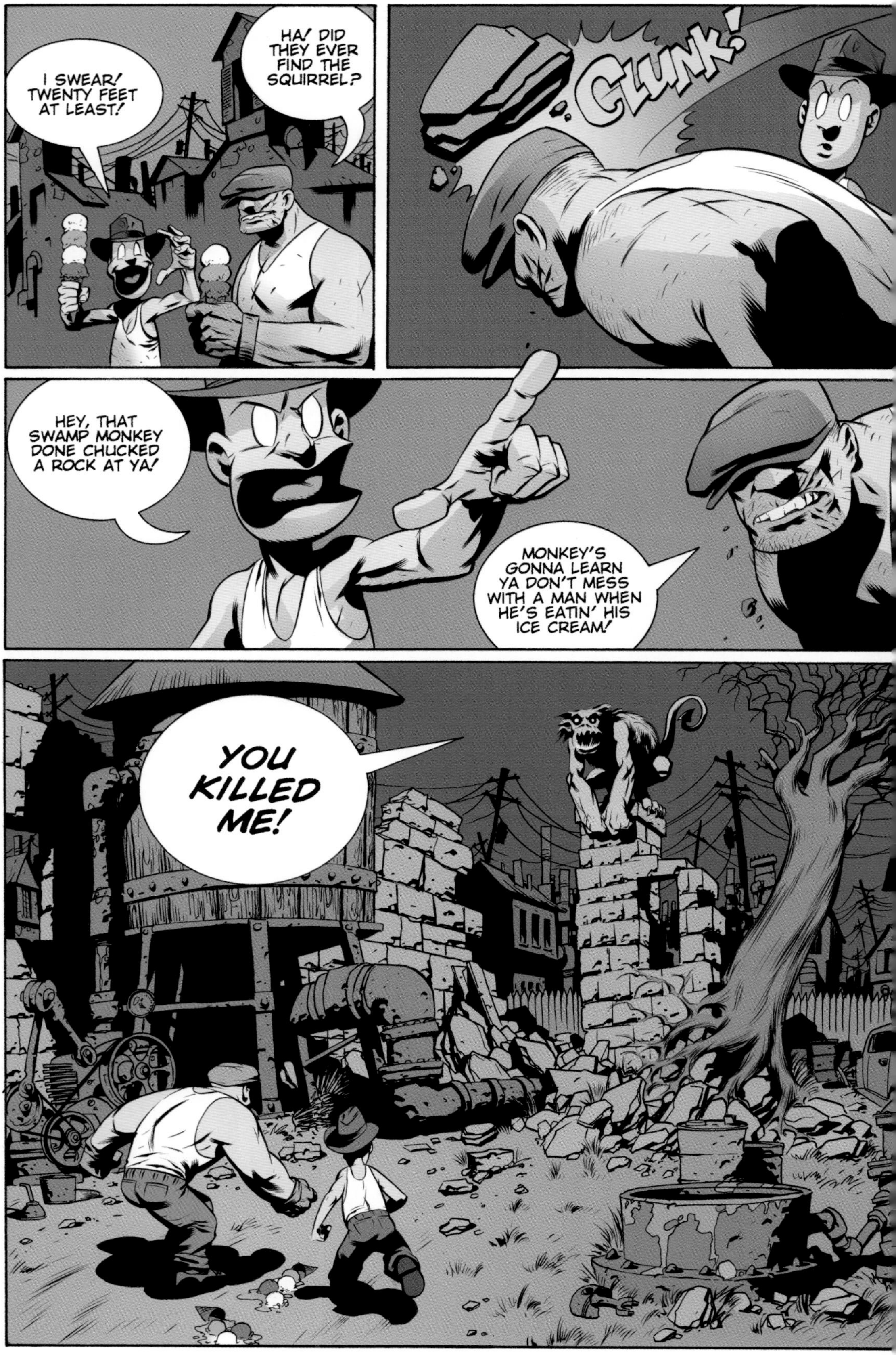
I SWEAR! TWENTY FEET AT LEAST!
HA! DID THEY EVER FIND THE SQUIRREL?
CLUNK!
HEY, THAT SWAMP MONKEY DONE CHUCKED A ROCK AT YA!
MONKEY'S GONNA LEARN YA DON'T MESS WITH A MAN WHEN HE'S EATIN' HIS ICE CREAM!
YOU KILLED ME!

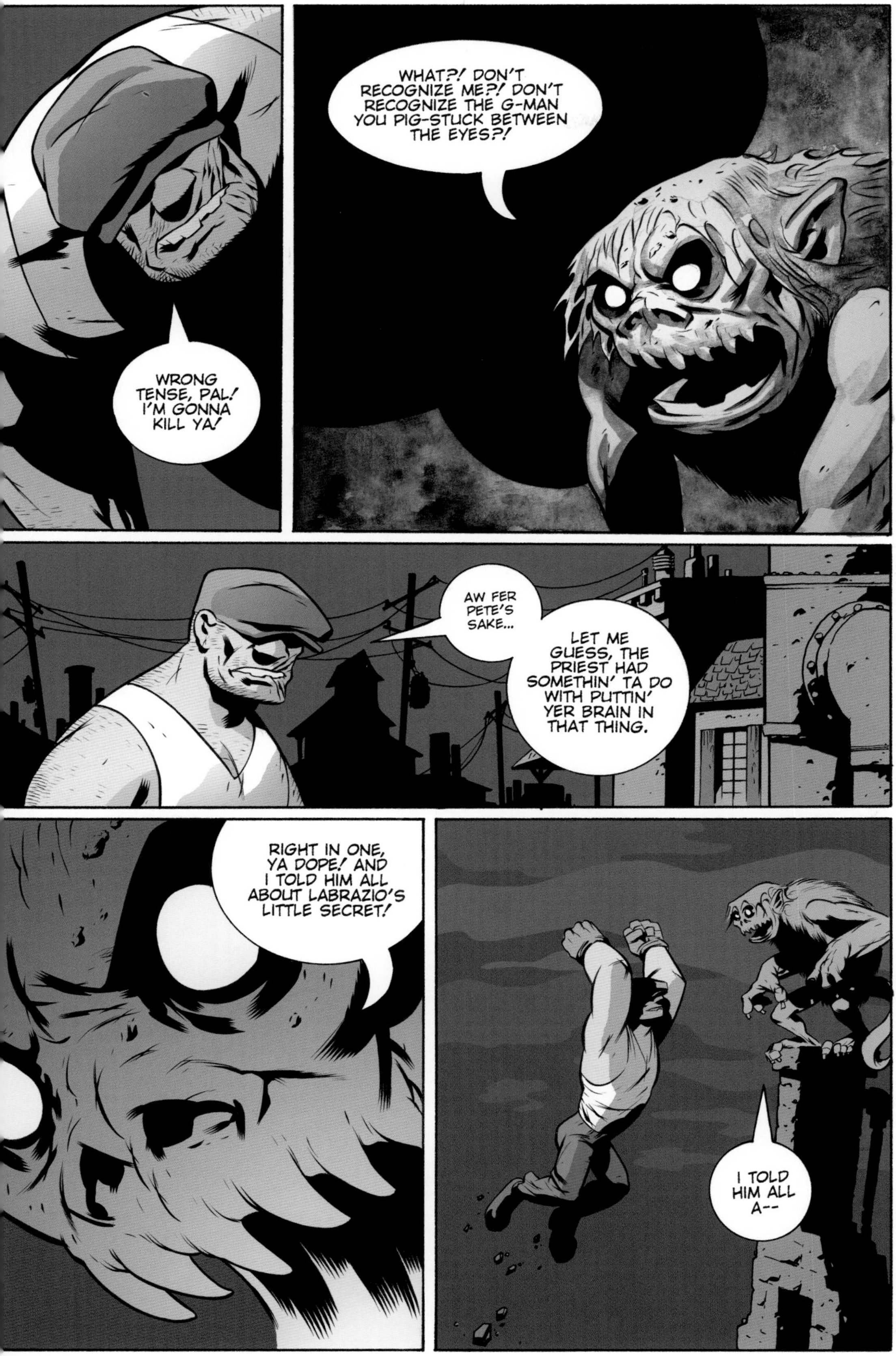
WHAT?! DON'T RECOGNIZE ME?! DON'T RECOGNIZE THE G-MAN YOU PIG-STUCK BETWEEN THE EYES?!
WRONG TENSE, PAL! I'M GONNA KILL YA!
AW FER PETE'S SAKE...
LET ME GUESS, THE PRIEST HAD SOMETHIN' TA DO WITH PUTTIN' YER BRAIN IN THAT THING.
RIGHT IN ONE, YA DOPE! AND I TOLD HIM ALL ABOUT LABRAZIO'S LITTLE SECRET!
I TOLD HIM ALL A--

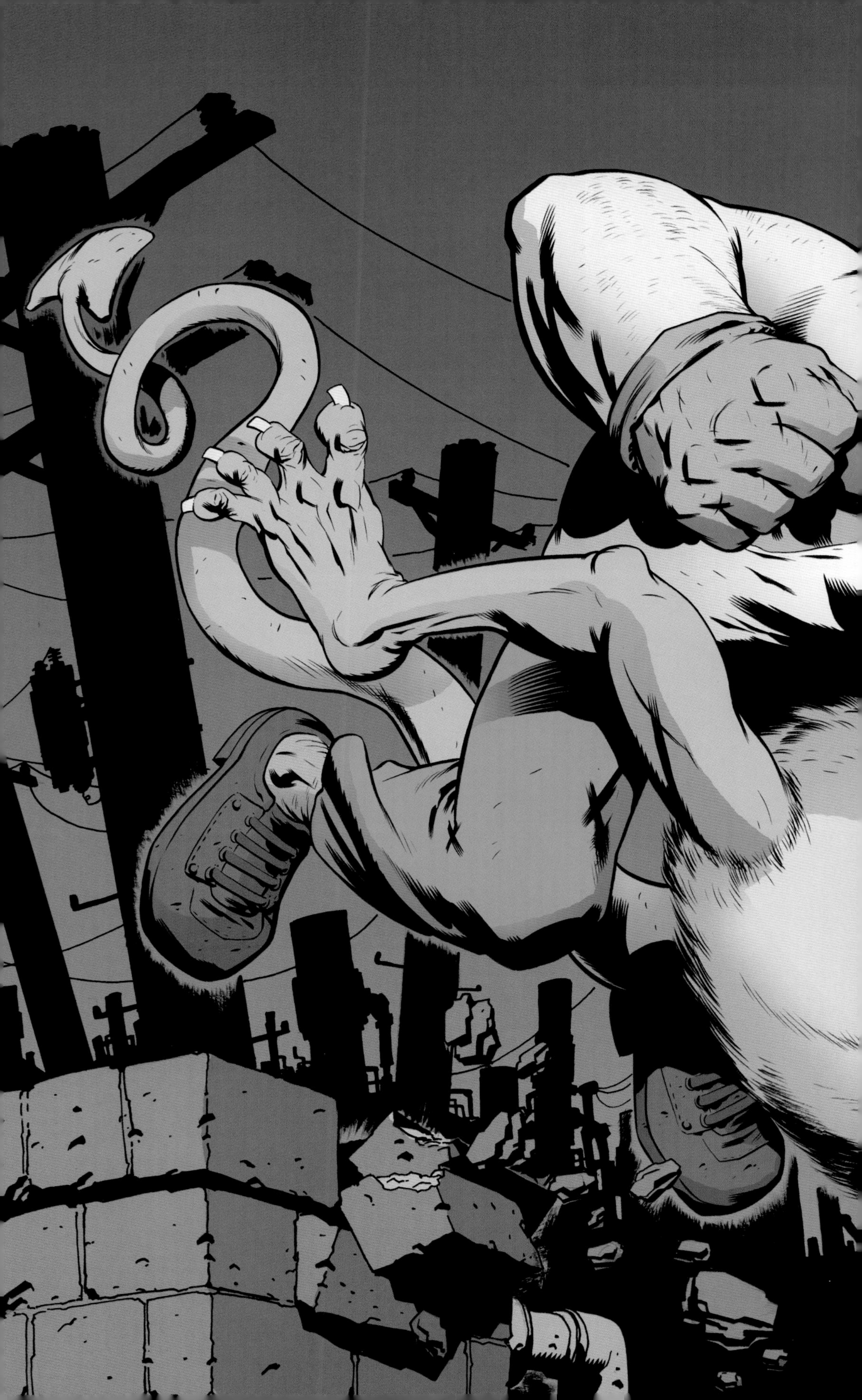

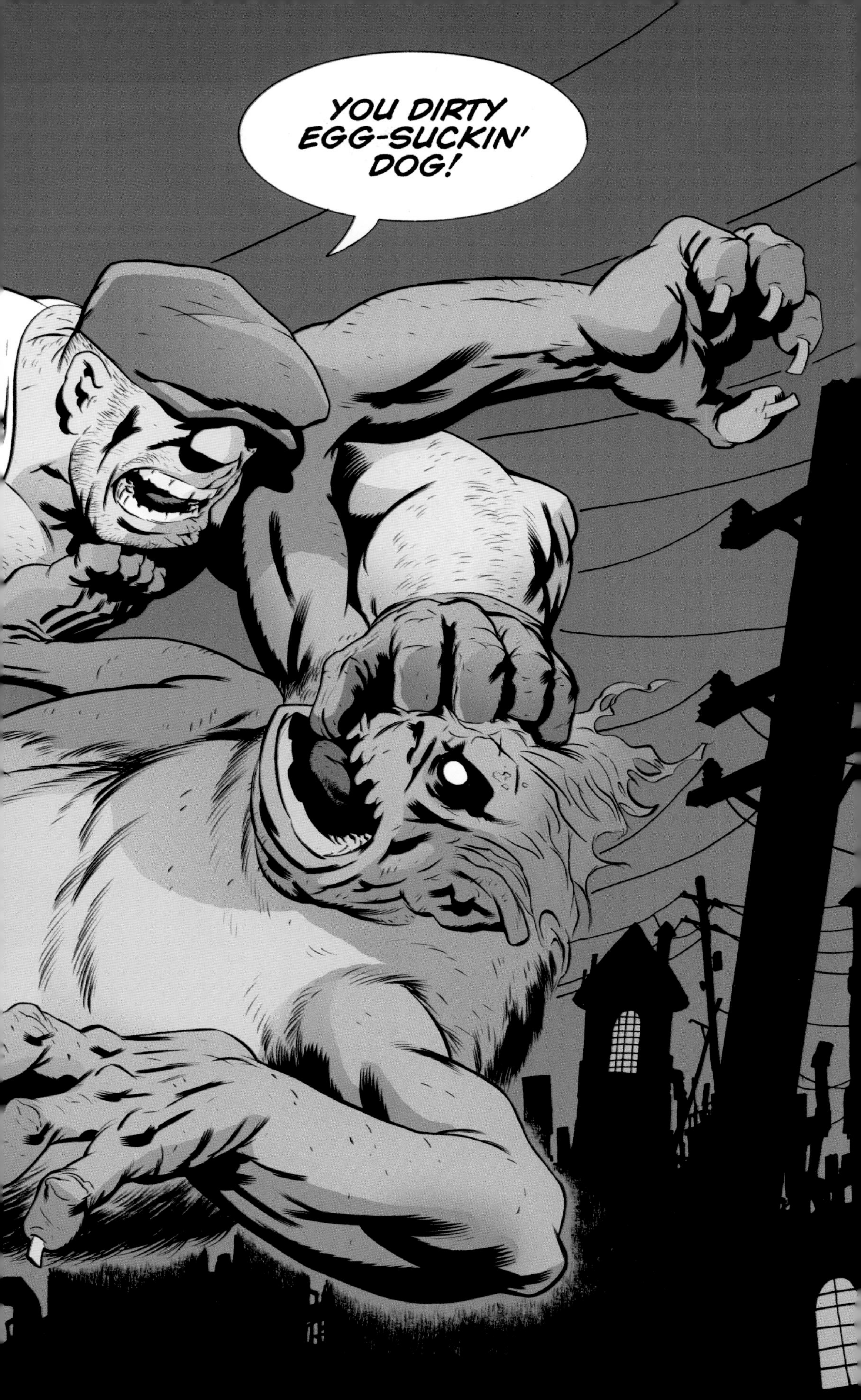
YOU DIRTY EGG-SUCKIN' DOG!

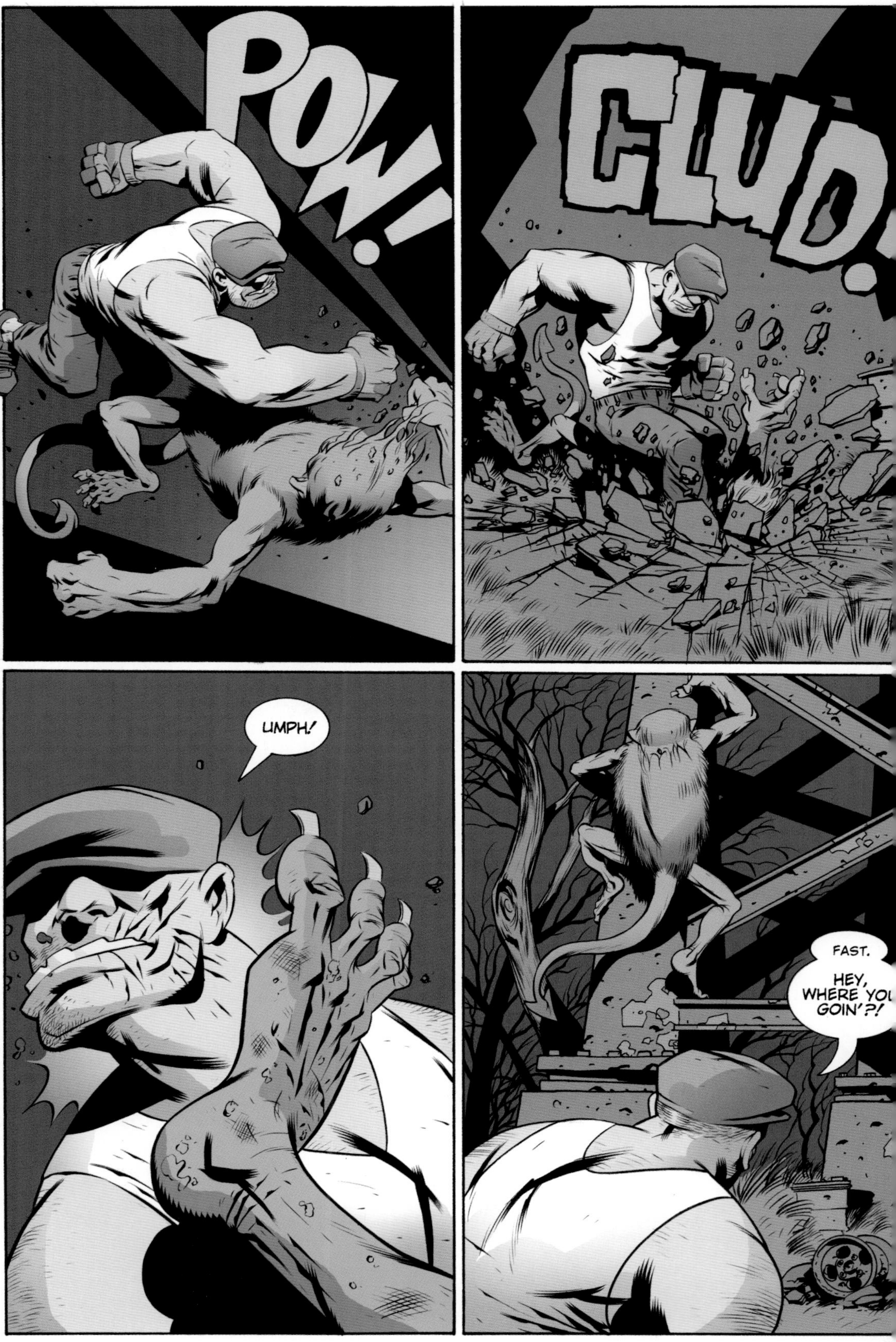
POW!
CLUD
UMPH!
FAST.
HEY, WHERE YOU GOIN'?!

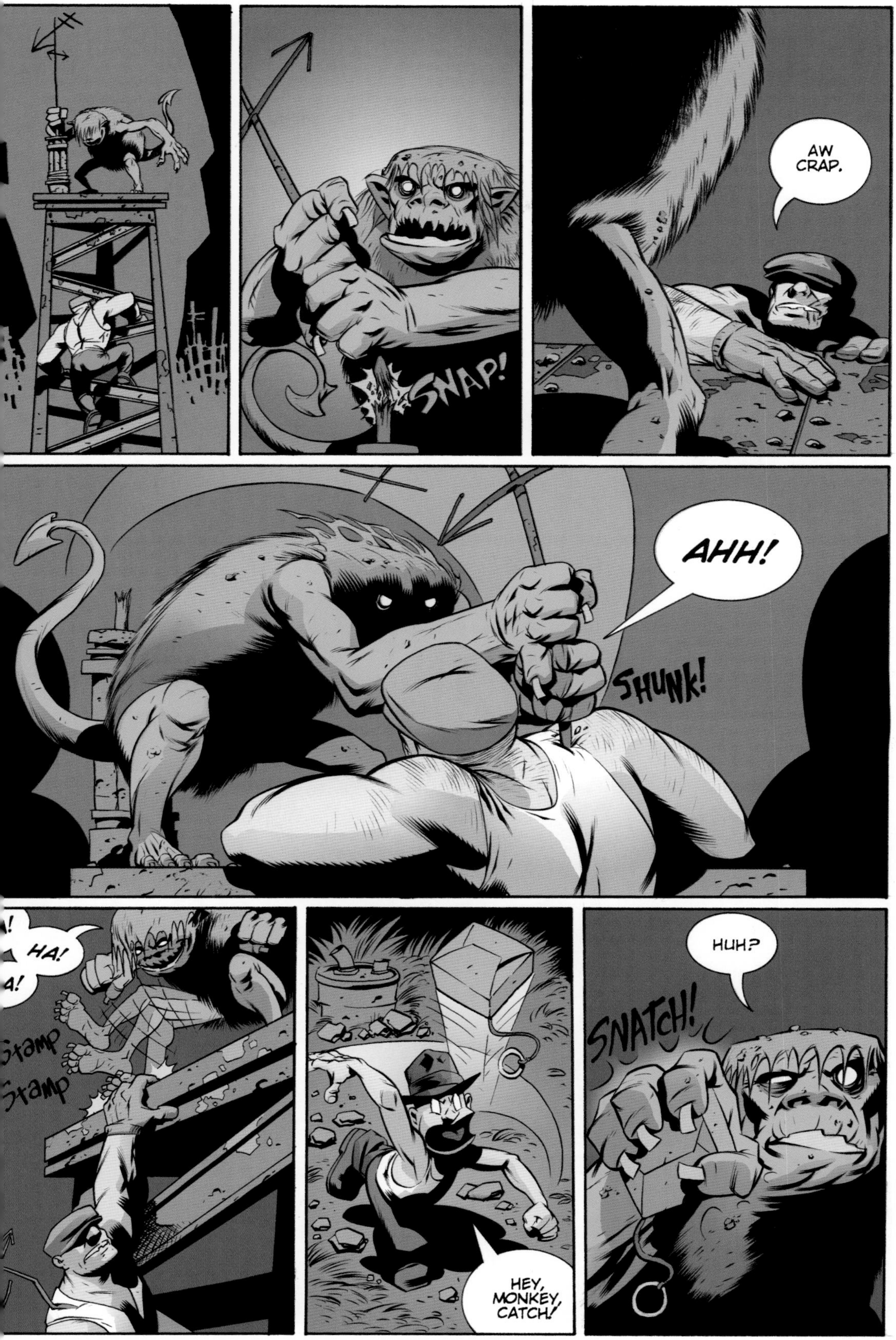
SNAP!
AW CRAP.
AHH!
SHUNK!
HA!
Stamp
Stamp
HEY, MONKEY, CATCH!
HUH?
SNATCH!

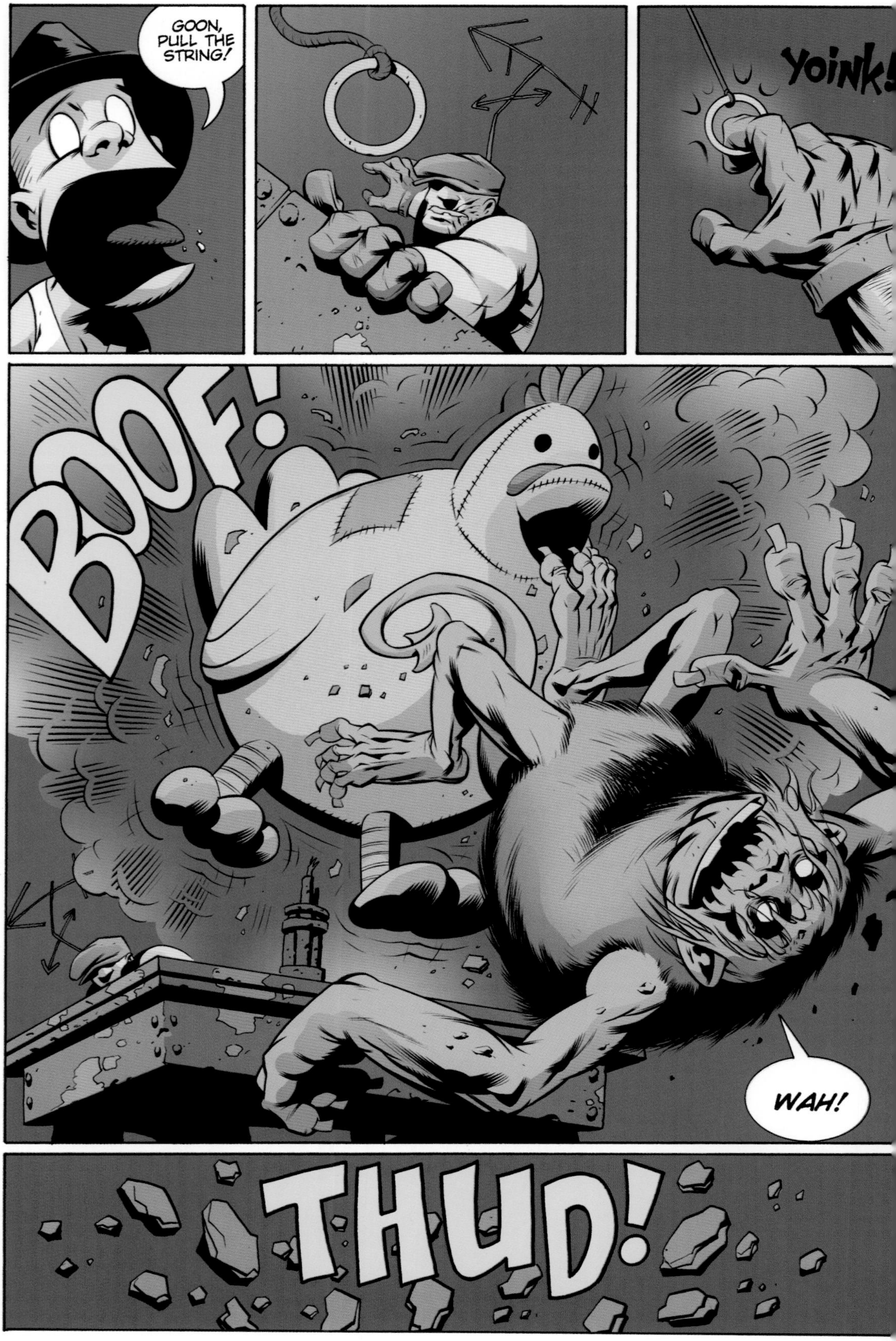
GOON, PULL THE STRING!
YOINK!
BOOF!
WAH!
THUD!

WELL, LOOKS LIKE FRANKY'S QUICK THINKIN' SAVES THE DAY AGAIN!

THUMP!

DON'T OWN 'N INFLATABLE CHICKEN?!

OH, SHUT UP!

WHEN YER DONE ULKIN' OVER THERE BOUT YER BLOW-UP OULTRY, HOW ABOUT ULLIN' THIS FRICKIN' ANTENNA OUTTA MY BACK!

SO, WHATTA WE GONNA DO ABOUT THIS LABRAZIO THING?

NUTHIN'.

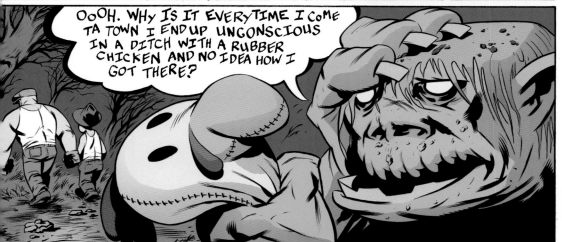

OOOH. WHY IS IT EVERYTIME I COME TA TOWN I END UP UNGONSCIOUS IN A DITCH WITH A RUBBER CHICKEN AND NO IDEA HOW I GOT THERE?

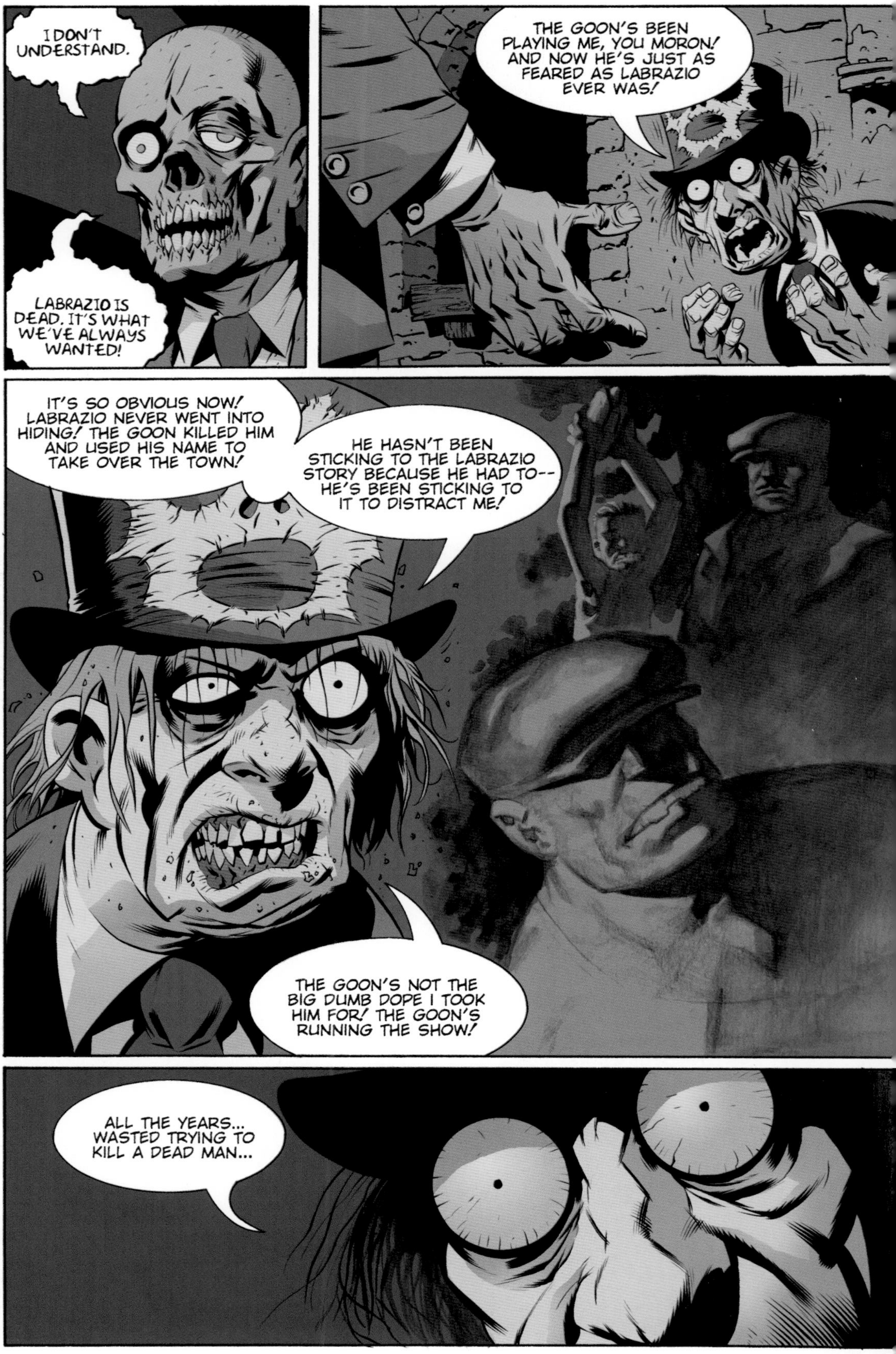
I DON'T UNDERSTAND.
LABRAZIO IS DEAD. IT'S WHAT WE'VE ALWAYS WANTED!
THE GOON'S BEEN PLAYING ME, YOU MORON! AND NOW HE'S JUST AS FEARED AS LABRAZIO EVER WAS!
IT'S SO OBVIOUS NOW! LABRAZIO NEVER WENT INTO HIDING! THE GOON KILLED HIM AND USED HIS NAME TO TAKE OVER THE TOWN!
HE HASN'T BEEN STICKING TO THE LABRAZIO STORY BECAUSE HE HAD TO-- HE'S BEEN STICKING TO IT TO DISTRACT ME!
THE GOON'S NOT THE BIG DUMB DOPE I TOOK HIM FOR! THE GOON'S RUNNING THE SHOW!
ALL THE YEARS... WASTED TRYING TO KILL A DEAD MAN...

MEGA BODY PILL!

OVER SIX HUNDRED BILLION UNITS SOLD IN KENTUCKY ALONE!

EGA BODY PILL!
NO EXERCISE...
NO DIET...
NO PROBLEM!

WHAT YOU WANT AND STILL
K GREAT IN A BATHING SUIT!

A METABOCORP PRODUCT

MEGA BODY

"I USED TO EAT RIGHT AND EXERCISE LIKE A SUCKER, BUT THANKS TO THE MEGA BODY PILL BY METABOCORP, I DO NOTHING BUT SIT ON MY BUTT ALL DAY EATING BACON AND ICE CREAM!"

TERRORISTS HATE THE MEGA BODY PILL!

THE NEW DIET DRUG TAKING AMERICA BY STORM!

WARNING!

SIDE EFFECTS INCLUDE NAUSEA, VOMITING, SWEATING, CHILLS, SORE THROAT, HAIR LOSS, TOOTH DECAY, UNCONTROLLABLE MOOD SWING, CRAMPS, BLINDNESS, MISCARRIAGE, RASH, HEART DISEASE, PNEUMONIA, RECTAL BLEEDING, DEPRESSION, BACK SPASMS, CANCER, IMPOTENCY, RETARDATION, HEARING LOSS, UNCONTROLLABLE FLATULENCE, DRY MOUTH, LIVER DISEASE, LOSS OF PRIMARY MOTOR SKILLS, DIABETES, DIARRHEA, HIVES, KIDNEY FAILURE, EPILEPSY, HEMORRHOIDS, LOSS OF MEMORY, LEUKEMIA, TESTICULAR HEMORRHAGE, MOUTH SORES, BONE-DENSITY LOSS, KIDNEY STONES, FOAMING AT THE MOUTH, HYPERTENSION, CONSTIPATION, GALLSTONES, ULCERS, SLURRED SPEECH, AND LOSS OF APPETITE.

CHAPTER 3

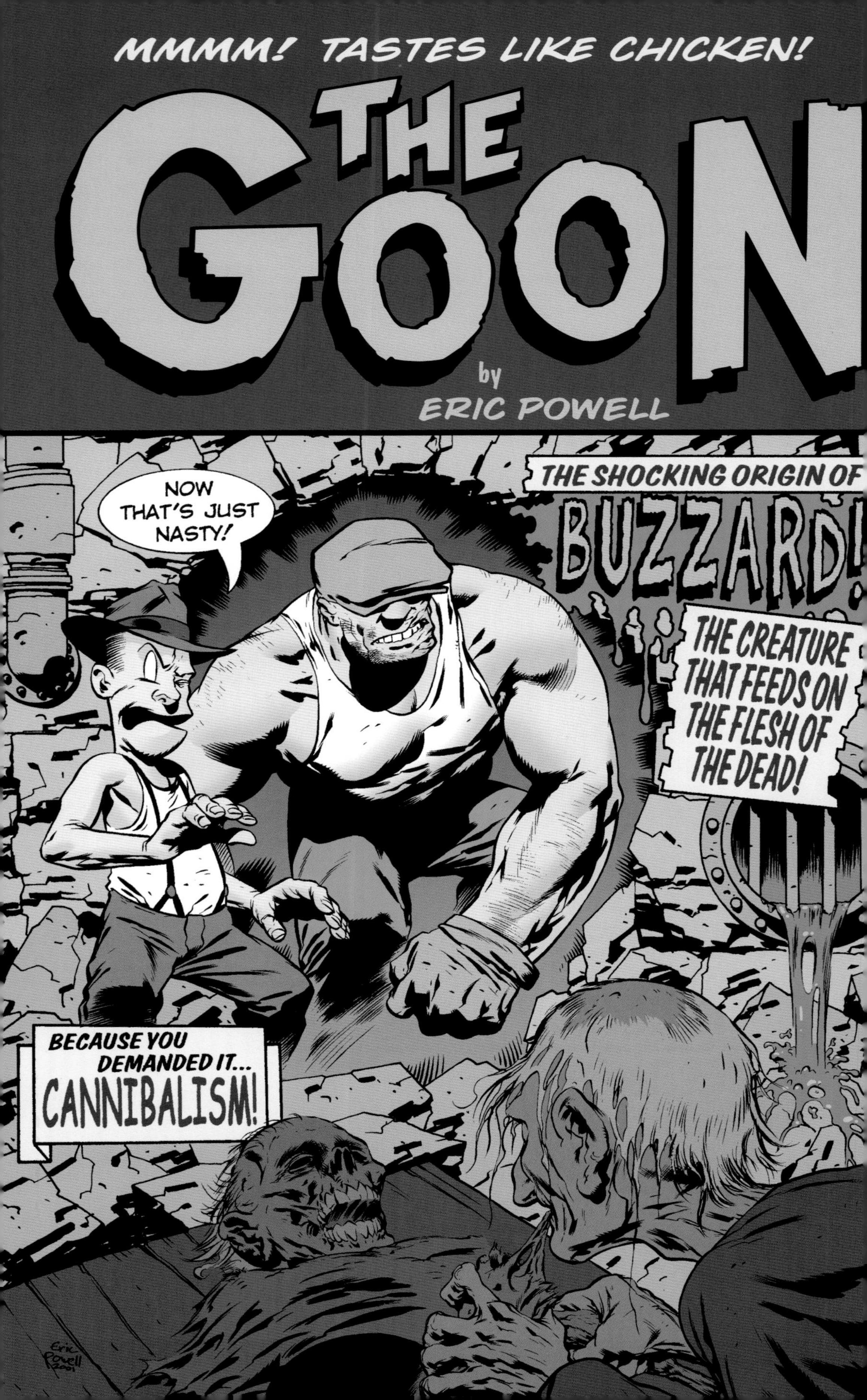

MMMM! TASTES LIKE CHICKEN!
THE GOON
by
ERIC POWELL
NOW THAT'S JUST NASTY!
THE SHOCKING ORIGIN OF
BUZZARD!
THE CREATURE THAT FEEDS ON THE FLESH OF THE DEAD!
BECAUSE YOU DEMANDED IT...
CANNIBALISM!

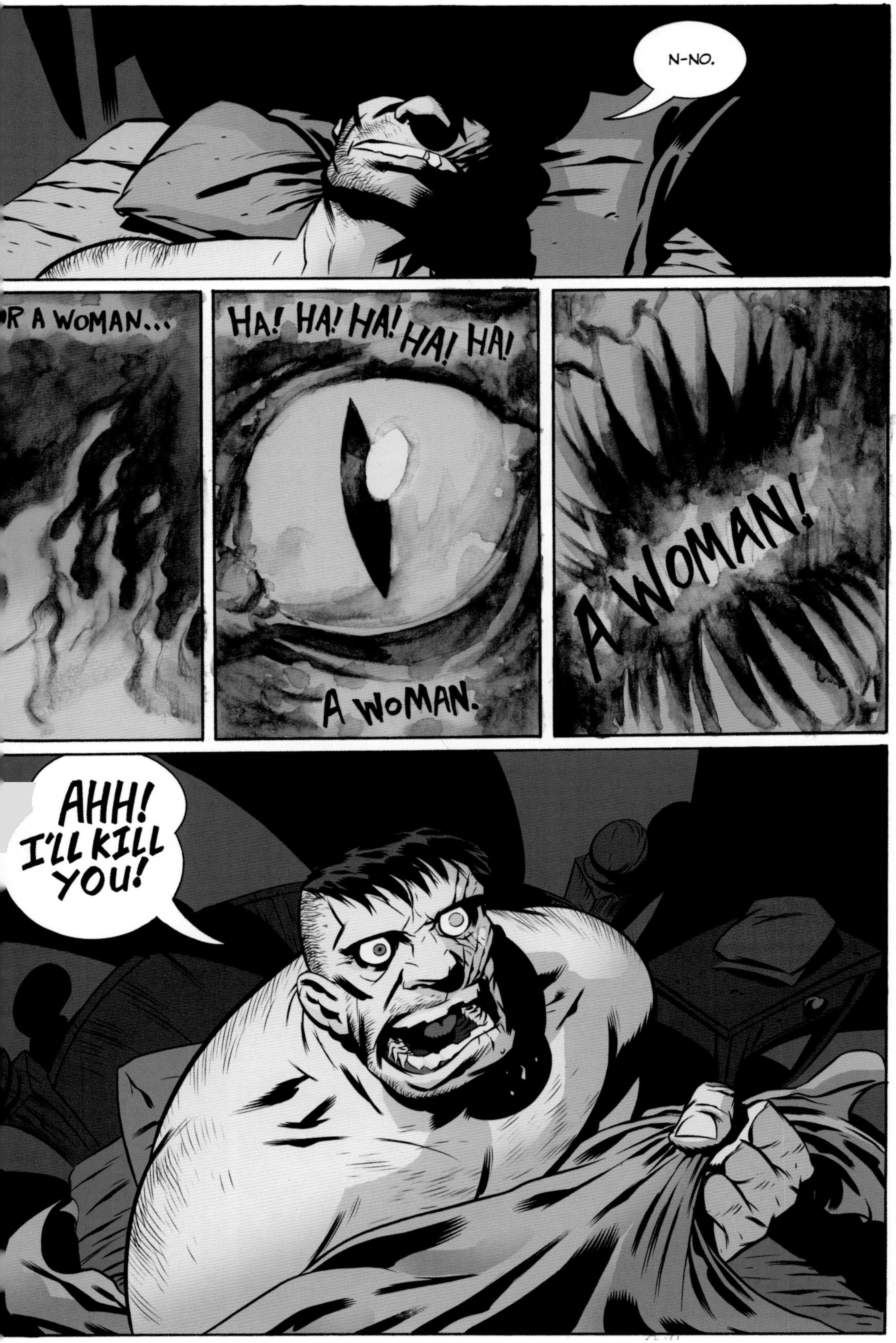
N-NO.
OR A WOMAN...
HA! HA! HA! HA! HA!
A WOMAN.
A WOMAN!
AHH! I'LL KILL YOU!

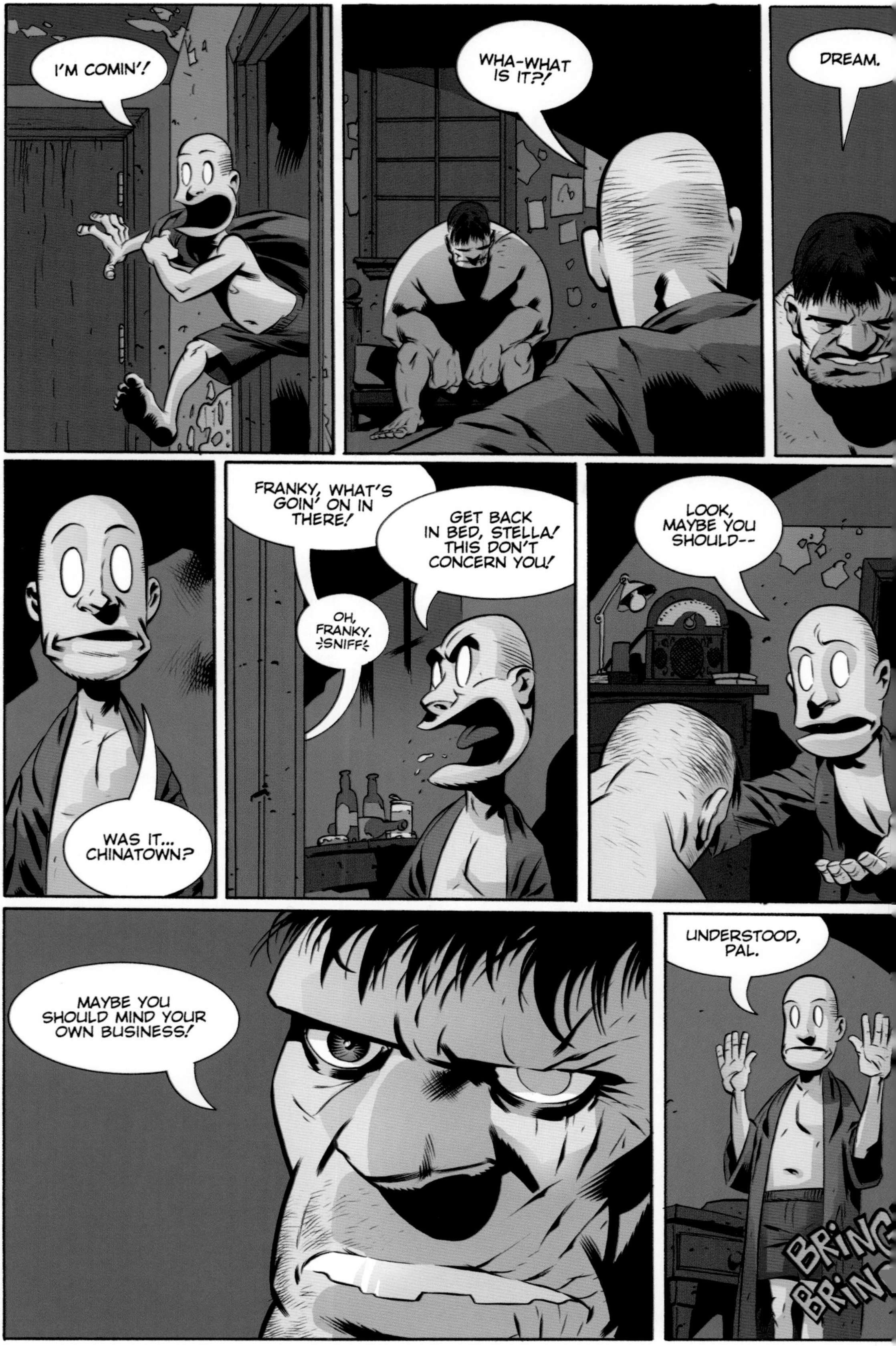
I'M COMIN'!
WHA-WHAT IS IT?!
DREAM.
WAS IT... CHINATOWN?
FRANKY, WHAT'S GOIN' ON IN THERE!
OH, FRANKY. -SNIFF-
GET BACK IN BED, STELLA! THIS DON'T CONCERN YOU!
LOOK, MAYBE YOU SHOULD--
MAYBE YOU SHOULD MIND YOUR OWN BUSINESS!
UNDERSTOOD, PAL.

YEAH, WHATTA YA WANT?!

HEY, GOON, MILO SAYS HE JUST SWIPED A TRUCK FULL OF MEXICAN PORN... WANTS TO KNOW IF WE CAN TAKE IT OFF HIS HANDS.

LET'S GO.

-L GIVE
U FIFTY
CKS FOR
E TRUCK.

BUT YOU GOTTA SEE THIS, GOON! ALL YOU GOTTA DO IS PARK THIS OUTSIDE A SCHOOL OR CHURCH AND THE MERCHANDISE WILL BE GONE IN AN HOUR! THOSE KIDS AND REPRESSED TYPES GO FOR THIS KINDA STUFF!

I'LL GIVE YOU FORTY BUCKS FOR THE TRUCK.

YOU JUST SAID YOU'D GIVE ME FIFTY!

I GOTTA COMPENSATE FOR MY TIME YER WASTIN' RUNNING YER MOUTH. KEEP YER MERCHANDISE... I'LL GIVE YOU THIRTY BUCKS FOR THE TRUCK.

NOW JUST HOLD ON A MINUTE, GOON! BEFORE YOU MAKE UP YOUR MIND, TAKE A LOOK AT THIS STUFF. YOU WON'T BELIEVE IT.

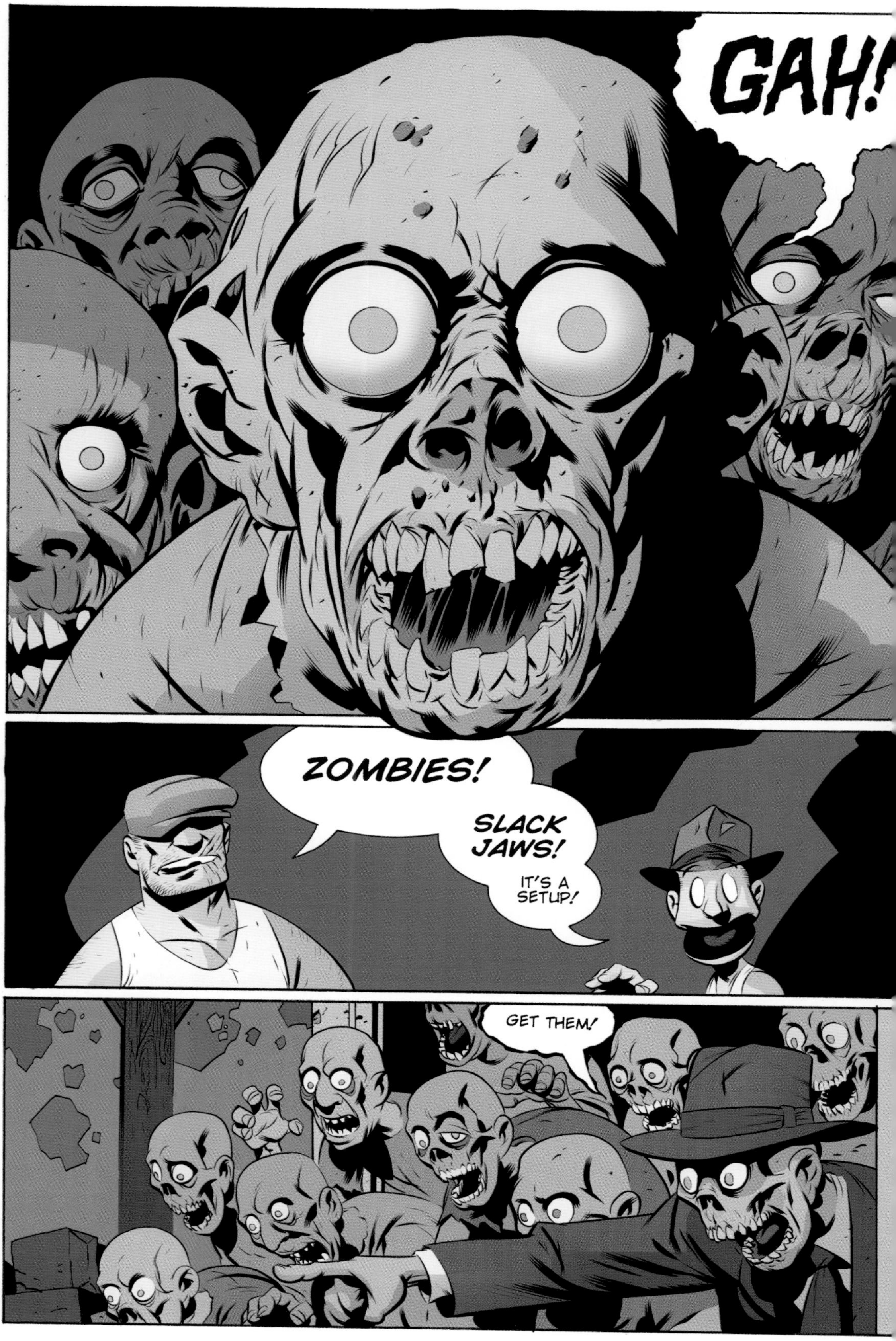
GAH!
ZOMBIES!
SLACK JAWS!
IT'S A SETUP!
GET THEM!

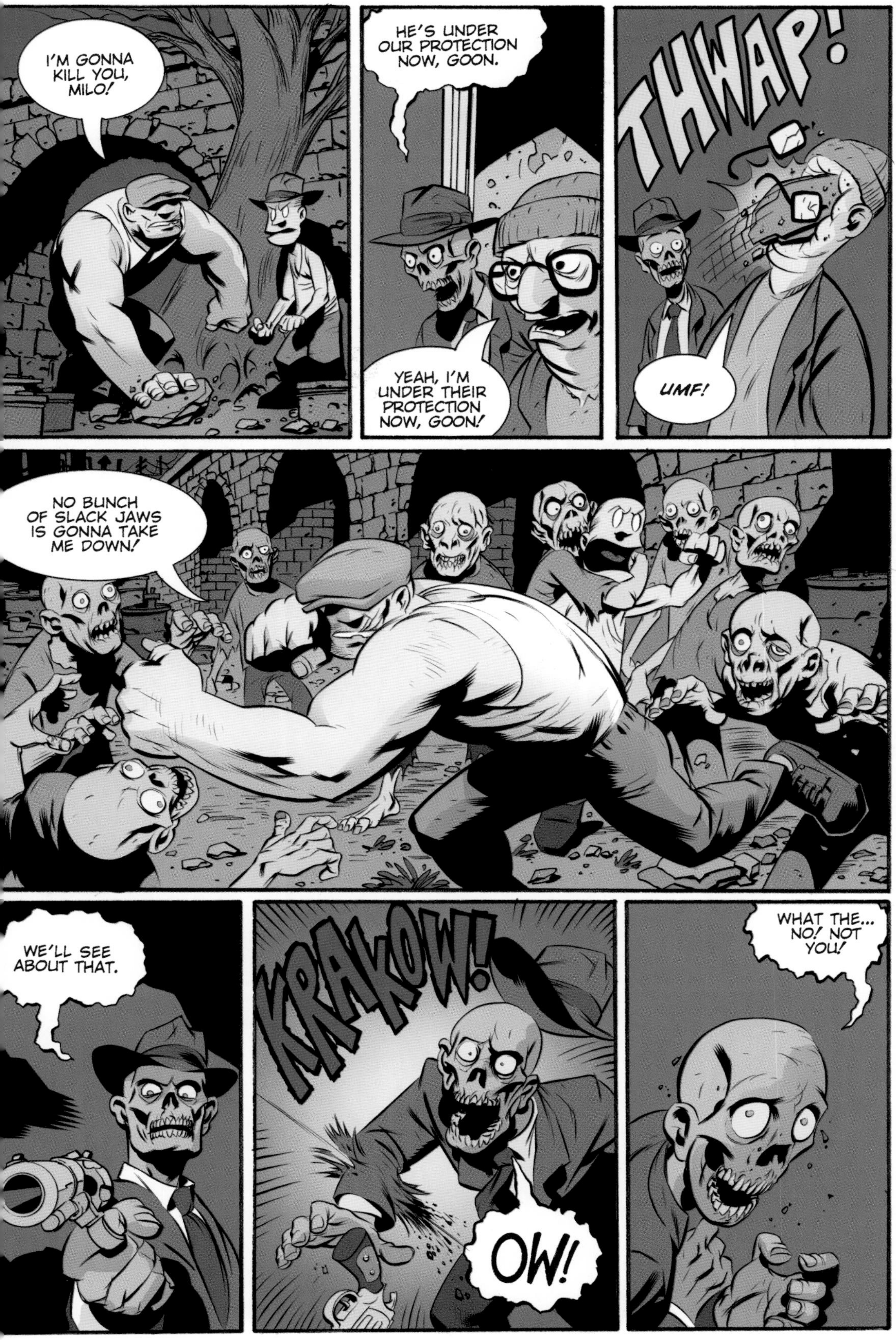
I'M GONNA KILL YOU, MILO!
HE'S UNDER OUR PROTECTION NOW, GOON.
YEAH, I'M UNDER THEIR PROTECTION NOW, GOON!
THWAP!
UMF!
NO BUNCH OF SLACK JAWS IS GONNA TAKE ME DOWN!
WE'LL SEE ABOUT THAT.
KRAKOW!
OW!
WHAT THE... NO! NOT YOU!

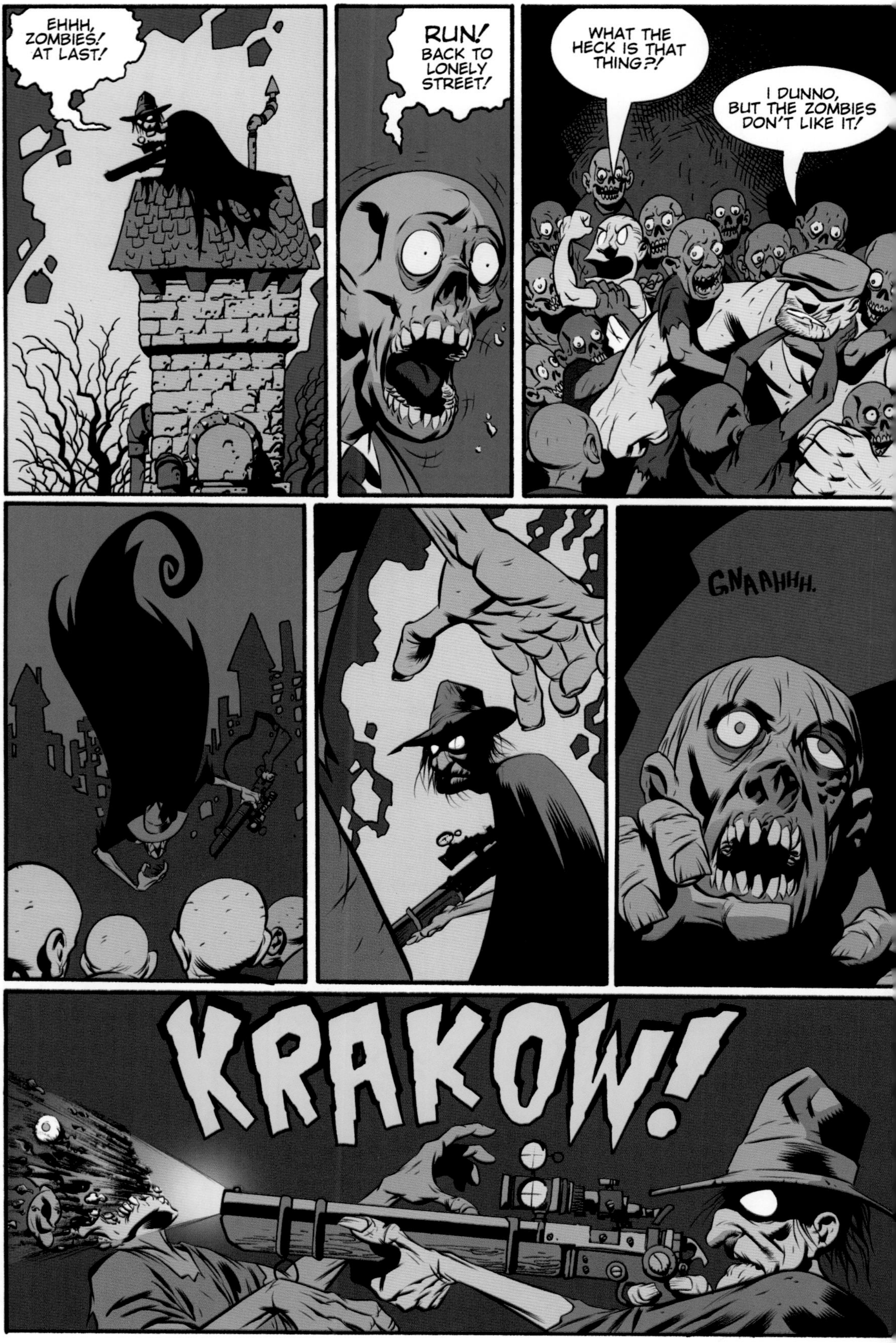
EHHH, ZOMBIES! AT LAST!
RUN! BACK TO LONELY STREET!
WHAT THE HECK IS THAT THING?!
I DUNNO, BUT THE ZOMBIES DON'T LIKE IT!
GNAAHHH.
KRAKOW!

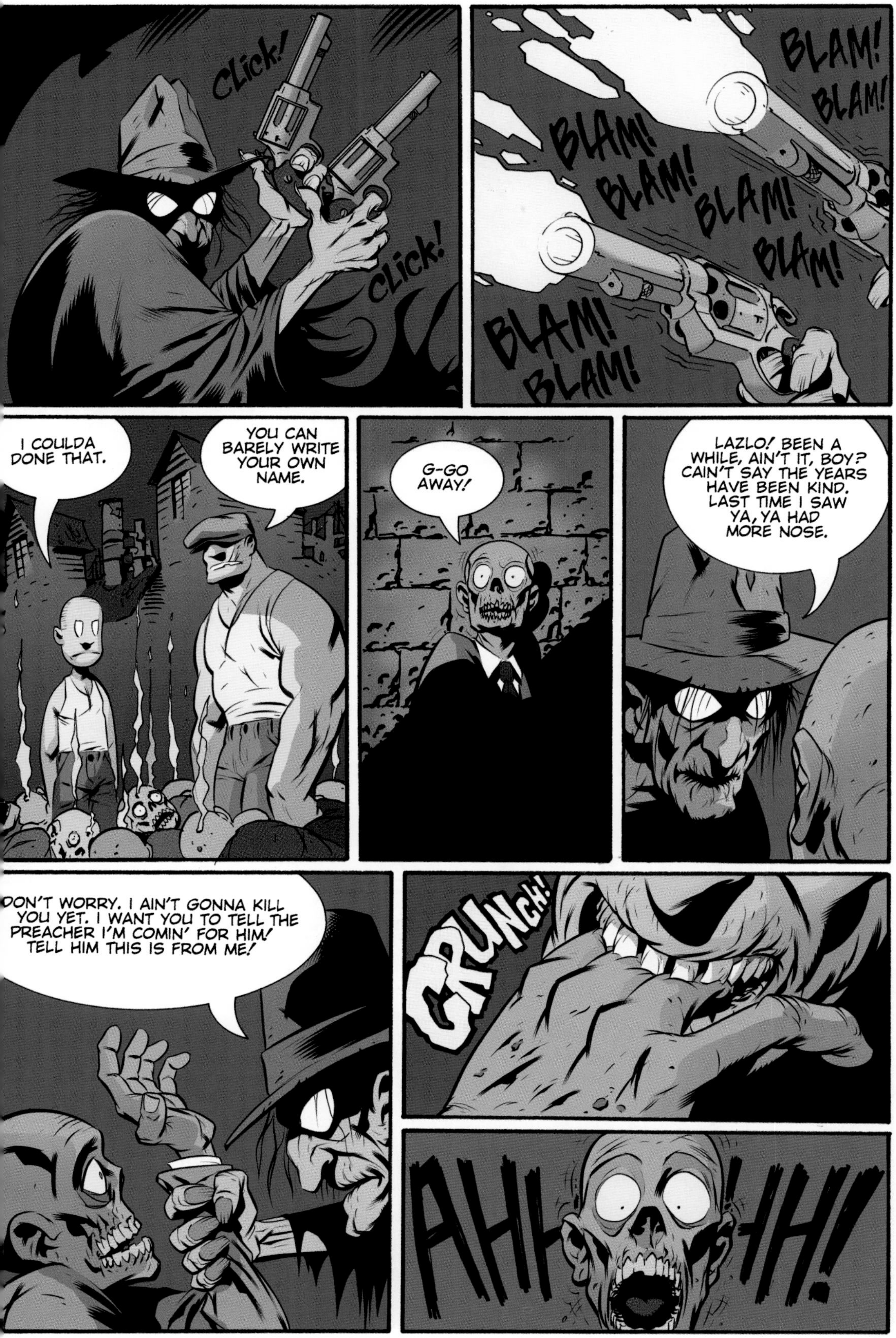
CLICK!
CLICK!
BLAM!
BLAM!
BLAM!
BLAM!
BLAM!
BLAM!
BLAM!
BLAM!
I COULDA DONE THAT.
YOU CAN BARELY WRITE YOUR OWN NAME.
G-GO AWAY!
LAZLO! BEEN A WHILE, AIN'T IT, BOY? CAIN'T SAY THE YEARS HAVE BEEN KIND. LAST TIME I SAW YA, YA HAD MORE NOSE.
DON'T WORRY. I AIN'T GONNA KILL YOU YET. I WANT YOU TO TELL THE PREACHER I'M COMIN' FOR HIM! TELL HIM THIS IS FROM ME!
CRUNCH!
AHHHH!

I'VE BEEN SHOT AND MY FINGERS BITTEN OFF! MY FINGERS BITTEN OFF AND I'VE BEEN SHOT!

YOU TASTE LIKE CRAP, LAZLO!

PREACHER??

I THINK HE'S TALKIN' 'BOUT THE ZOMBIE PRIEST.

I KNEW THAT!

CRUNCH! CRUNCH!

EEEH, A LIVE 'UN!

NAAH.

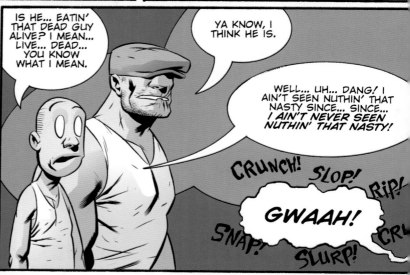

IS HE... EATIN' THAT DEAD GUY ALIVE? I MEAN... LIVE... DEAD... YOU KNOW WHAT I MEAN.

YA KNOW, I THINK HE IS.

WELL... UH... DANG! I AIN'T SEEN NUTHIN' THAT NASTY SINCE... SINCE... I AIN'T NEVER SEEN NUTHIN' THAT NASTY!

CRUNCH! SLOP! RIP!

GWAAH!

SNAP! CRU

SLURP!

HI THERE, ER, FELLA, EH, HA-HA, GOT A LITTLE INTESTINE HANGIN' OFF YER CHIN THERE. THANKS FOR HELPIN' US OUT WITH THOSE, UH, ZOMBIES.

DON'T MENTION IT. THE NAME'S... I DON'T RECKON I REMEMBER MY RIGHT NAME, BUT I REMEMBERS SOME FOLKS CALLS ME BUZZARD.

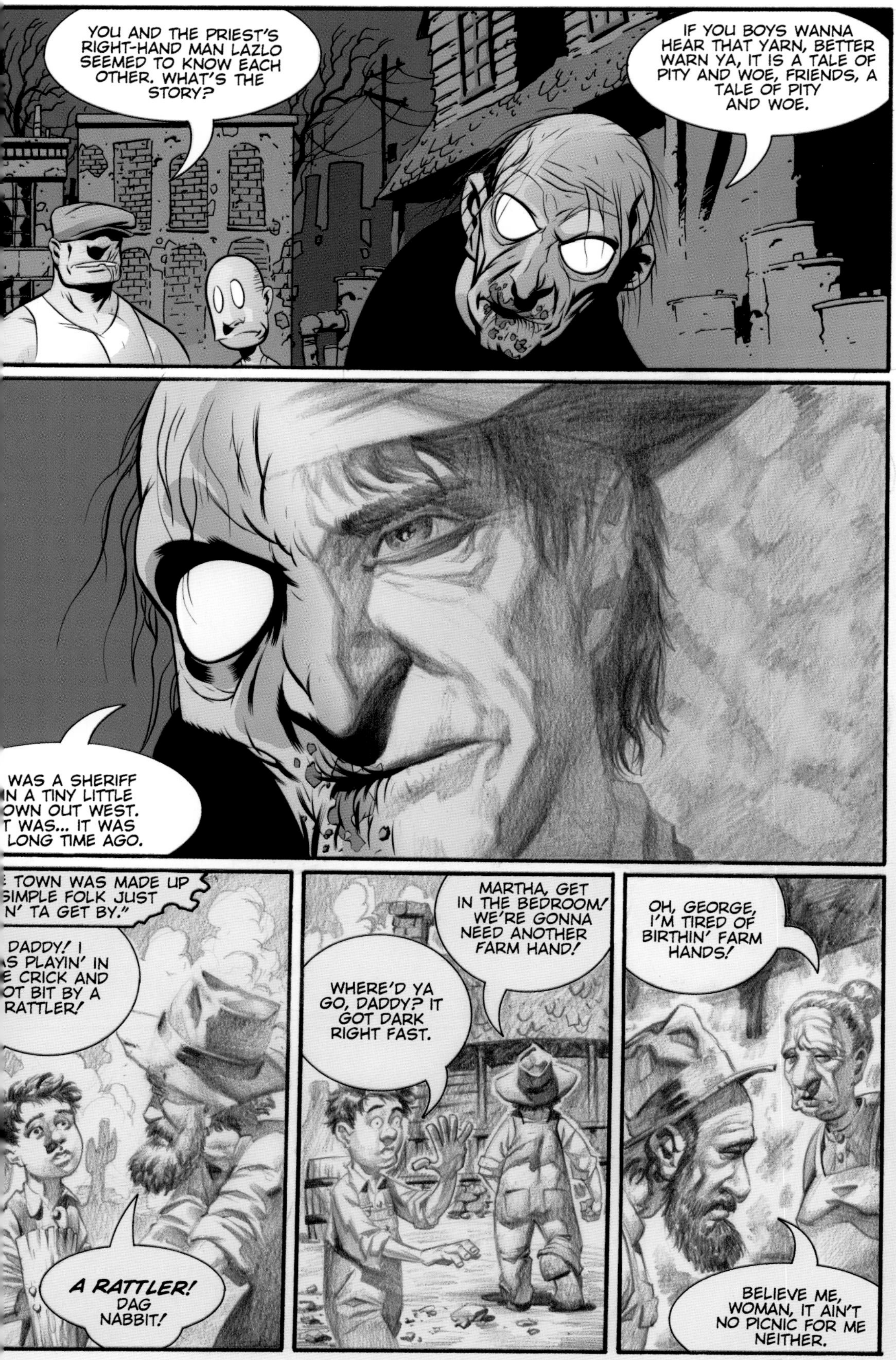
YOU AND THE PRIEST'S RIGHT-HAND MAN LAZLO SEEMED TO KNOW EACH OTHER. WHAT'S THE STORY?
IF YOU BOYS WANNA HEAR THAT YARN, BETTER WARN YA, IT IS A TALE OF PITY AND WOE, FRIENDS, A TALE OF PITY AND WOE.
WAS A SHERIFF N A TINY LITTLE OWN OUT WEST. T WAS... IT WAS LONG TIME AGO.
E TOWN WAS MADE UP SIMPLE FOLK JUST N' TA GET BY."
DADDY! I S PLAYIN' IN E CRICK AND OT BIT BY A RATTLER!
A RATTLER! DAG NABBIT!
MARTHA, GET IN THE BEDROOM! WE'RE GONNA NEED ANOTHER FARM HAND!
WHERE'D YA GO, DADDY? IT GOT DARK RIGHT FAST.
OH, GEORGE, I'M TIRED OF BIRTHIN' FARM HANDS!
BELIEVE ME, WOMAN, IT AIN'T NO PICNIC FOR ME NEITHER.

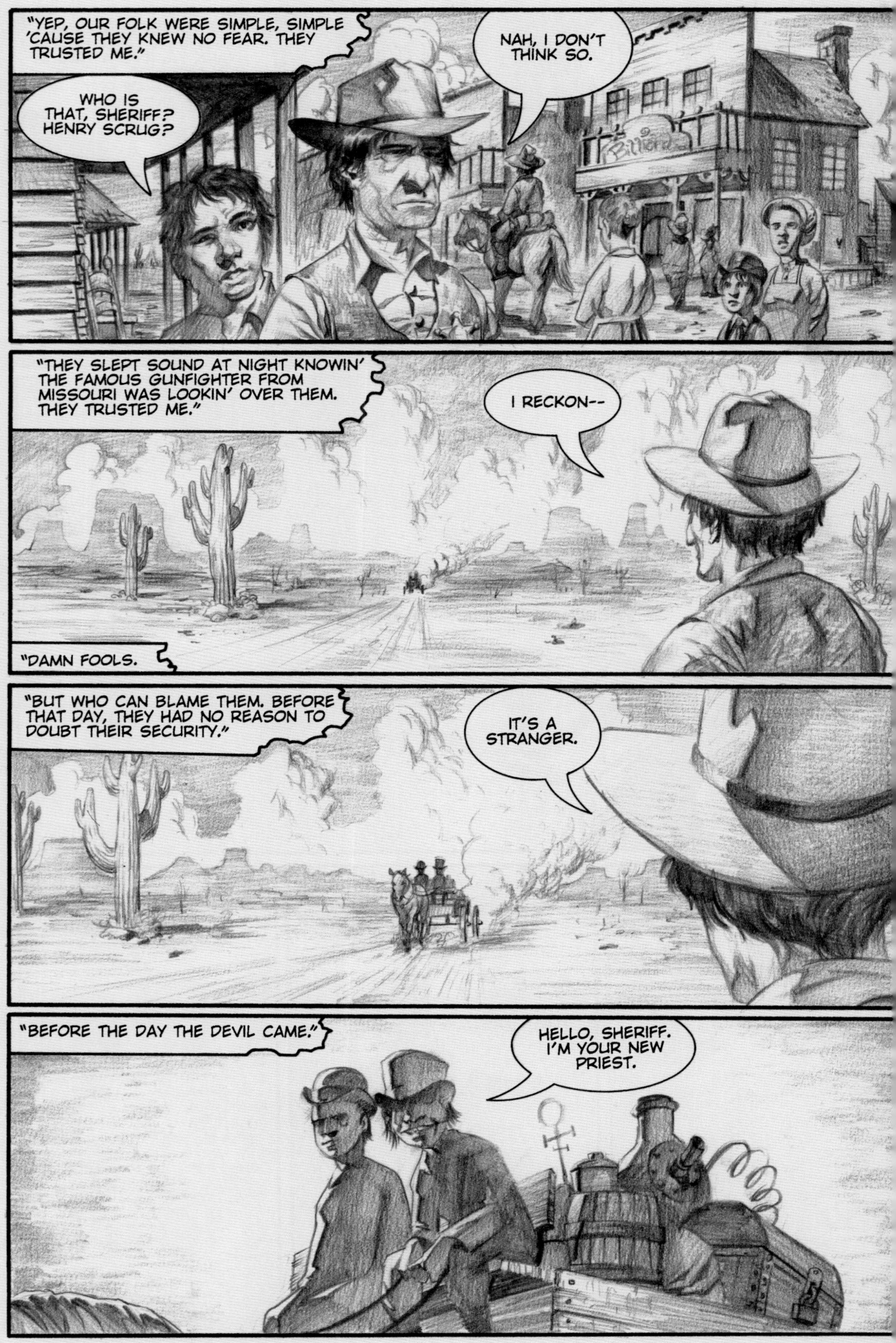
"YEP, OUR FOLK WERE SIMPLE, SIMPLE 'CAUSE THEY KNEW NO FEAR. THEY TRUSTED ME."
WHO IS THAT, SHERIFF? HENRY SCRUG?
NAH, I DON'T THINK SO.
"THEY SLEPT SOUND AT NIGHT KNOWIN' THE FAMOUS GUNFIGHTER FROM MISSOURI WAS LOOKIN' OVER THEM. THEY TRUSTED ME."
I RECKON--
"DAMN FOOLS.
"BUT WHO CAN BLAME THEM. BEFORE THAT DAY, THEY HAD NO REASON TO DOUBT THEIR SECURITY."
IT'S A STRANGER.
"BEFORE THE DAY THE DEVIL CAME."
HELLO, SHERIFF. I'M YOUR NEW PRIEST.

SORRY, FELLA, BUT WE AIN'T SENT FOR NO PREACHER.

OH, THE GOOD BROTHER LAZLO AND I ROAM WHERE THE WINDS BLOW US.

THAT'S SOME MIGHTY ODD GEAR FOR A PREACHER, AIN'T IT?

I'M ALSO A MEDICAL DOCTOR.

YEAH, WELL, WE ALREADY GOT A SAWBONES.

WE WON'T BE ANY BURDEN, GOOD SHERIFF. WE'LL JUST SET UP OUR TENT ON THE OUTSKIRTS, AND MOVE ON WHEN WE'RE FINISHED SPREADING THE GOOD WORD.

WELL, I RECKON THAT'D BE OKAY.

"THAT'S WHEN I KNEW SOMETHIN' WAS WRONG. THE CREEP THAT WENT UP MY SPINE WHEN I TOUCHED HIS SKIN... I WANTED TO CHUCK HIM RIGHT BACK IN THAT WAGON! IF ONLY I HAD."

FINE, FINE.

YOU GOT TWO WEEKS. THEN I WANT YOU OUTTA HERE!

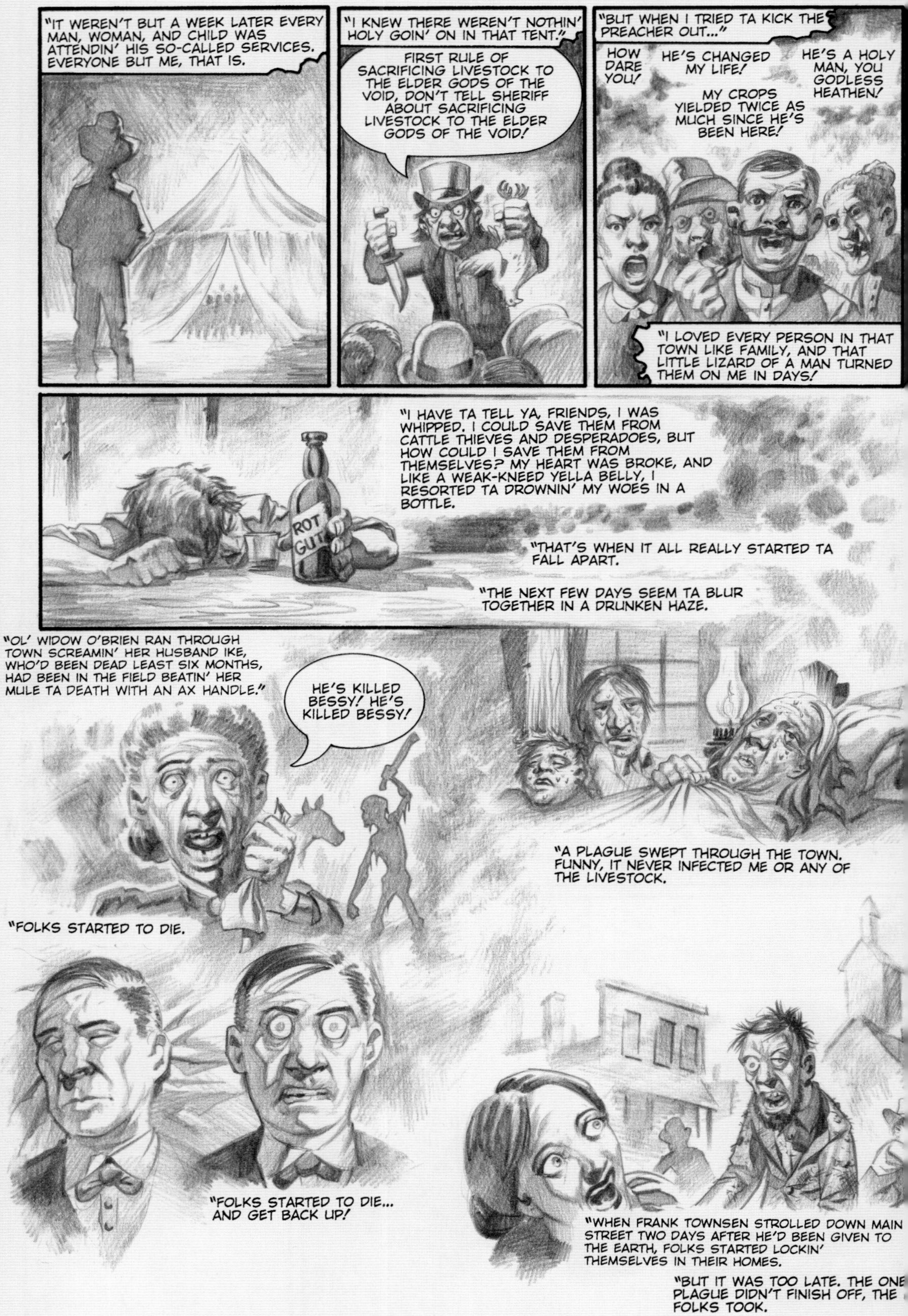
"IT WEREN'T BUT A WEEK LATER EVERY MAN, WOMAN, AND CHILD WAS ATTENDIN' HIS SO-CALLED SERVICES. EVERYONE BUT ME, THAT IS.
"I KNEW THERE WEREN'T NOTHIN' HOLY GOIN' ON IN THAT TENT."
FIRST RULE OF SACRIFICING LIVESTOCK TO THE ELDER GODS OF THE VOID, DON'T TELL SHERIFF ABOUT SACRIFICING LIVESTOCK TO THE ELDER GODS OF THE VOID!
"BUT WHEN I TRIED TA KICK THE PREACHER OUT..."
HOW DARE YOU!
HE'S CHANGED MY LIFE!
HE'S A HOLY MAN, YOU GODLESS HEATHEN!
MY CROPS YIELDED TWICE AS MUCH SINCE HE'S BEEN HERE!
"I LOVED EVERY PERSON IN THAT TOWN LIKE FAMILY, AND THAT LITTLE LIZARD OF A MAN TURNED THEM ON ME IN DAYS!
"I HAVE TA TELL YA, FRIENDS, I WAS WHIPPED. I COULD SAVE THEM FROM CATTLE THIEVES AND DESPERADOES, BUT HOW COULD I SAVE THEM FROM THEMSELVES? MY HEART WAS BROKE, AND LIKE A WEAK-KNEED YELLA BELLY, I RESORTED TA DROWNIN' MY WOES IN A BOTTLE.
ROT GUT
"THAT'S WHEN IT ALL REALLY STARTED TA FALL APART.
"THE NEXT FEW DAYS SEEM TA BLUR TOGETHER IN A DRUNKEN HAZE.
"OL' WIDOW O'BRIEN RAN THROUGH TOWN SCREAMIN' HER HUSBAND IKE, WHO'D BEEN DEAD LEAST SIX MONTHS, HAD BEEN IN THE FIELD BEATIN' HER MULE TA DEATH WITH AN AX HANDLE."
HE'S KILLED BESSY! HE'S KILLED BESSY!
"A PLAGUE SWEPT THROUGH THE TOWN. FUNNY, IT NEVER INFECTED ME OR ANY OF THE LIVESTOCK.
"FOLKS STARTED TO DIE.
"FOLKS STARTED TO DIE... AND GET BACK UP!
"WHEN FRANK TOWNSEN STROLLED DOWN MAIN STREET TWO DAYS AFTER HE'D BEEN GIVEN TO THE EARTH, FOLKS STARTED LOCKIN' THEMSELVES IN THEIR HOMES.
"BUT IT WAS TOO LATE. THE ONE PLAGUE DIDN'T FINISH OFF, THE FOLKS TOOK.

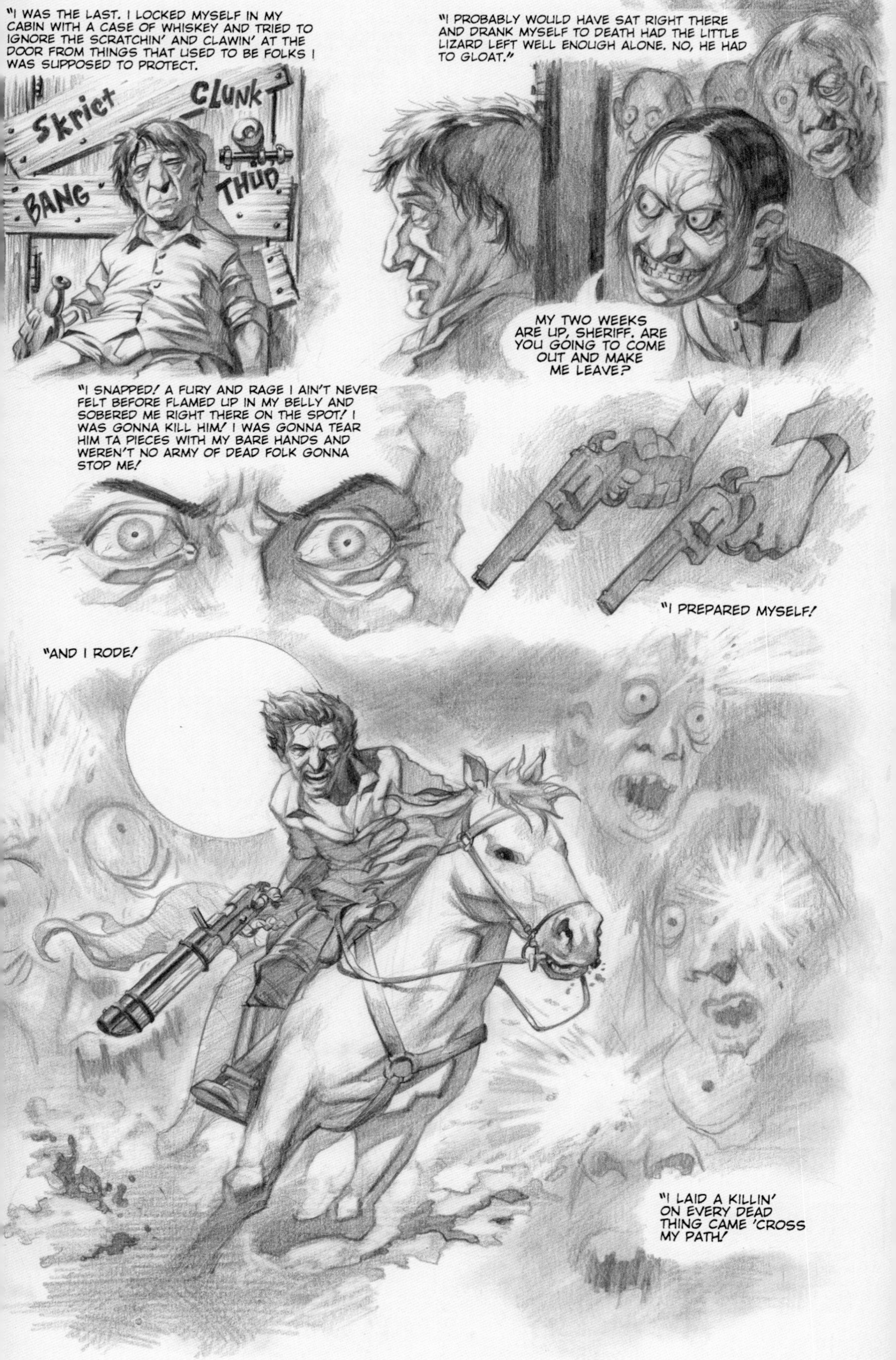
"I WAS THE LAST. I LOCKED MYSELF IN MY CABIN WITH A CASE OF WHISKEY AND TRIED TO IGNORE THE SCRATCHIN' AND CLAWIN' AT THE DOOR FROM THINGS THAT USED TO BE FOLKS I WAS SUPPOSED TO PROTECT.
Skrict
CLUNK
BANG
THUD
"I PROBABLY WOULD HAVE SAT RIGHT THERE AND DRANK MYSELF TO DEATH HAD THE LITTLE LIZARD LEFT WELL ENOUGH ALONE. NO, HE HAD TO GLOAT."
MY TWO WEEKS ARE UP, SHERIFF. ARE YOU GOING TO COME OUT AND MAKE ME LEAVE?
"I SNAPPED! A FURY AND RAGE I AIN'T NEVER FELT BEFORE FLAMED UP IN MY BELLY AND SOBERED ME RIGHT THERE ON THE SPOT! I WAS GONNA KILL HIM! I WAS GONNA TEAR HIM TA PIECES WITH MY BARE HANDS AND WEREN'T NO ARMY OF DEAD FOLK GONNA STOP ME!
"I PREPARED MYSELF!
"AND I RODE!
"I LAID A KILLIN' ON EVERY DEAD THING CAME 'CROSS MY PATH!

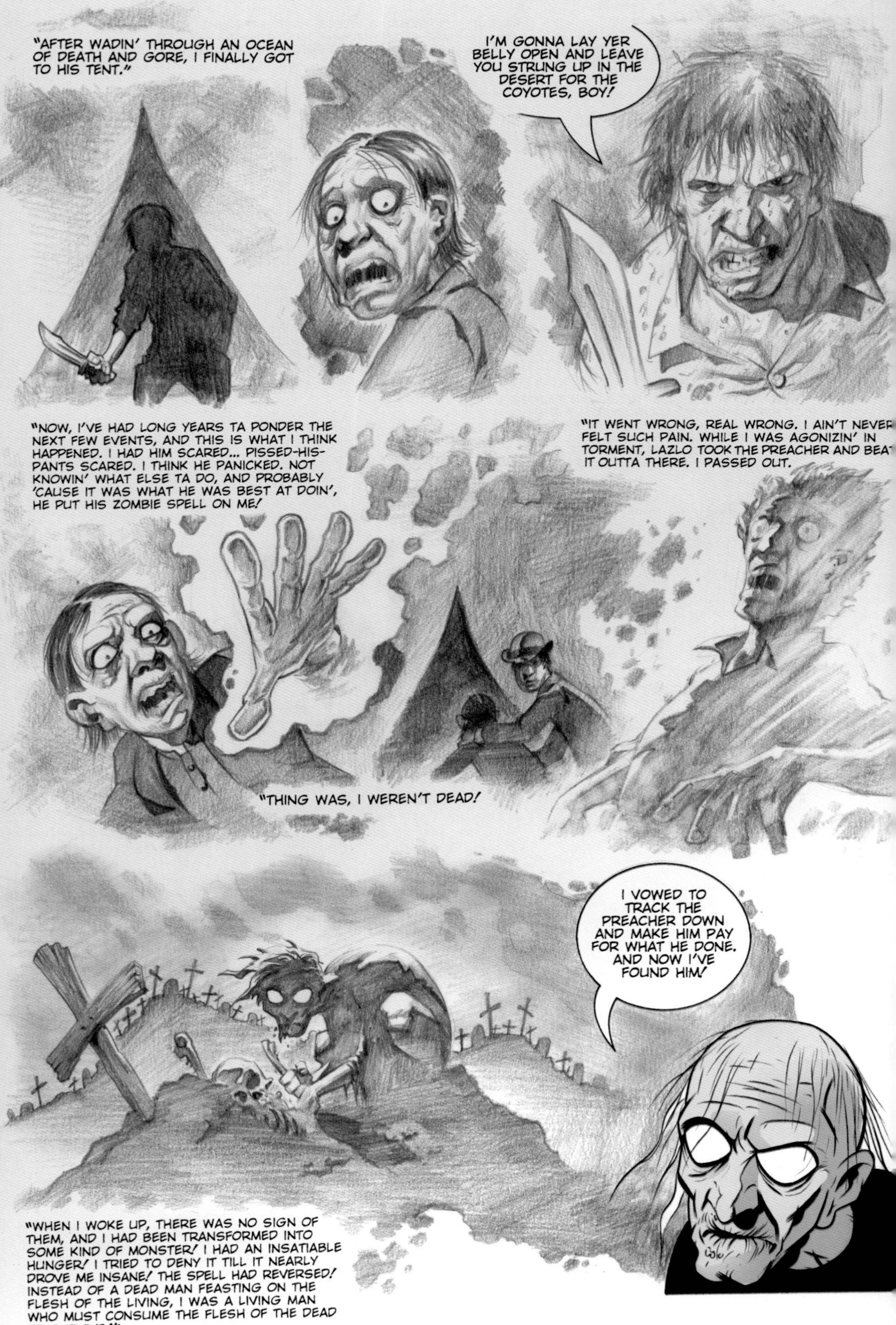
"AFTER WADIN' THROUGH AN OCEAN OF DEATH AND GORE, I FINALLY GOT TO HIS TENT."
I'M GONNA LAY YER BELLY OPEN AND LEAVE YOU STRUNG UP IN THE DESERT FOR THE COYOTES, BOY!
"NOW, I'VE HAD LONG YEARS TA PONDER THE NEXT FEW EVENTS, AND THIS IS WHAT I THINK HAPPENED. I HAD HIM SCARED... PISSED-HIS-PANTS SCARED. I THINK HE PANICKED. NOT KNOWIN' WHAT ELSE TA DO, AND PROBABLY 'CAUSE IT WAS WHAT HE WAS BEST AT DOIN', HE PUT HIS ZOMBIE SPELL ON ME!
"THING WAS, I WEREN'T DEAD!
"IT WENT WRONG, REAL WRONG. I AIN'T NEVER FELT SUCH PAIN. WHILE I WAS AGONIZIN' IN TORMENT, LAZLO TOOK THE PREACHER AND BEAT IT OUTTA THERE. I PASSED OUT.
"WHEN I WOKE UP, THERE WAS NO SIGN OF THEM, AND I HAD BEEN TRANSFORMED INTO SOME KIND OF MONSTER! I HAD AN INSATIABLE HUNGER! I TRIED TO DENY IT TILL IT NEARLY DROVE ME INSANE! THE SPELL HAD REVERSED! INSTEAD OF A DEAD MAN FEASTING ON THE FLESH OF THE LIVING, I WAS A LIVING MAN WHO MUST CONSUME THE FLESH OF THE DEAD TO SURVIVE!"
I VOWED TO TRACK THE PREACHER DOWN AND MAKE HIM PAY FOR WHAT HE DONE. AND NOW I'VE FOUND HIM!

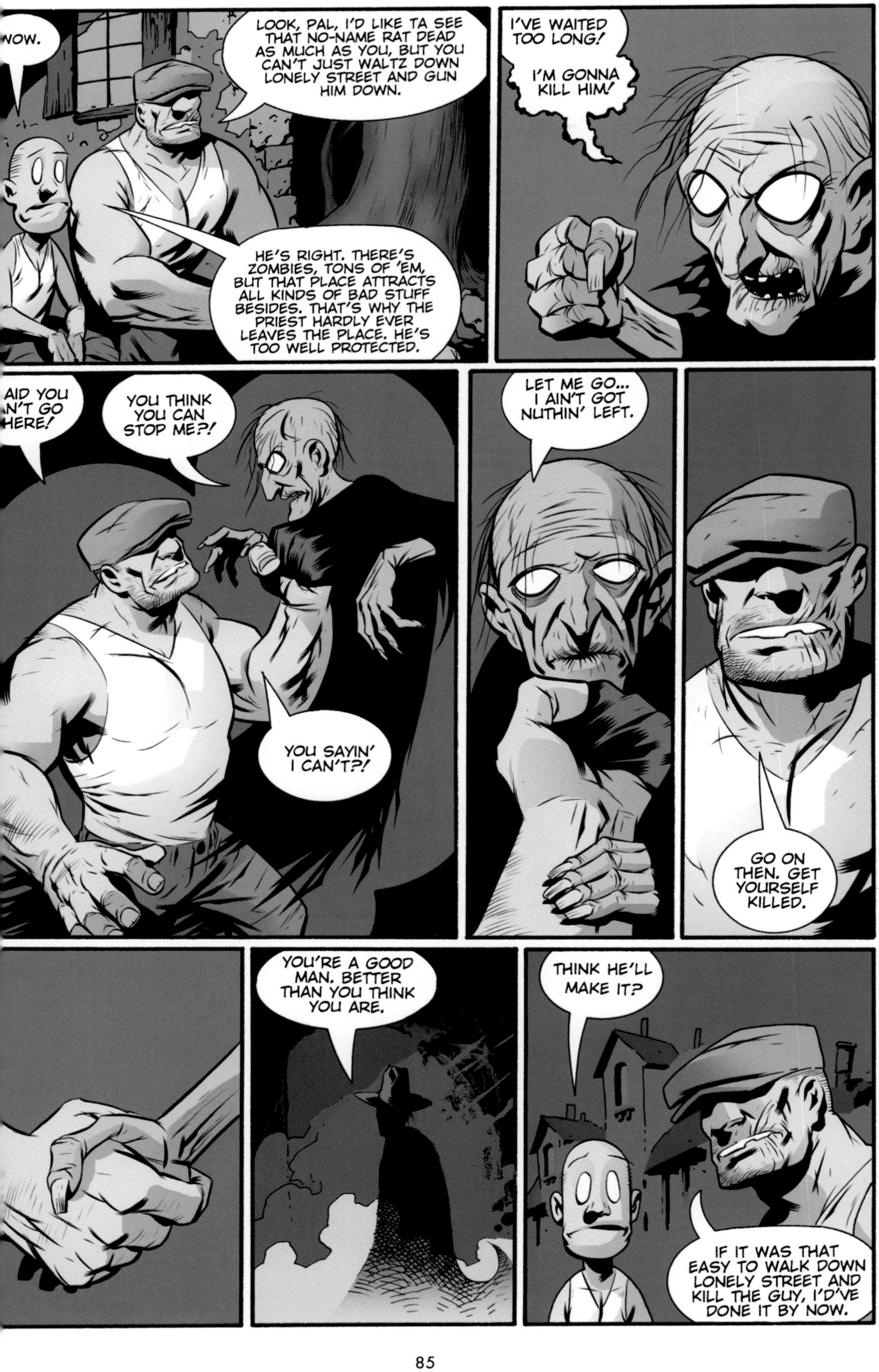
NOW.
LOOK, PAL, I'D LIKE TA SEE THAT NO-NAME RAT DEAD AS MUCH AS YOU, BUT YOU CAN'T JUST WALTZ DOWN LONELY STREET AND GUN HIM DOWN.
HE'S RIGHT. THERE'S ZOMBIES, TONS OF 'EM, BUT THAT PLACE ATTRACTS ALL KINDS OF BAD STUFF BESIDES. THAT'S WHY THE PRIEST HARDLY EVER LEAVES THE PLACE. HE'S TOO WELL PROTECTED.
I'VE WAITED TOO LONG!
I'M GONNA KILL HIM!
AID YOU N'T GO HERE!
YOU THINK YOU CAN STOP ME?!
YOU SAYIN' I CAN'T?!
LET ME GO... I AIN'T GOT NUTHIN' LEFT.
GO ON THEN. GET YOURSELF KILLED.
YOU'RE A GOOD MAN. BETTER THAN YOU THINK YOU ARE.
THINK HE'LL MAKE IT?
IF IT WAS THAT EASY TO WALK DOWN LONELY STREET AND KILL THE GUY, I'D'VE DONE IT BY NOW.

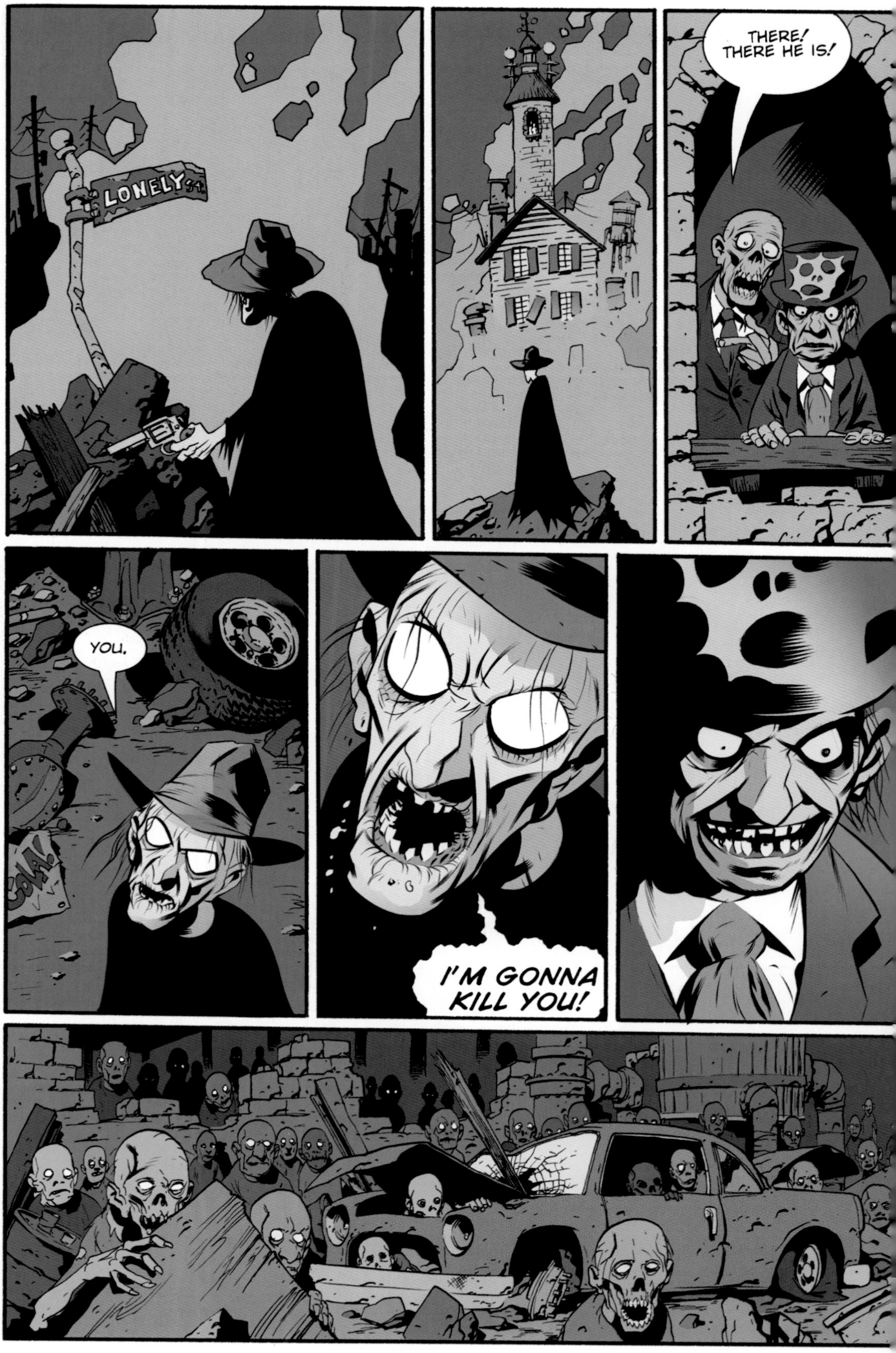
LONELY ST.
THERE! THERE HE IS!
YOU.
I'M GONNA KILL YOU!

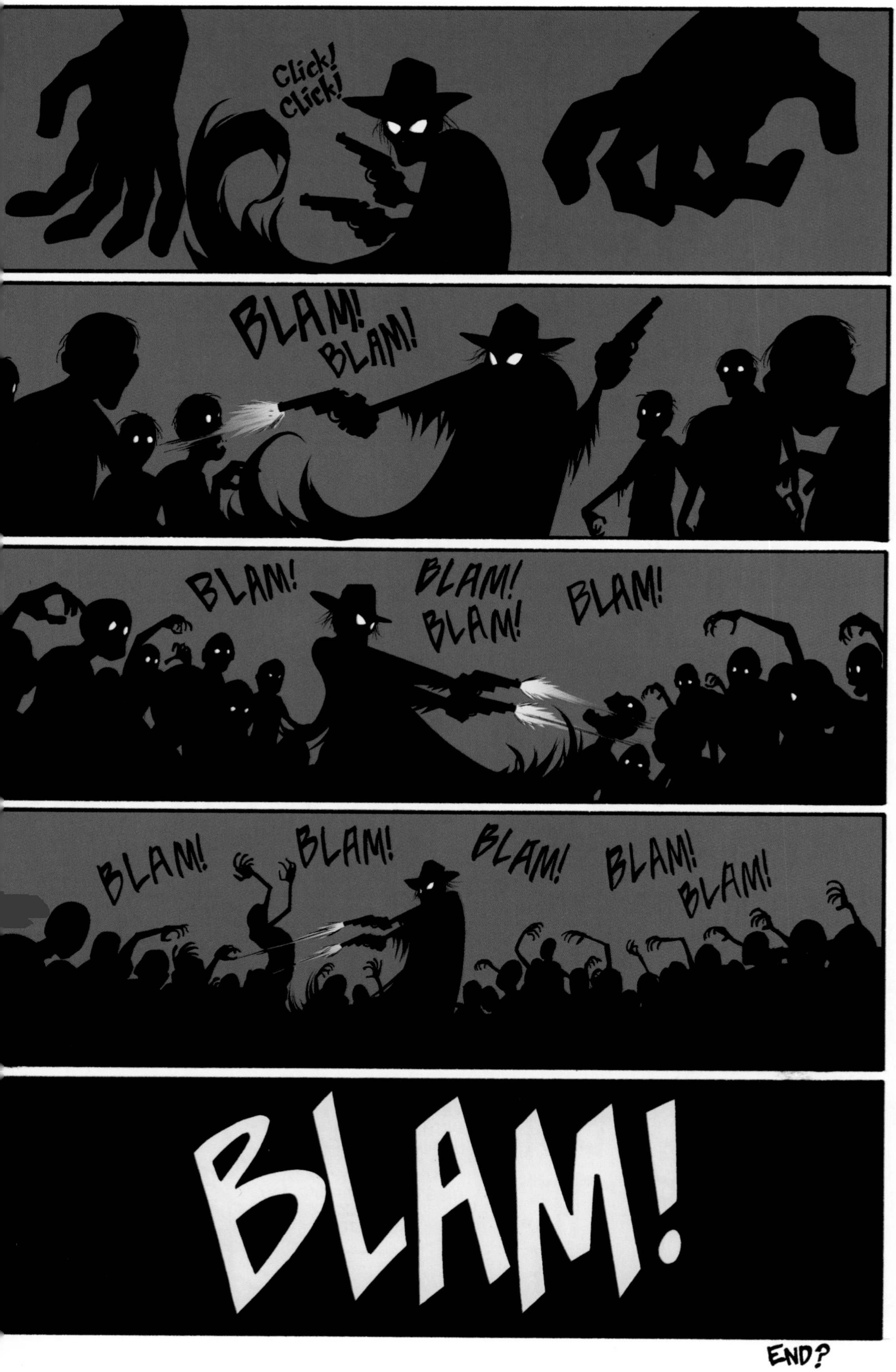
Click!
Click!
BLAM!
BLAM!
BLAM!
BLAM!
BLAM!
BLAM!
BLAM!
BLAM!
BLAM!
BLAM!
BLAM!
BLAM!

END?

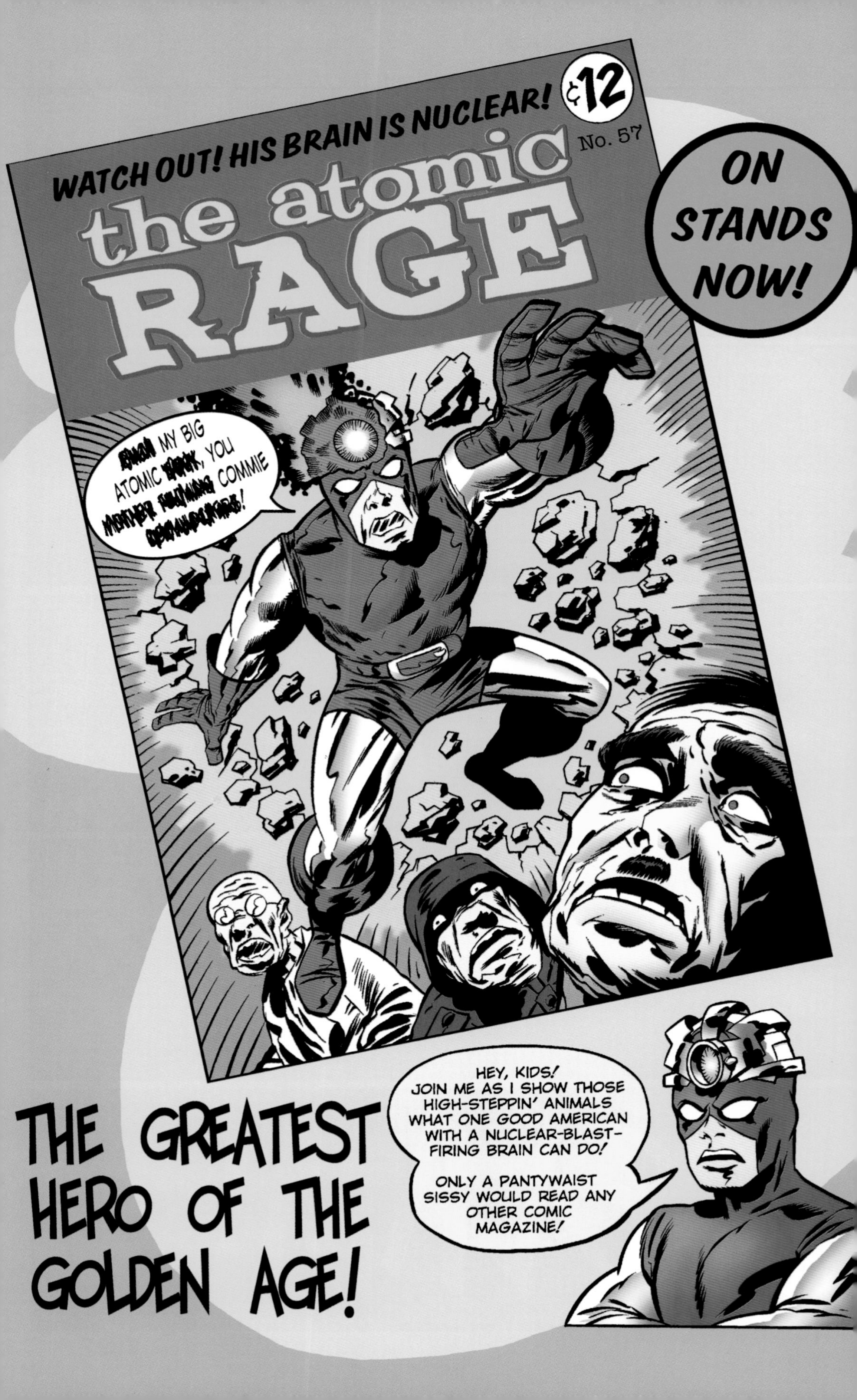
WATCH OUT! HIS BRAIN IS NUCLEAR!
¢12
No. 57
the atomic RAGE
[redacted] MY BIG
ATOMIC [redacted], YOU
[redacted] COMMIE
[redacted]!
ON STANDS NOW!
THE GREATEST HERO OF THE GOLDEN AGE!
HEY, KIDS! JOIN ME AS I SHOW THOSE HIGH-STEPPIN' ANIMALS WHAT ONE GOOD AMERICAN WITH A NUCLEAR-BLAST-FIRING BRAIN CAN DO!
ONLY A PANTYWAIST SISSY WOULD READ ANY OTHER COMIC MAGAZINE!

CHAPTER 4

THE GOON™

A Christmas Story

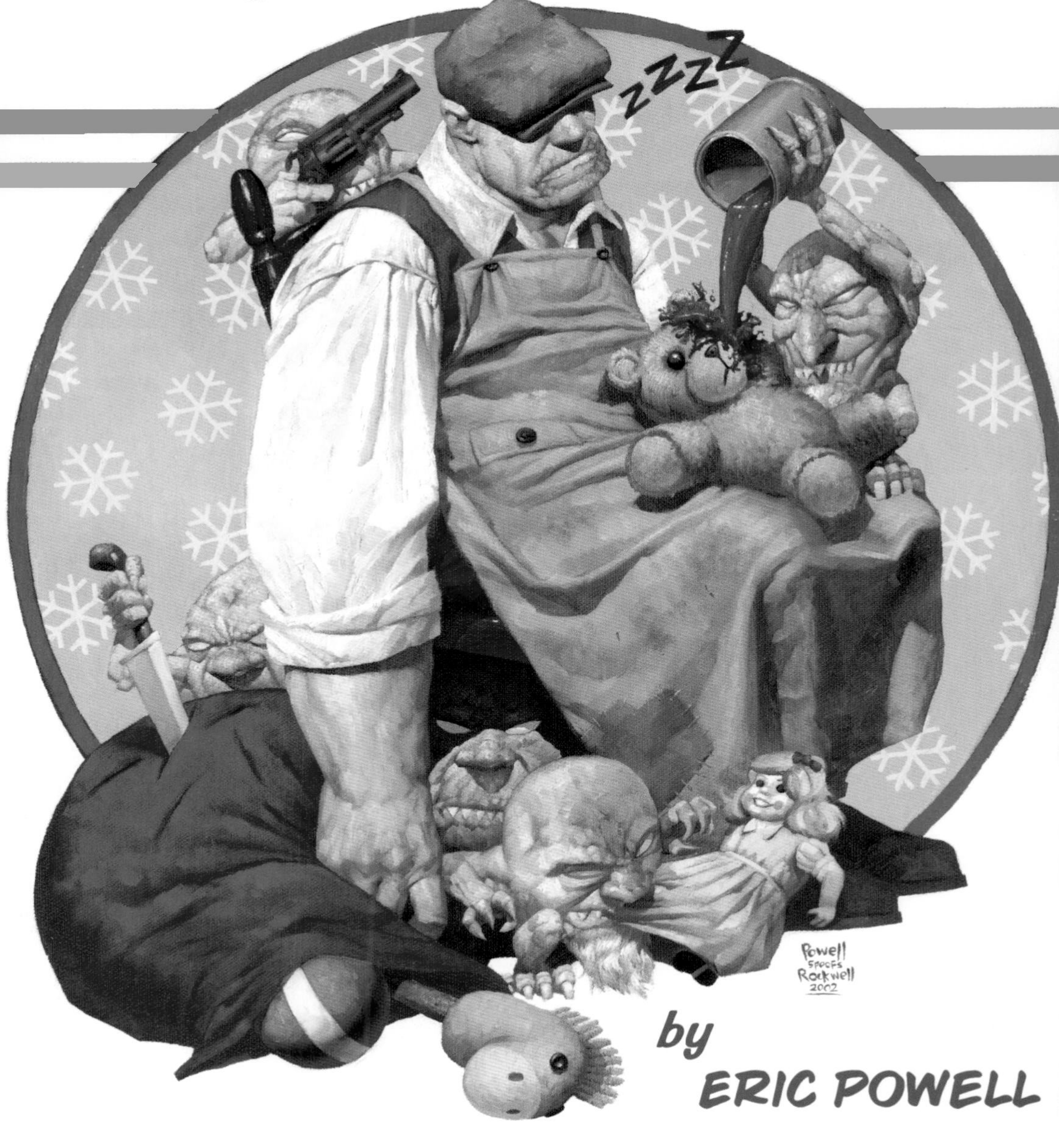

zzzz
Powell spoofs Rockwell 2002

by

ERIC POWELL

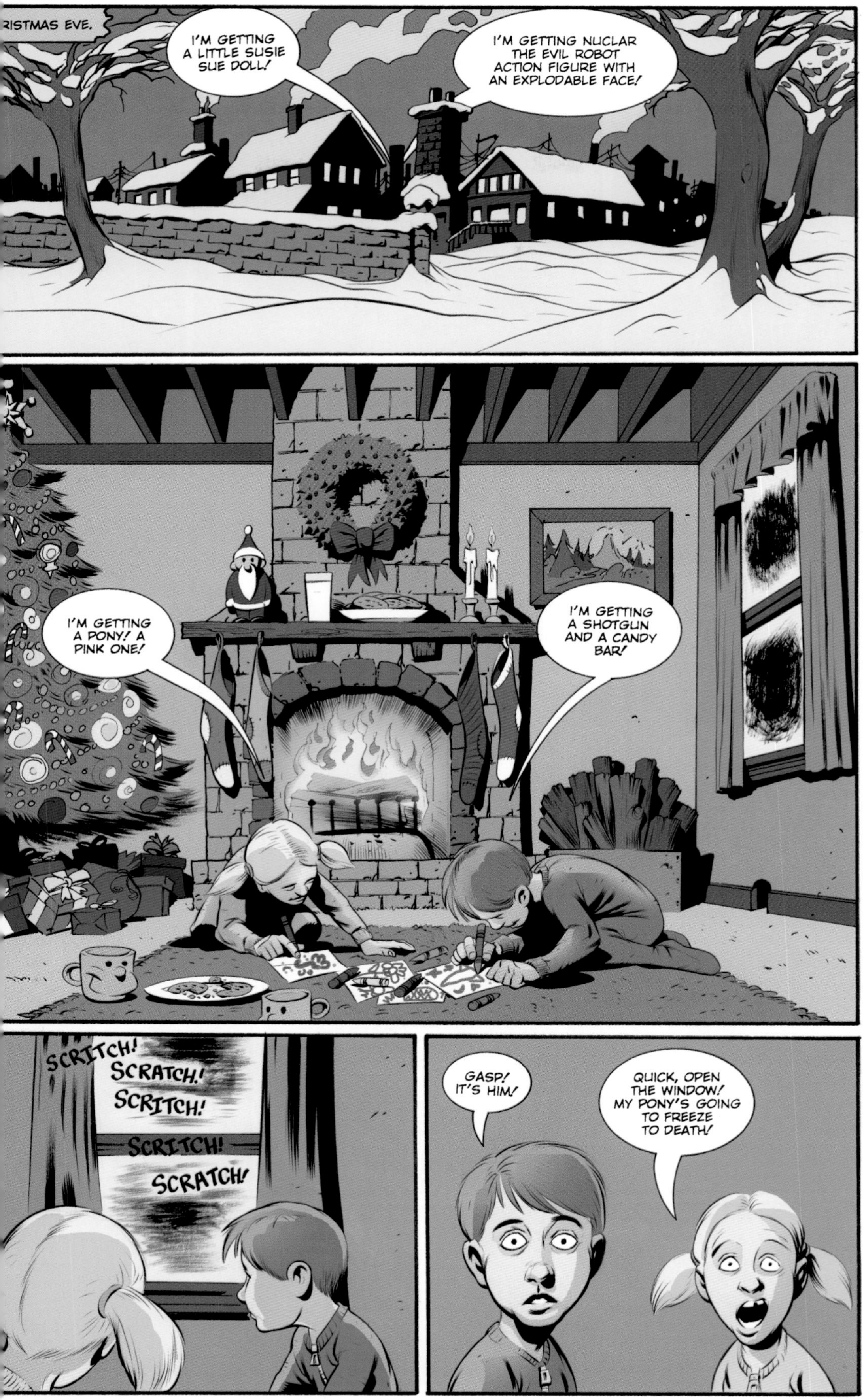

RISTMAS EVE.
I'M GETTING A LITTLE SUSIE SUE DOLL!
I'M GETTING NUCLAR THE EVIL ROBOT ACTION FIGURE WITH AN EXPLODABLE FACE!
I'M GETTING A PONY! A PINK ONE!
I'M GETTING A SHOTGUN AND A CANDY BAR!
SCRITCH! SCRATCH! SCRITCH!
SCRITCH! SCRATCH!
GASP! IT'S HIM!
QUICK, OPEN THE WINDOW! MY PONY'S GOING TO FREEZE TO DEATH!

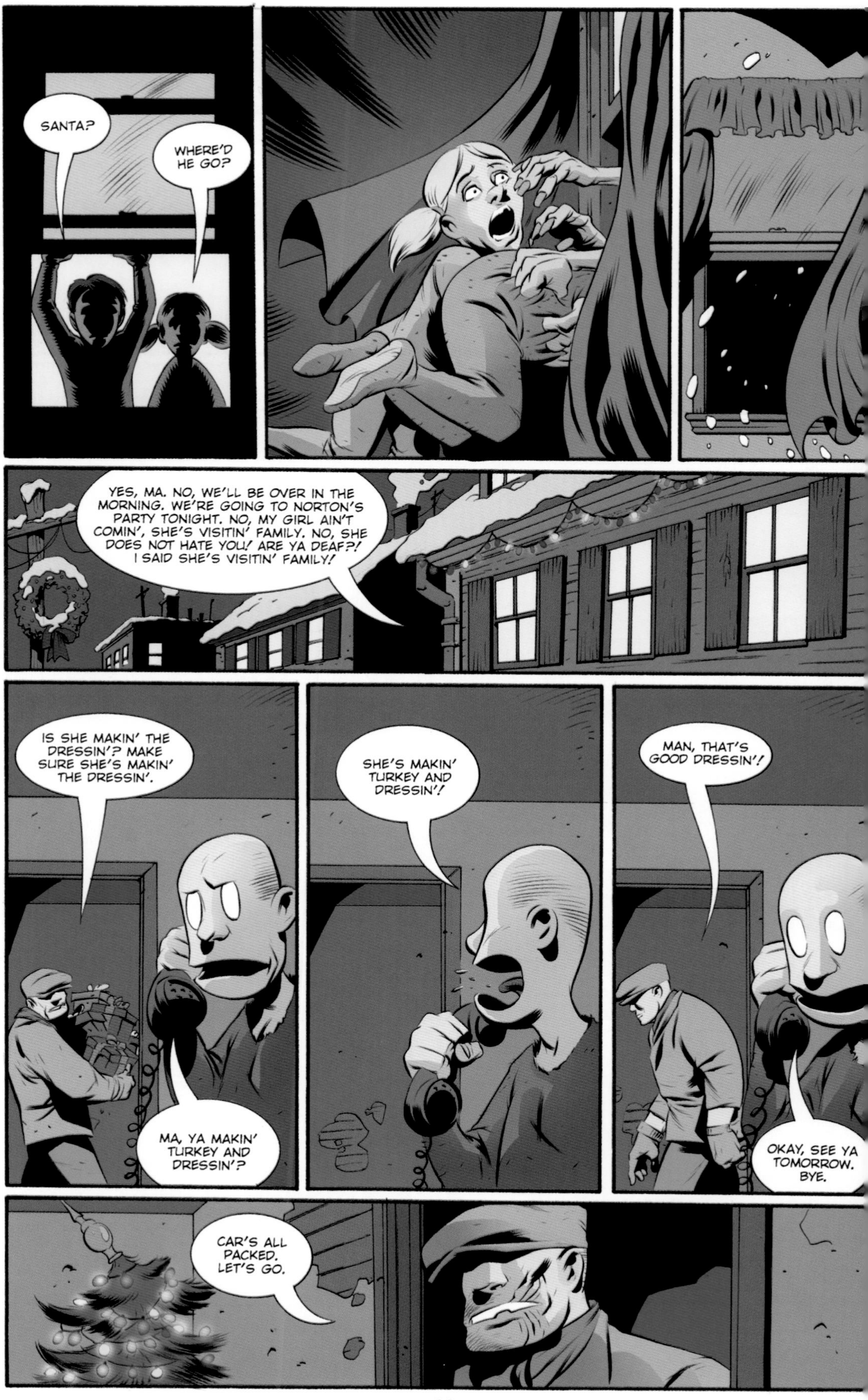
SANTA?
WHERE'D HE GO?
YES, MA. NO, WE'LL BE OVER IN THE MORNING. WE'RE GOING TO NORTON'S PARTY TONIGHT. NO, MY GIRL AIN'T COMIN', SHE'S VISITIN' FAMILY. NO, SHE DOES NOT HATE YOU! ARE YA DEAF?! I SAID SHE'S VISITIN' FAMILY!
IS SHE MAKIN' THE DRESSIN'? MAKE SURE SHE'S MAKIN' THE DRESSIN'.
MA, YA MAKIN' TURKEY AND DRESSIN'?
SHE'S MAKIN' TURKEY AND DRESSIN'!
MAN, THAT'S GOOD DRESSIN'!
OKAY, SEE YA TOMORROW. BYE.
CAR'S ALL PACKED. LET'S GO.

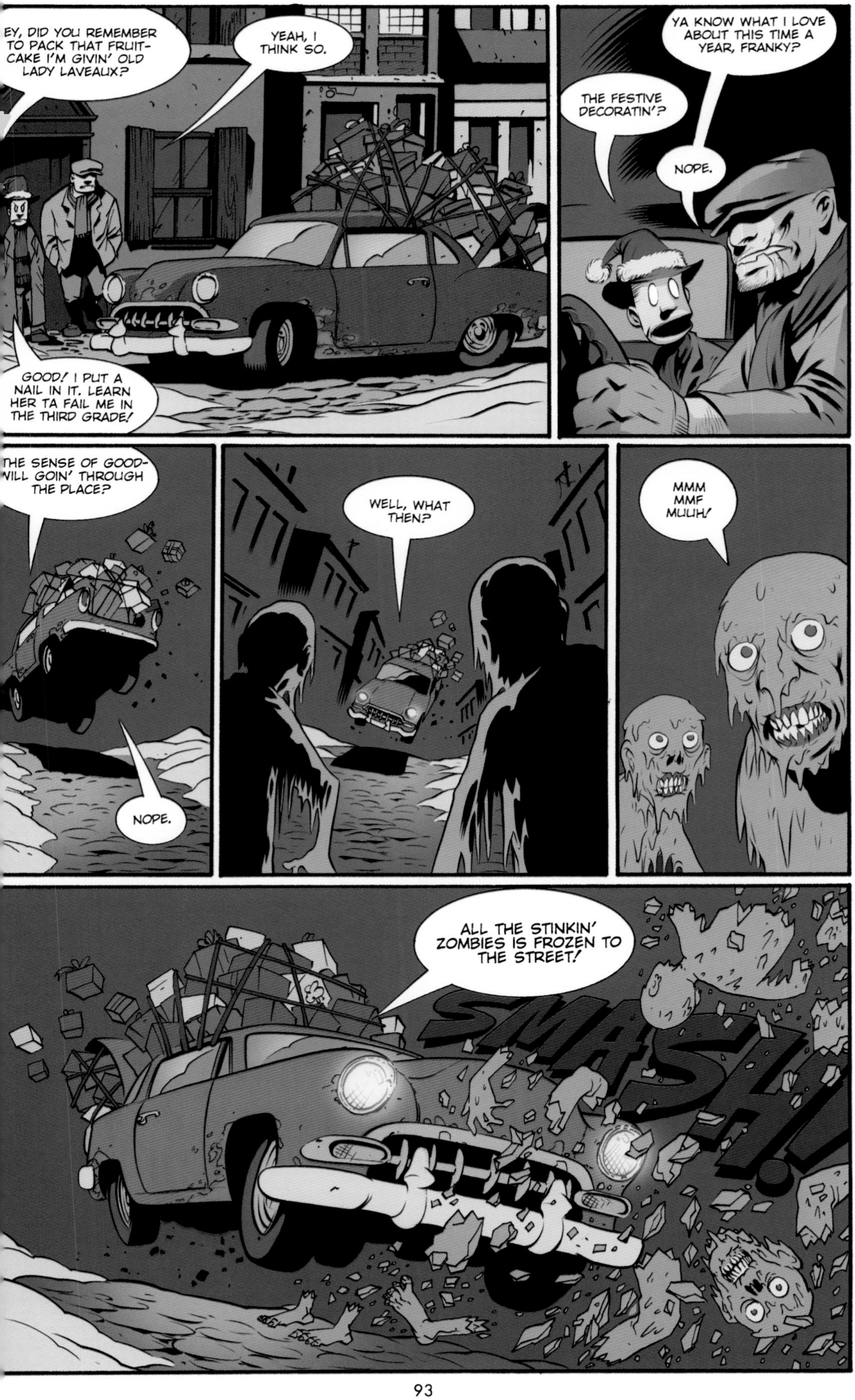
EY, DID YOU REMEMBER TO PACK THAT FRUIT-CAKE I'M GIVIN' OLD LADY LAVEAUX?
YEAH, I THINK SO.
GOOD! I PUT A NAIL IN IT. LEARN HER TA FAIL ME IN THE THIRD GRADE!
YA KNOW WHAT I LOVE ABOUT THIS TIME A YEAR, FRANKY?
THE FESTIVE DECORATIN'?
NOPE.
THE SENSE OF GOOD-WILL GOIN' THROUGH THE PLACE?
NOPE.
WELL, WHAT THEN?
MMM MMF MUUH!
ALL THE STINKIN' ZOMBIES IS FROZEN TO THE STREET!
SMASH!

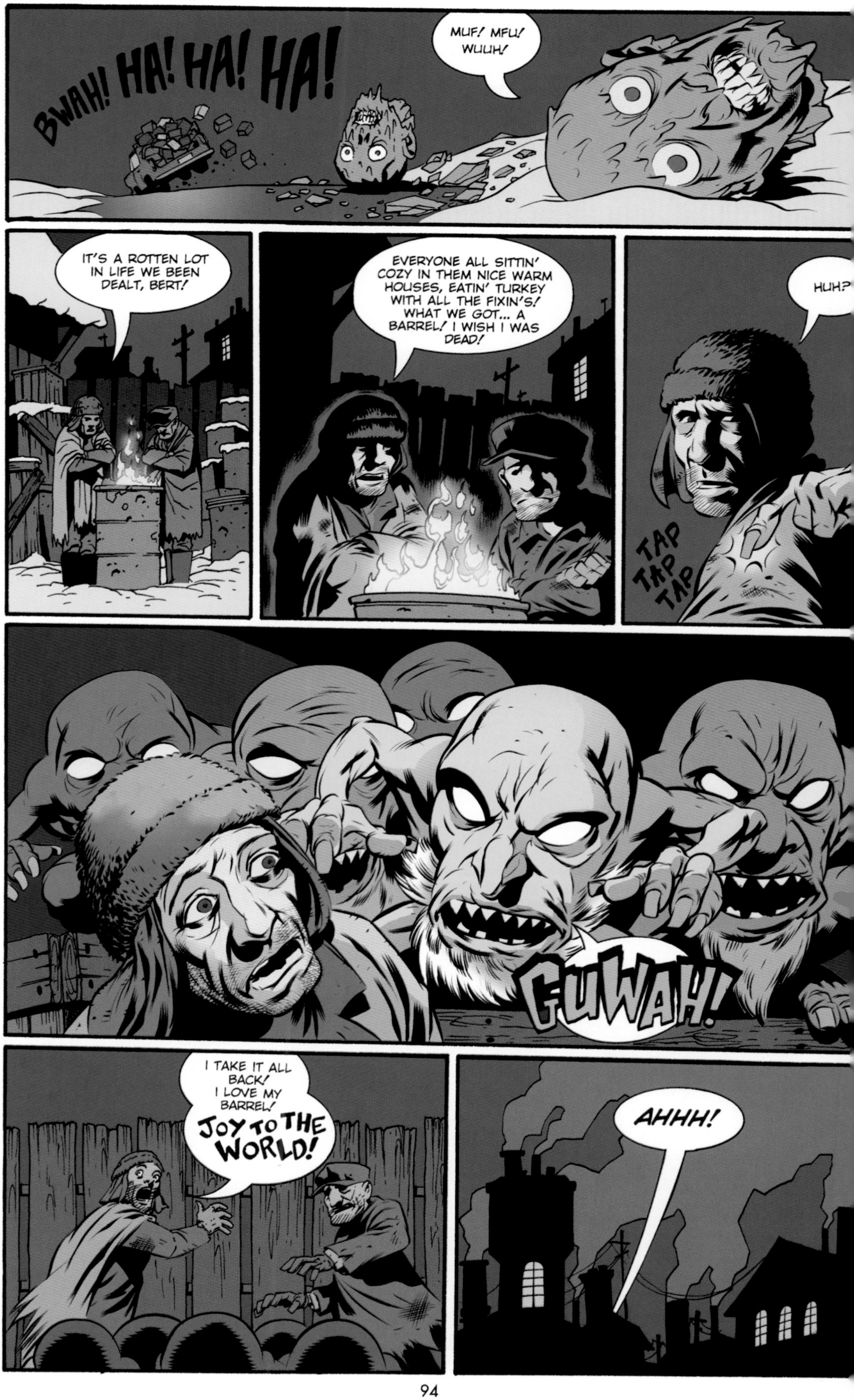
BWAH! HA! HA! HA!
MUF! MFU! WUUH!
IT'S A ROTTEN LOT IN LIFE WE BEEN DEALT, BERT!
EVERYONE ALL SITTIN' COZY IN THEM NICE WARM HOUSES, EATIN' TURKEY WITH ALL THE FIXIN'S! WHAT WE GOT... A BARREL! I WISH I WAS DEAD!
HUH?
TAP TAP TAP
GUWAH!
I TAKE IT ALL BACK! I LOVE MY BARREL! JOY TO THE WORLD!
AHHH!

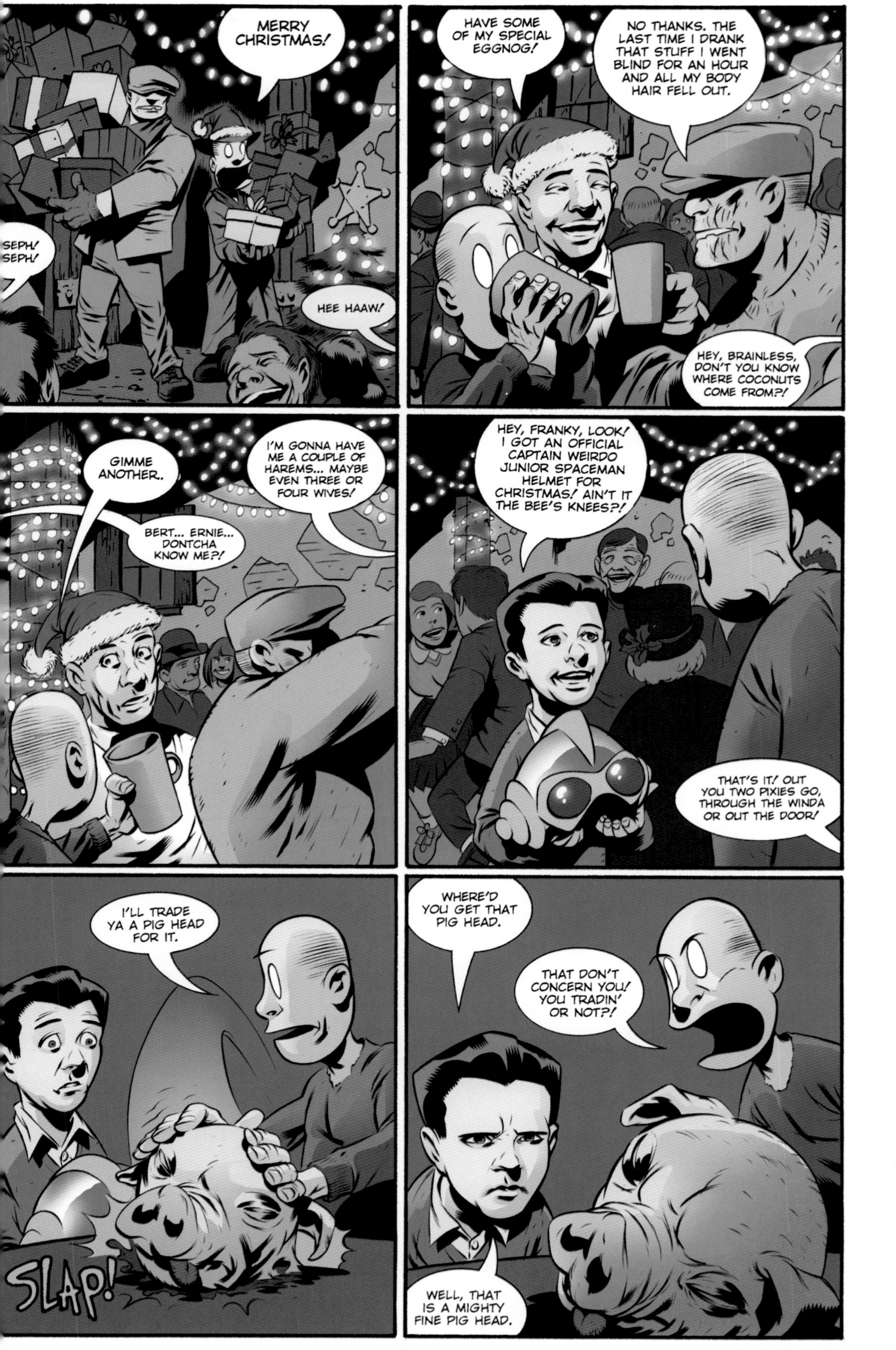
MERRY CHRISTMAS!
SEPH! SEPH!
HEE HAAW!
HAVE SOME OF MY SPECIAL EGGNOG!
NO THANKS. THE LAST TIME I DRANK THAT STUFF I WENT BLIND FOR AN HOUR AND ALL MY BODY HAIR FELL OUT.
HEY, BRAINLESS, DON'T YOU KNOW WHERE COCONUTS COME FROM?!
GIMME ANOTHER.
I'M GONNA HAVE ME A COUPLE OF HAREMS... MAYBE EVEN THREE OR FOUR WIVES!
BERT... ERNIE... DONTCHA KNOW ME?!
HEY, FRANKY, LOOK! I GOT AN OFFICIAL CAPTAIN WEIRDO JUNIOR SPACEMAN HELMET FOR CHRISTMAS! AIN'T IT THE BEE'S KNEES?!
THAT'S IT! OUT YOU TWO PIXIES GO, THROUGH THE WINDA OR OUT THE DOOR!
I'LL TRADE YA A PIG HEAD FOR IT.
SLAP!
WHERE'D YOU GET THAT PIG HEAD.
THAT DON'T CONCERN YOU! YOU TRADIN' OR NOT?!
WELL, THAT IS A MIGHTY FINE PIG HEAD.

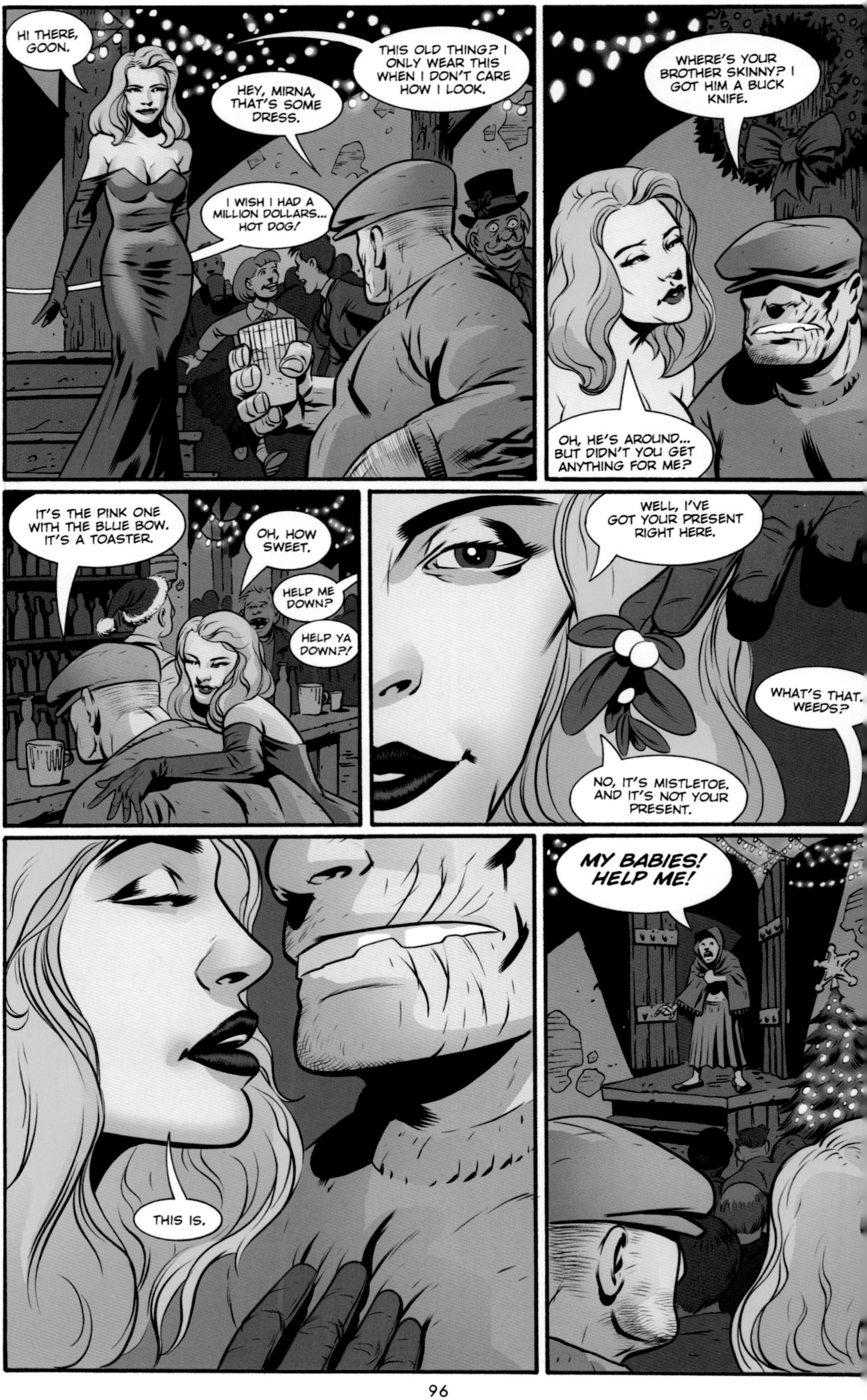
HI THERE, GOON.
HEY, MIRNA, THAT'S SOME DRESS.
THIS OLD THING? I ONLY WEAR THIS WHEN I DON'T CARE HOW I LOOK.
I WISH I HAD A MILLION DOLLARS... HOT DOG!
WHERE'S YOUR BROTHER SKINNY? I GOT HIM A BUCK KNIFE.
OH, HE'S AROUND... BUT DIDN'T YOU GET ANYTHING FOR ME?
IT'S THE PINK ONE WITH THE BLUE BOW. IT'S A TOASTER.
OH, HOW SWEET.
HELP ME DOWN?
HELP YA DOWN?!
WELL, I'VE GOT YOUR PRESENT RIGHT HERE.
WHAT'S THAT. WEEDS?
NO, IT'S MISTLETOE. AND IT'S NOT YOUR PRESENT.
THIS IS.
MY BABIES! HELP ME!

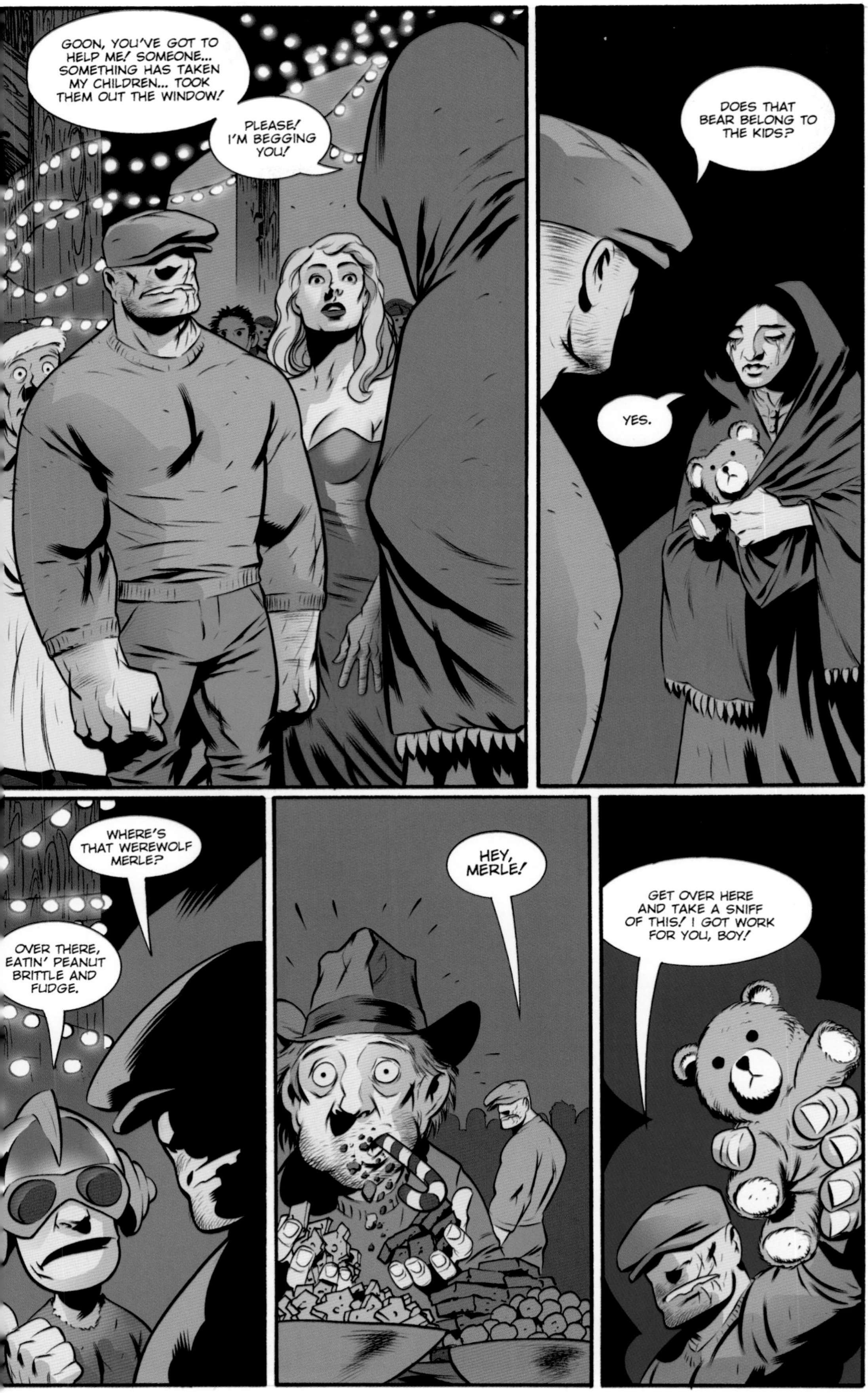
GOON, YOU'VE GOT TO HELP ME! SOMEONE... SOMETHING HAS TAKEN MY CHILDREN... TOOK THEM OUT THE WINDOW!
PLEASE! I'M BEGGING YOU!
DOES THAT BEAR BELONG TO THE KIDS?
YES.
WHERE'S THAT WEREWOLF MERLE?
OVER THERE, EATIN' PEANUT BRITTLE AND FUDGE.
HEY, MERLE!
GET OVER HERE AND TAKE A SNIFF OF THIS! I GOT WORK FOR YOU, BOY!

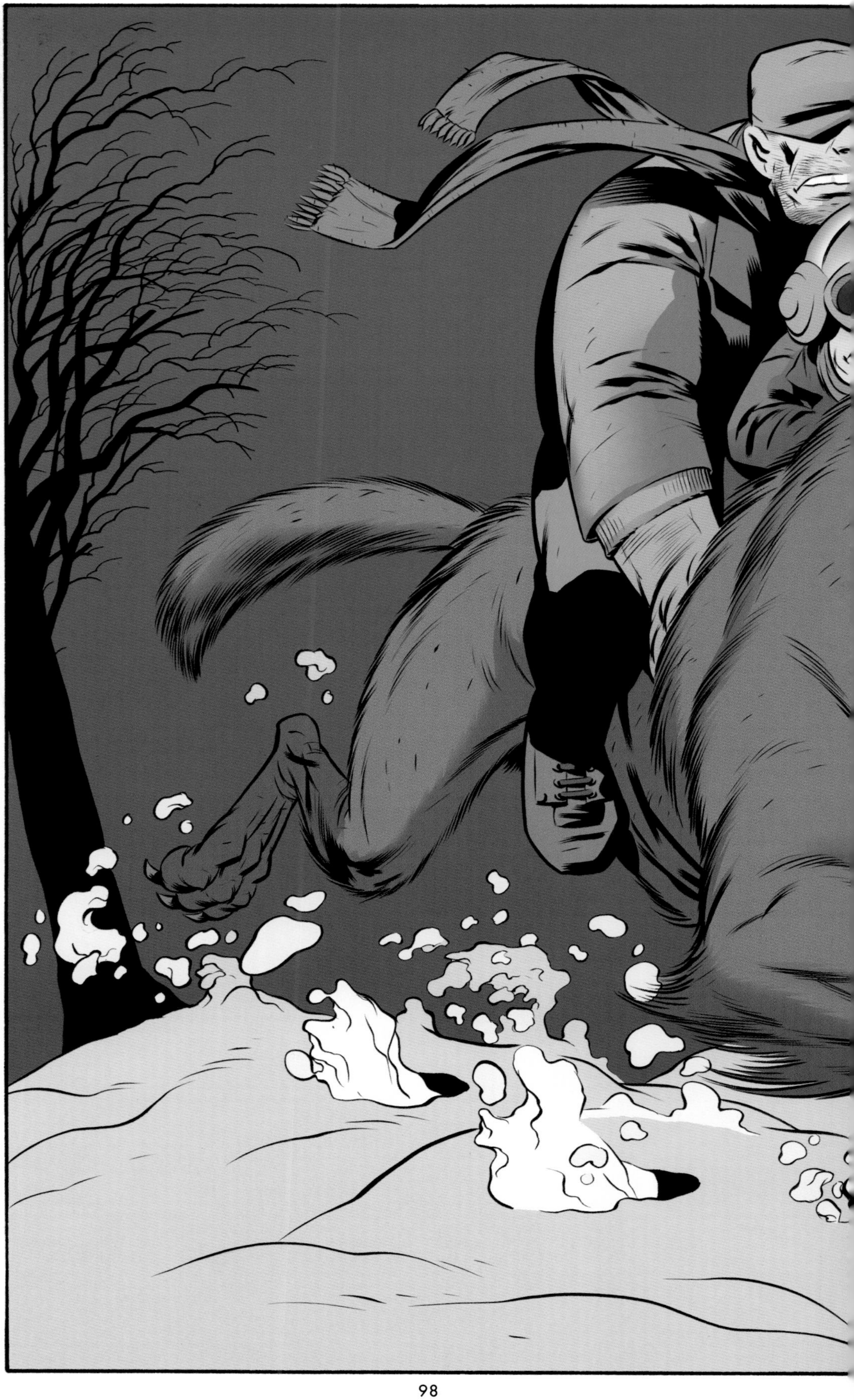

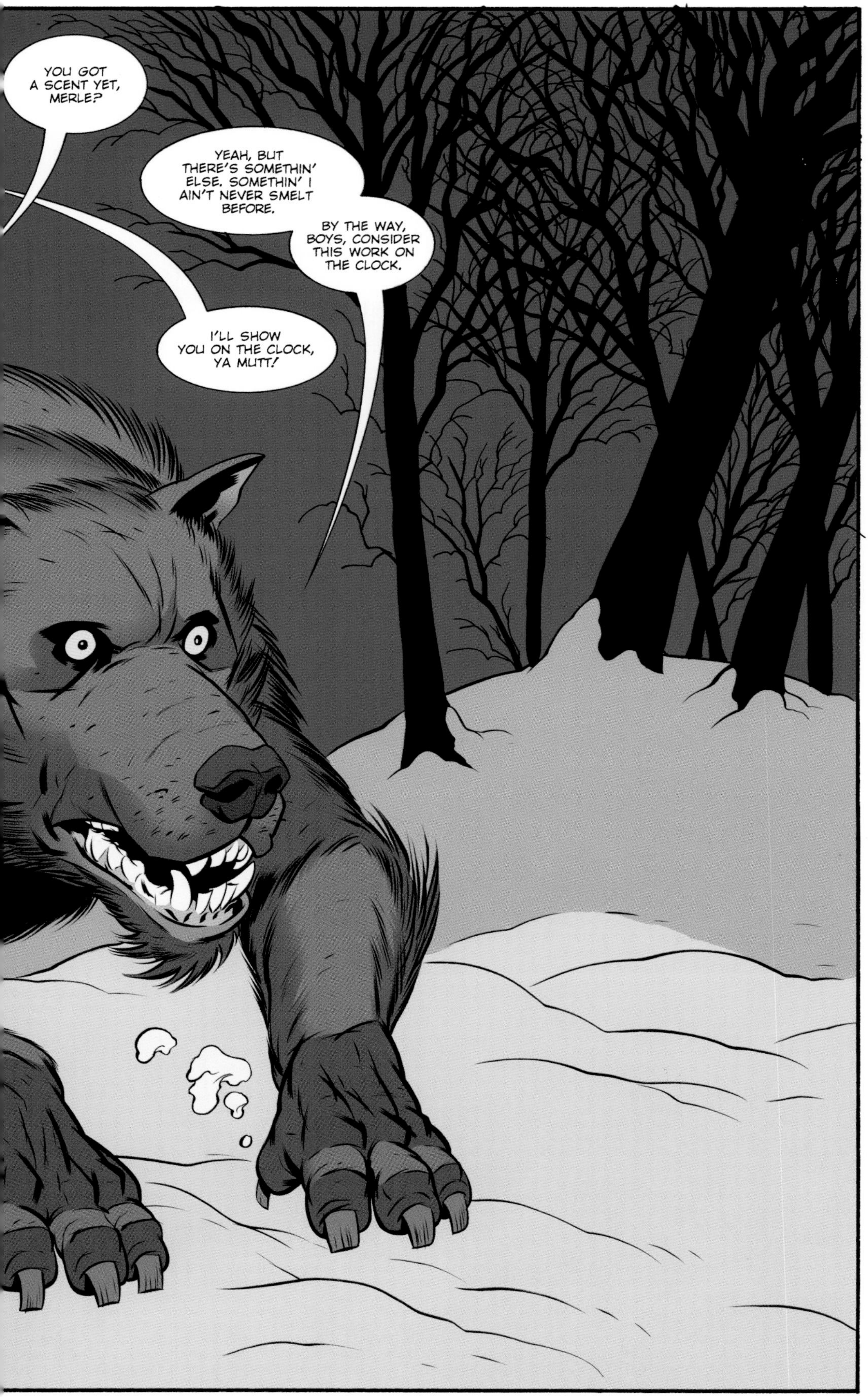
YOU GOT A SCENT YET, MERLE?
YEAH, BUT THERE'S SOMETHIN' ELSE. SOMETHIN' I AIN'T NEVER SMELT BEFORE.
BY THE WAY, BOYS, CONSIDER THIS WORK ON THE CLOCK.
I'LL SHOW YOU ON THE CLOCK, YA MUTT!

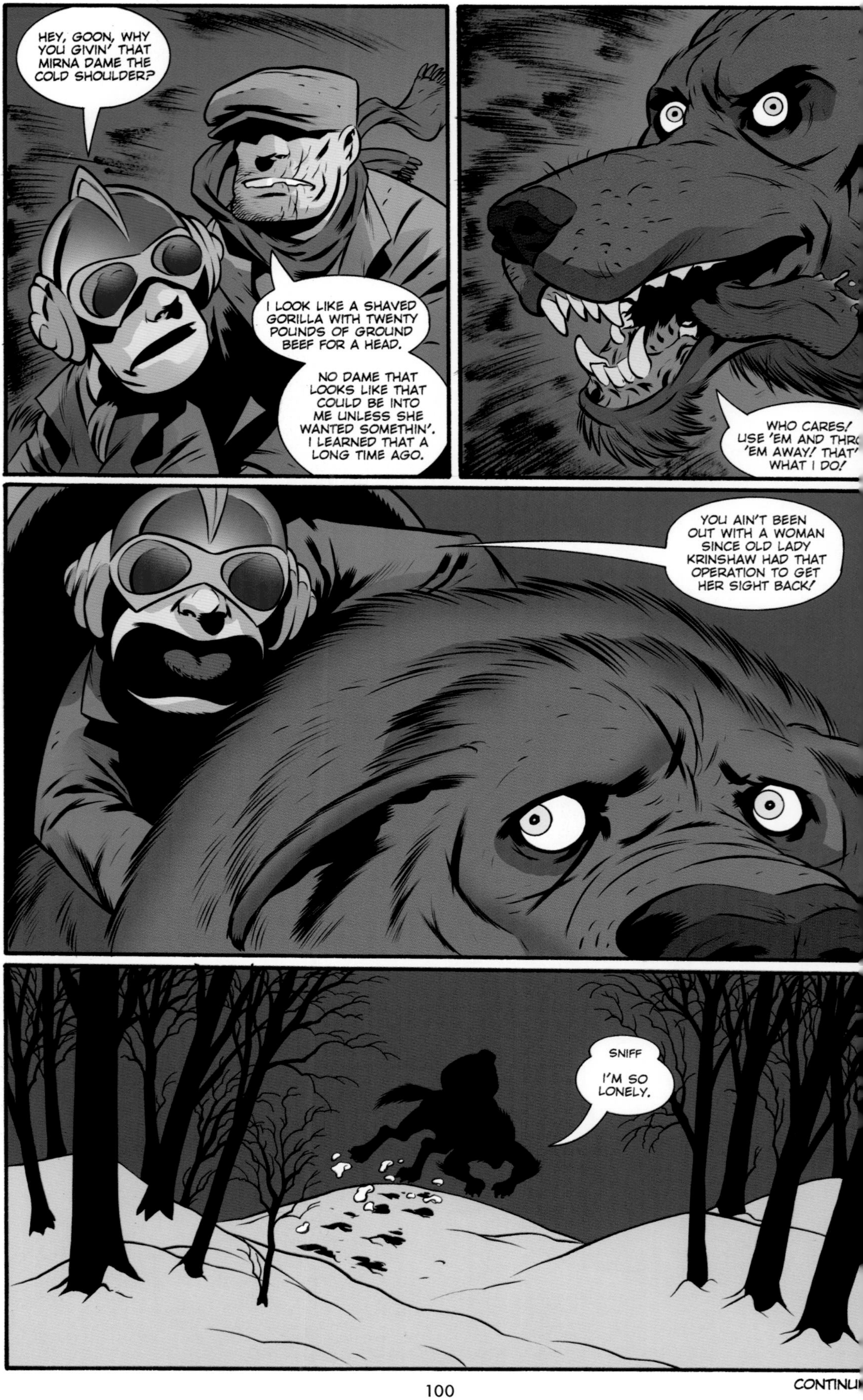

HEY, GOON, WHY YOU GIVIN' THAT MIRNA DAME THE COLD SHOULDER?
I LOOK LIKE A SHAVED GORILLA WITH TWENTY POUNDS OF GROUND BEEF FOR A HEAD.
NO DAME THAT LOOKS LIKE THAT COULD BE INTO ME UNLESS SHE WANTED SOMETHIN'. I LEARNED THAT A LONG TIME AGO.
WHO CARES! USE 'EM AND THR 'EM AWAY! THAT' WHAT I DO!
YOU AIN'T BEEN OUT WITH A WOMAN SINCE OLD LADY KRINSHAW HAD THAT OPERATION TO GET HER SIGHT BACK!
SNIFF
I'M SO LONELY.

CONTINU

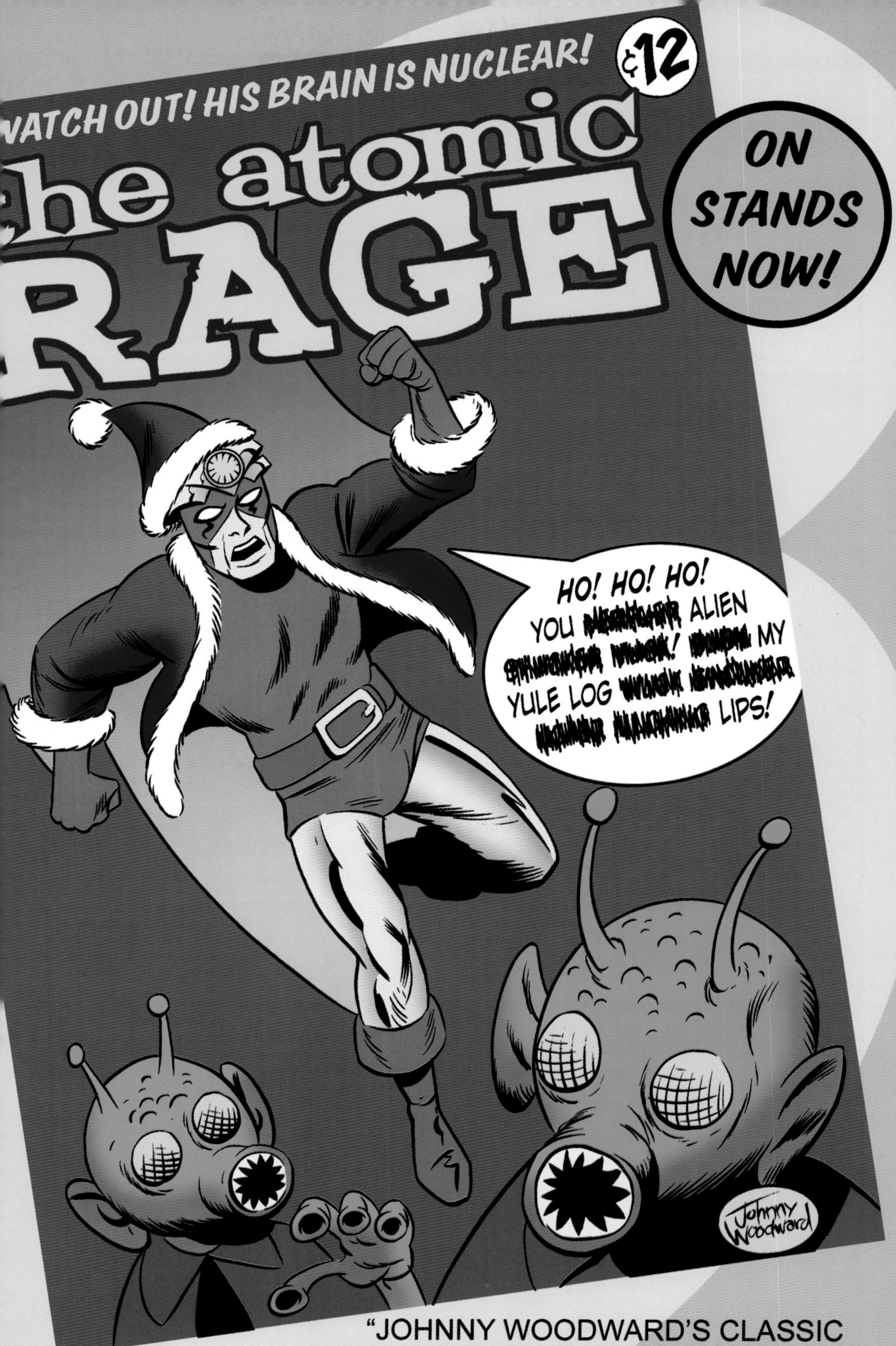

WATCH OUT! HIS BRAIN IS NUCLEAR!
¢12
the atomic RAGE
ON STANDS NOW!
HO! HO! HO! YOU [redacted] ALIEN [redacted] MY YULE LOG [redacted] LIPS!
Johnny Woodward

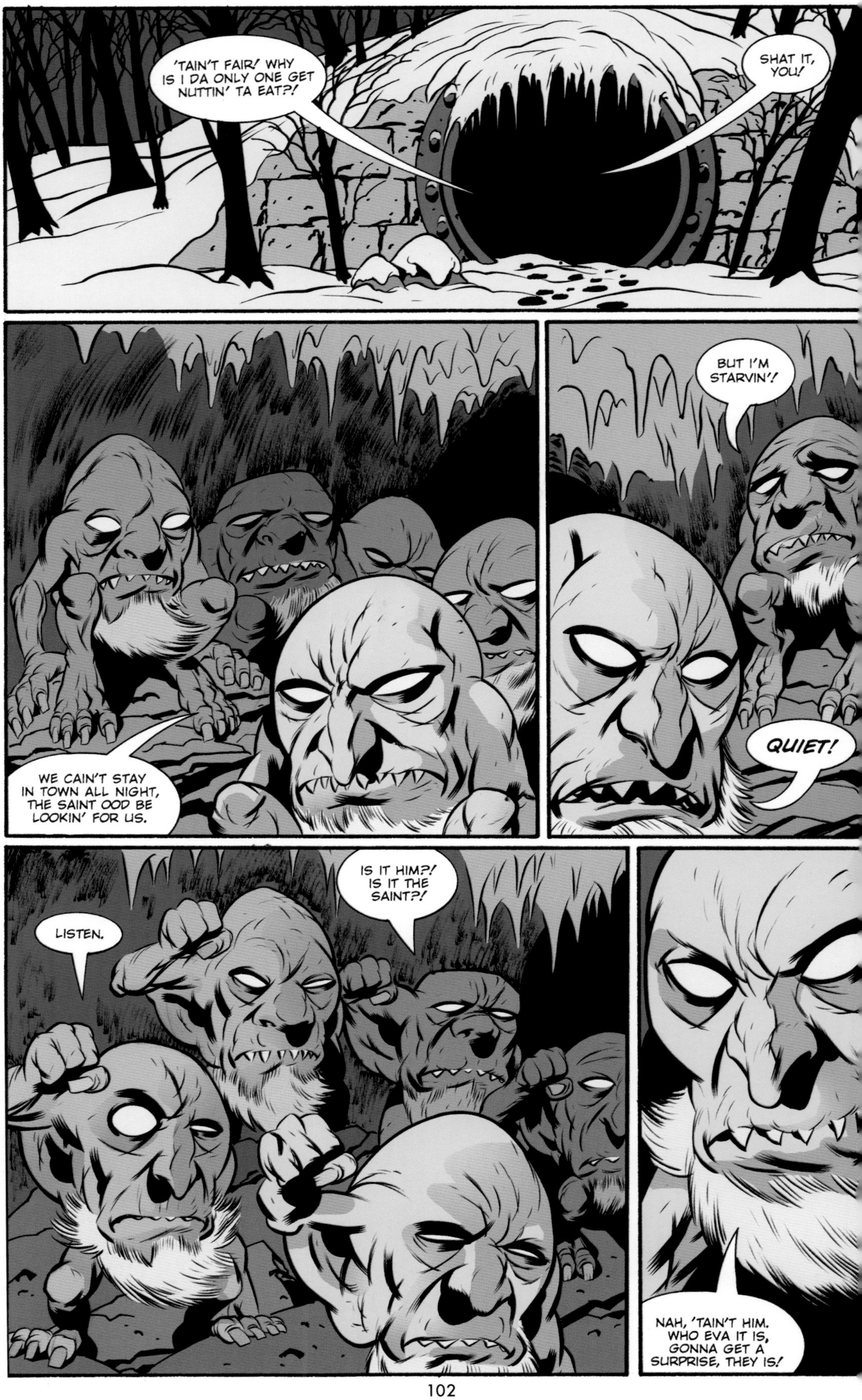
'TAIN'T FAIR! WHY IS I DA ONLY ONE GET NUTTIN' TA EAT?!
SHAT IT, YOU!
WE CAIN'T STAY IN TOWN ALL NIGHT, THE SAINT OOD BE LOOKIN' FOR US.
BUT I'M STARVIN'!
QUIET!
LISTEN.
IS IT HIM?! IS IT THE SAINT?!
NAH, 'TAIN'T HIM. WHO EVA IT IS, GONNA GET A SURPRISE, THEY IS!

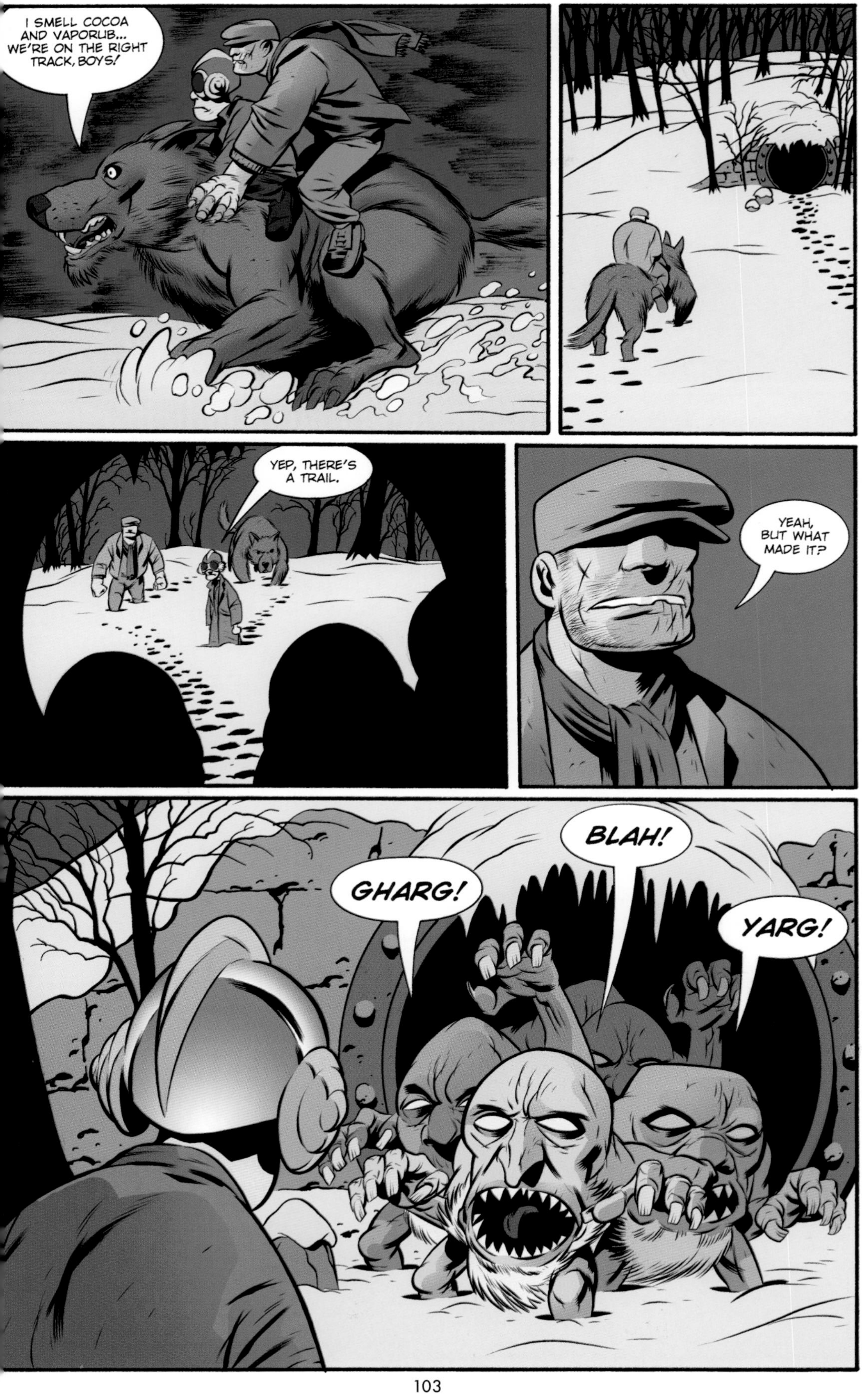

I SMELL COCOA AND VAPORUB... WE'RE ON THE RIGHT TRACK, BOYS!
YEP, THERE'S A TRAIL.
YEAH, BUT WHAT MADE IT?
GHARG!
BLAH!
YARG!

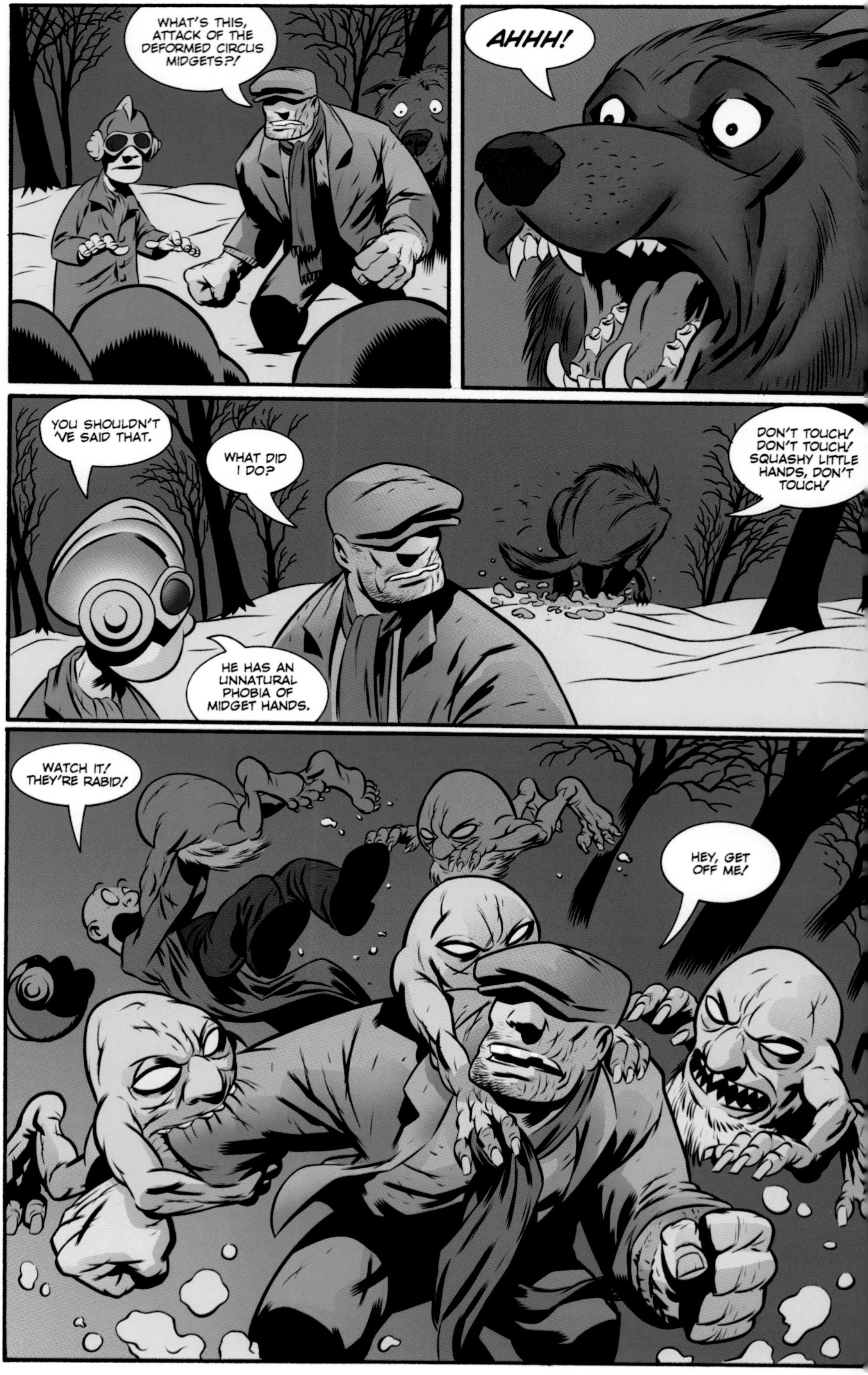
WHAT'S THIS, ATTACK OF THE DEFORMED CIRCUS MIDGETS?!
AHHH!
YOU SHOULDN'T 'VE SAID THAT.
WHAT DID I DO?
DON'T TOUCH! DON'T TOUCH! SQUASHY LITTLE HANDS, DON'T TOUCH!
HE HAS AN UNNATURAL PHOBIA OF MIDGET HANDS.
WATCH IT! THEY'RE RABID!
HEY, GET OFF ME!

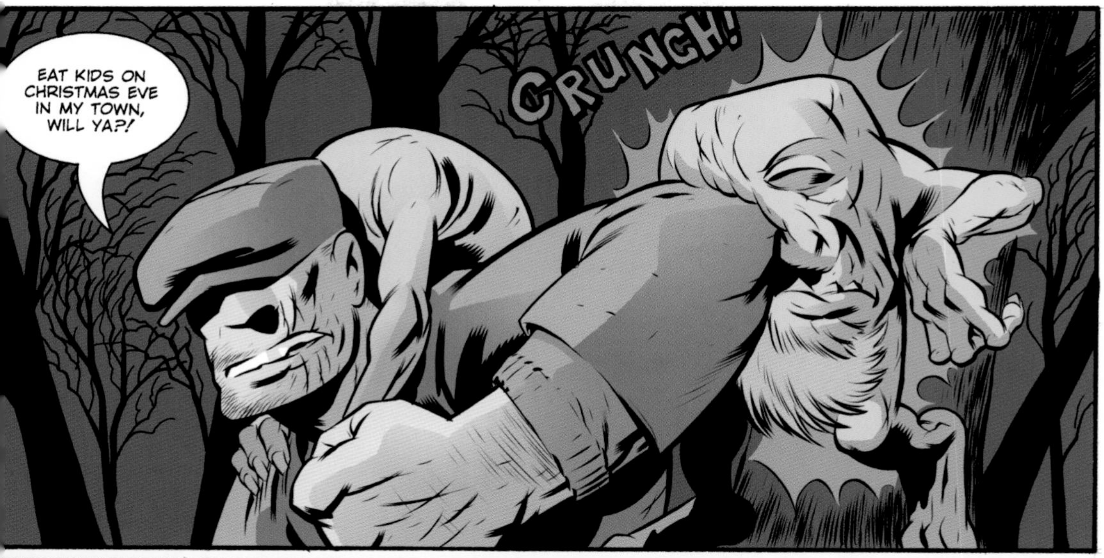
EAT KIDS ON CHRISTMAS EVE IN MY TOWN, WILL YA?!
CRUNCH!

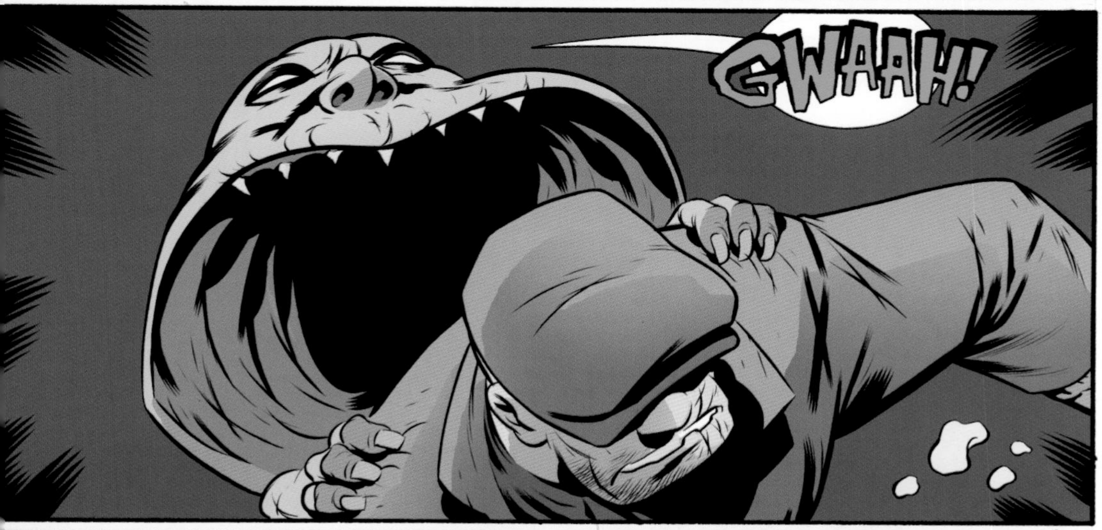
GWAAH!

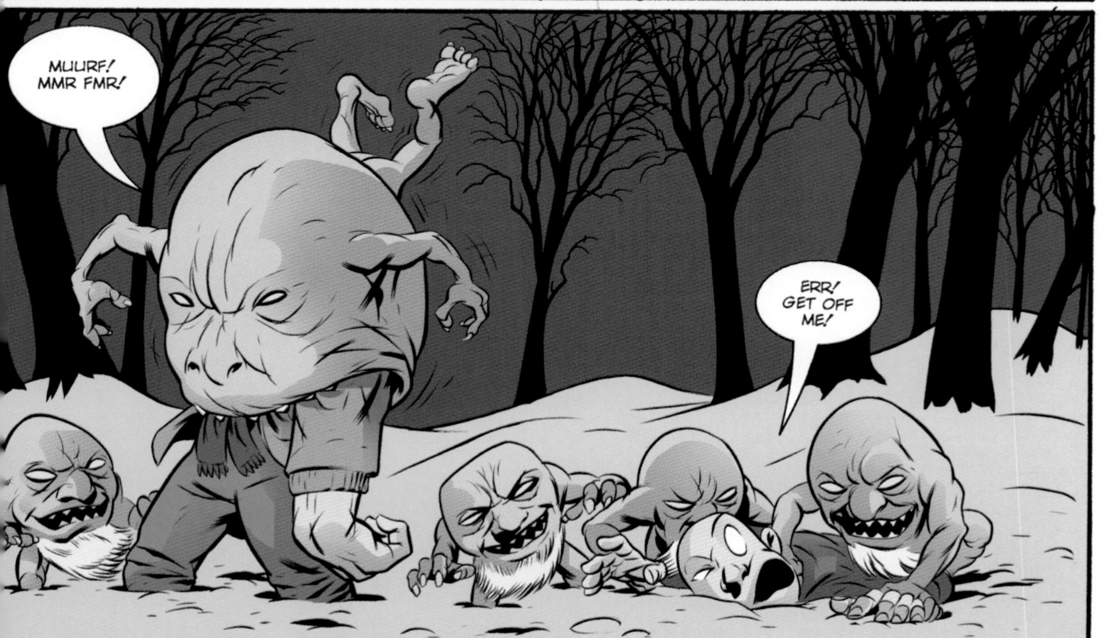
MUURF! MMR FMR!
ERR! GET OFF ME!

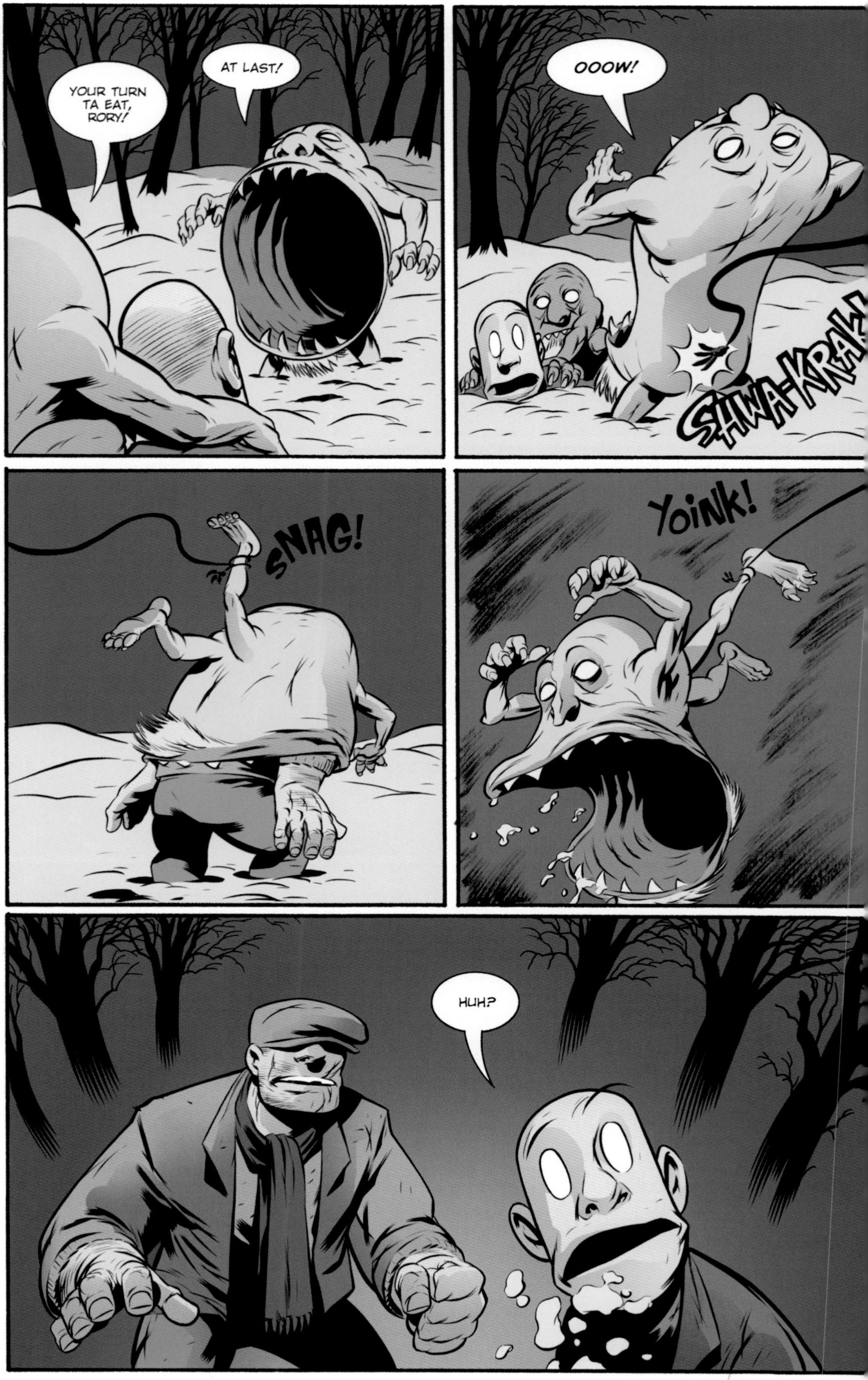
YOUR TURN TA EAT, RORY!
AT LAST!
OOOW!
SHWAH-KRAK!
SNAG!
YOINK!
HUH?

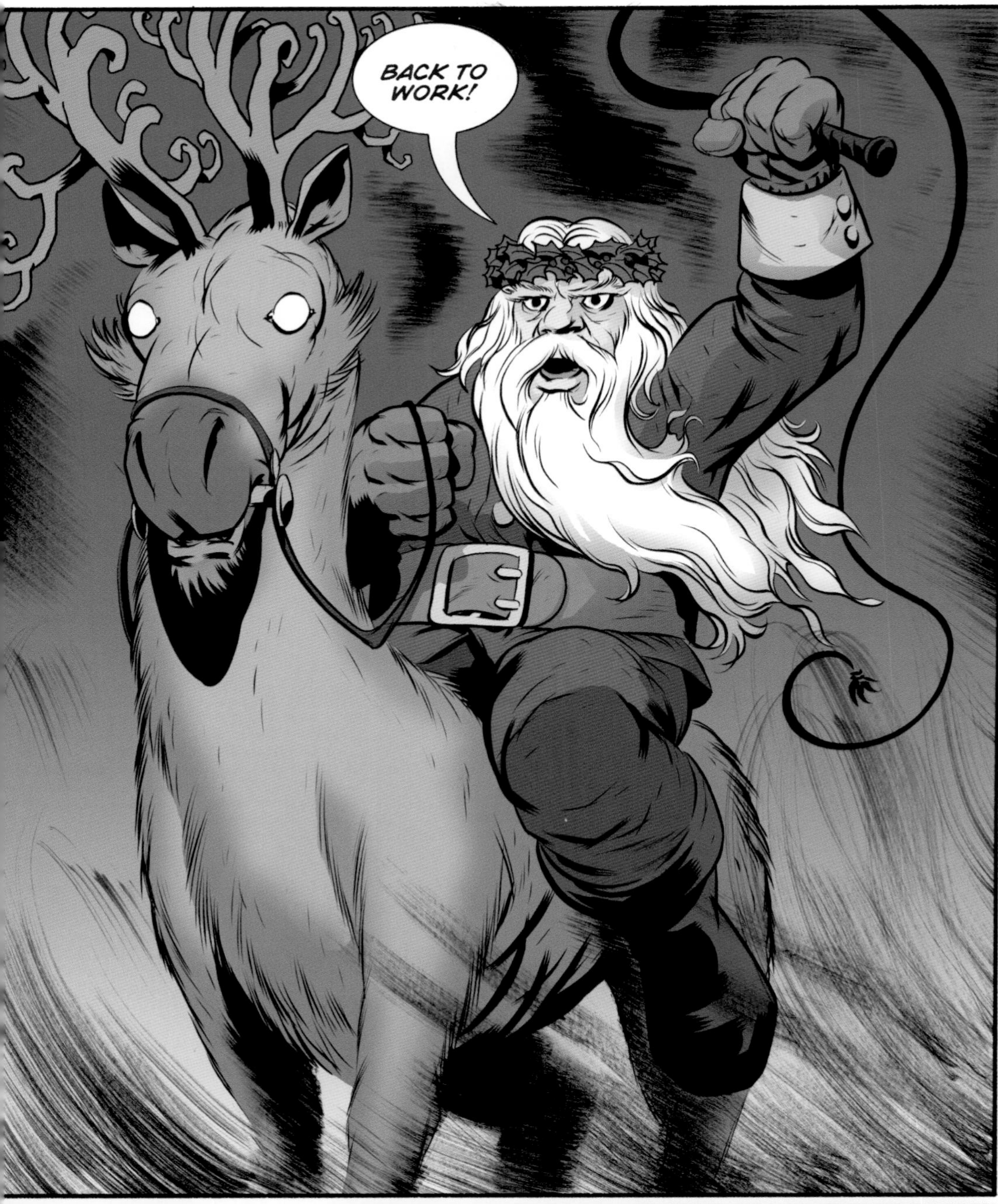
BACK TO WORK!

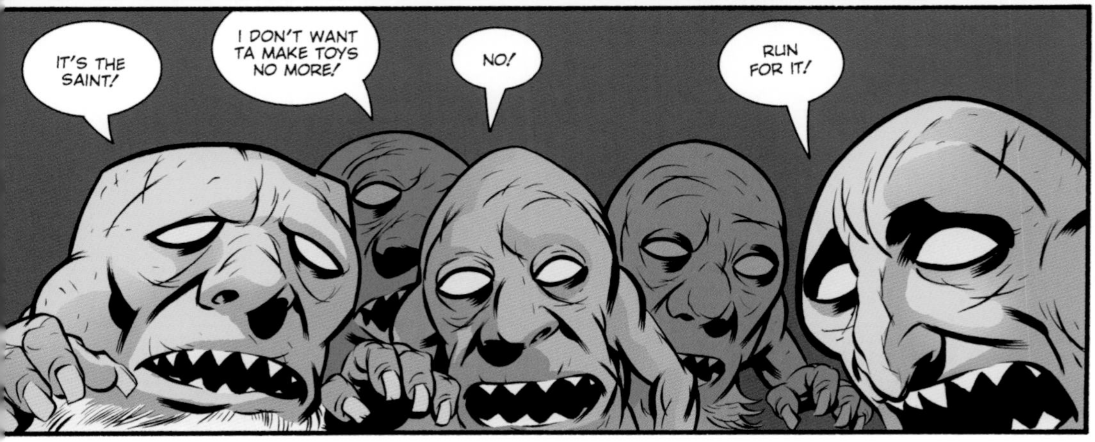
IT'S THE SAINT!
I DON'T WANT TA MAKE TOYS NO MORE!
NO!
RUN FOR IT!

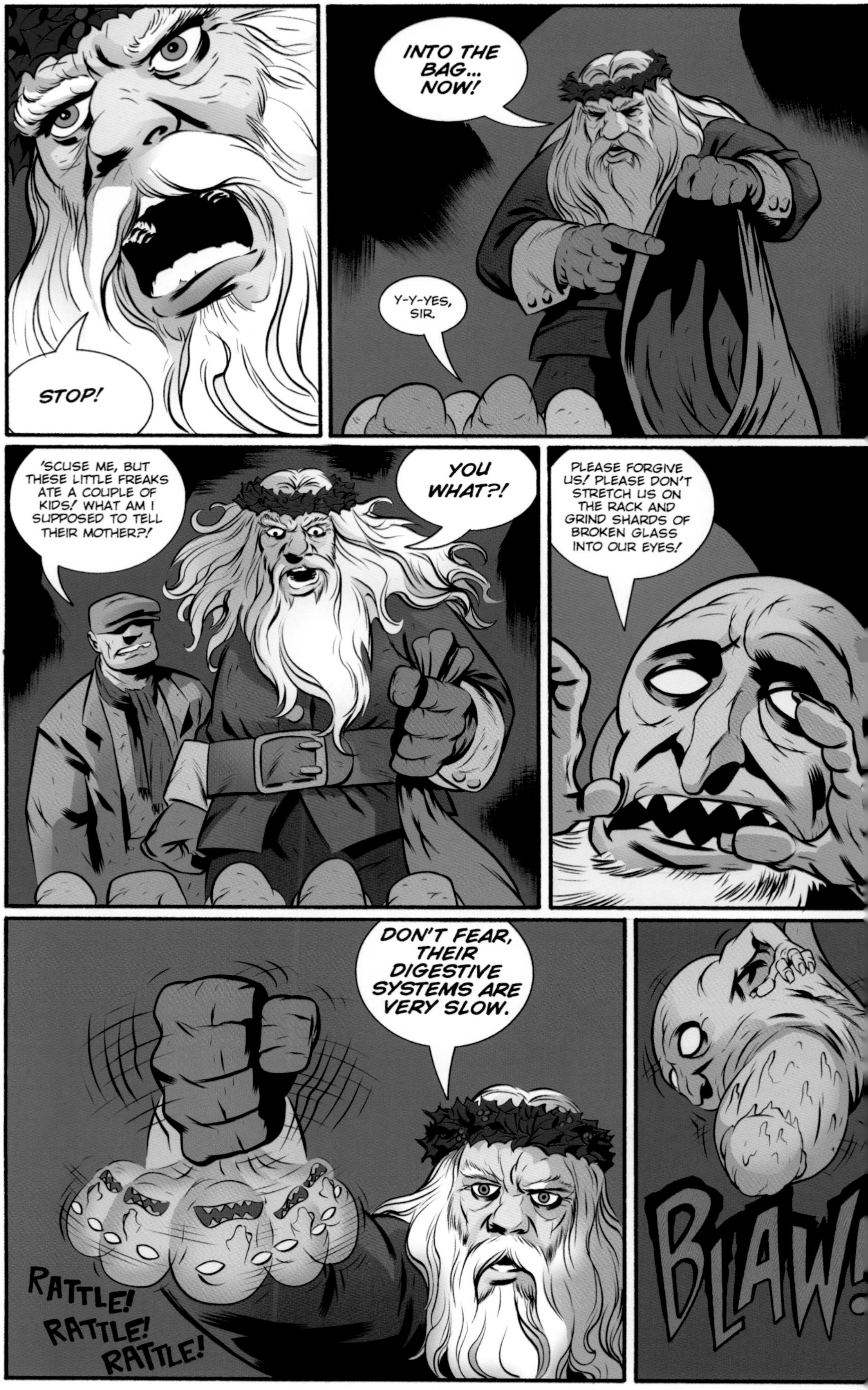
STOP!
INTO THE BAG... NOW!
Y-Y-YES, SIR.
'SCUSE ME, BUT THESE LITTLE FREAKS ATE A COUPLE OF KIDS! WHAT AM I SUPPOSED TO TELL THEIR MOTHER?!
YOU WHAT?!
PLEASE FORGIVE US! PLEASE DON'T STRETCH US ON THE RACK AND GRIND SHARDS OF BROKEN GLASS INTO OUR EYES!
DON'T FEAR, THEIR DIGESTIVE SYSTEMS ARE VERY SLOW.
RATTLE! RATTLE! RATTLE!
BLAW!

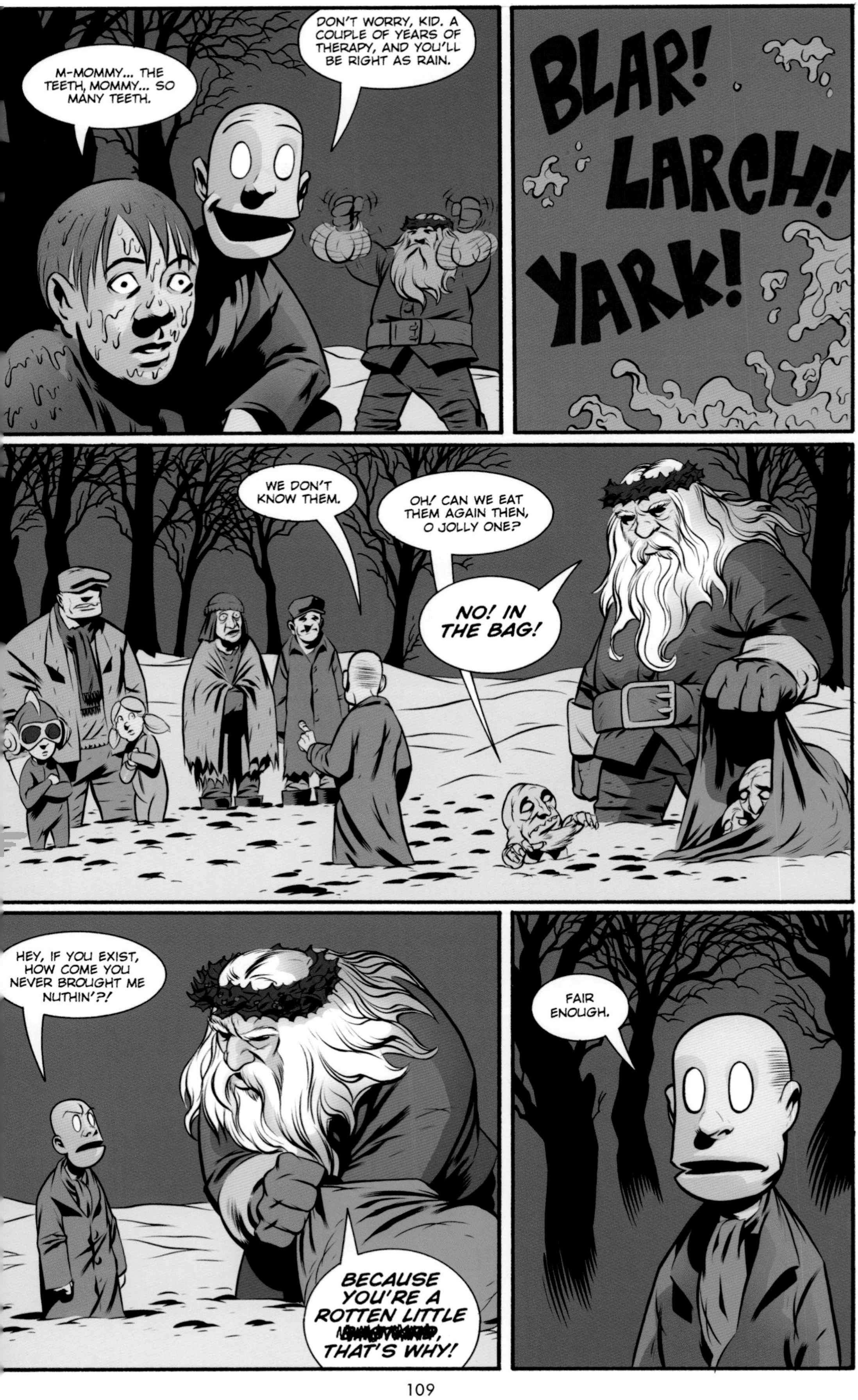
M-MOMMY... THE TEETH, MOMMY... SO MANY TEETH.
DON'T WORRY, KID. A COUPLE OF YEARS OF THERAPY, AND YOU'LL BE RIGHT AS RAIN.
BLAR! LARCH! YARK!
WE DON'T KNOW THEM.
OH! CAN WE EAT THEM AGAIN THEN, O JOLLY ONE?
NO! IN THE BAG!
HEY, IF YOU EXIST, HOW COME YOU NEVER BROUGHT ME NUTHIN'?!
BECAUSE YOU'RE A ROTTEN LITTLE [redacted], THAT'S WHY!
FAIR ENOUGH.

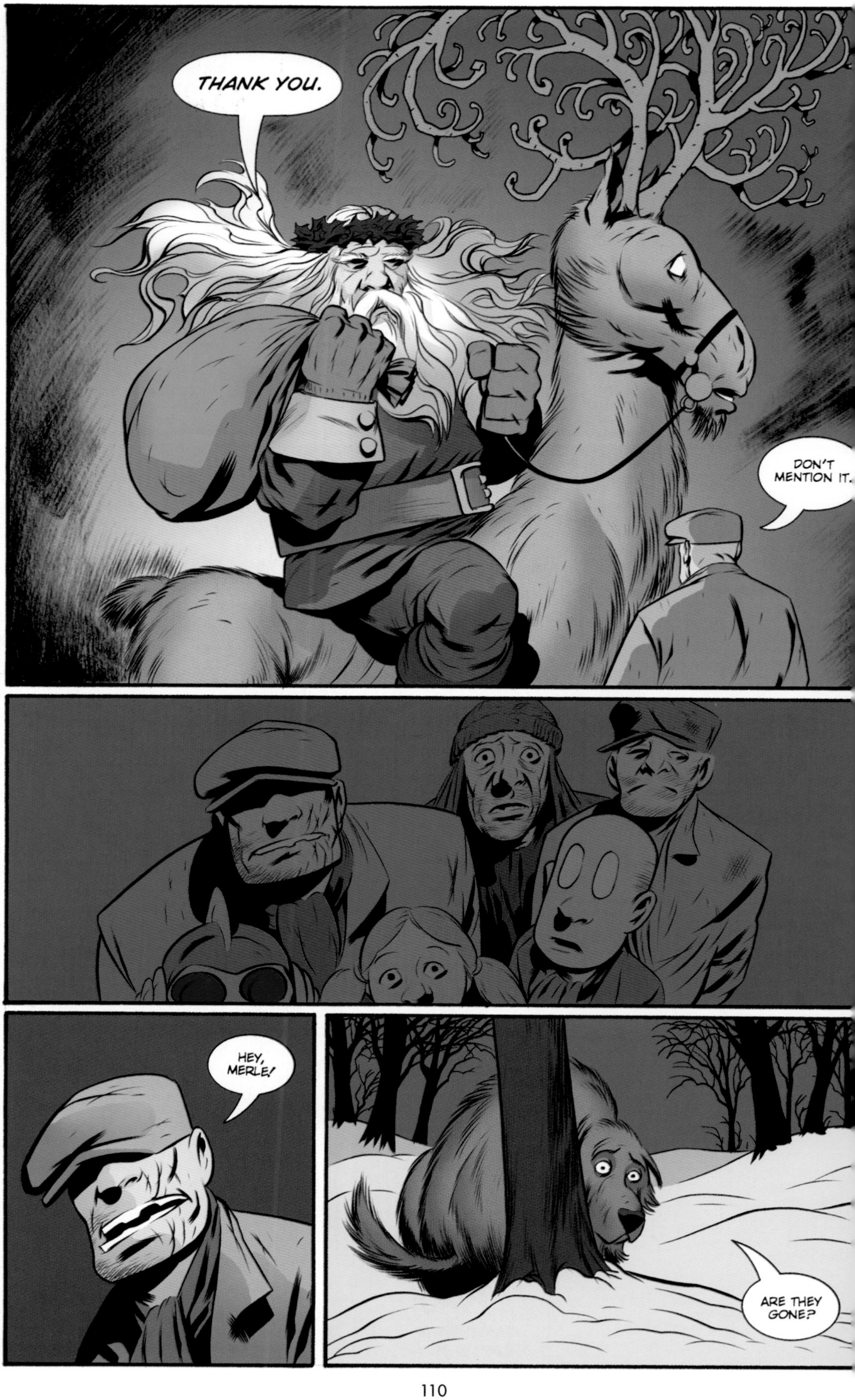
THANK YOU.
DON'T MENTION IT.
HEY, MERLE!
ARE THEY GONE?

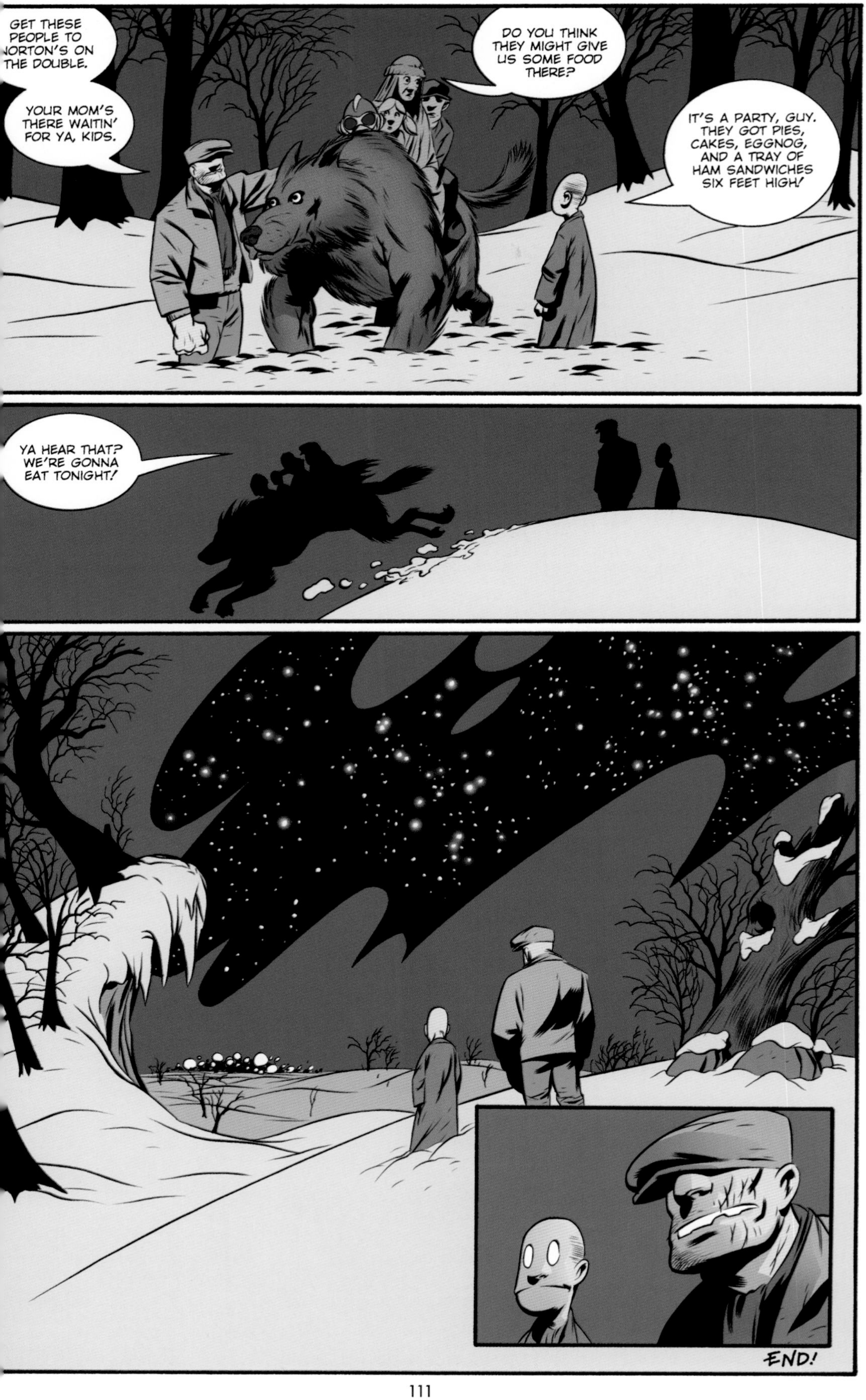
GET THESE PEOPLE TO NORTON'S ON THE DOUBLE.
YOUR MOM'S THERE WAITIN' FOR YA, KIDS.
DO YOU THINK THEY MIGHT GIVE US SOME FOOD THERE?
IT'S A PARTY, GUY. THEY GOT PIES, CAKES, EGGNOG, AND A TRAY OF HAM SANDWICHES SIX FEET HIGH!
YA HEAR THAT? WE'RE GONNA EAT TONIGHT!
END!

CHAPTER 5

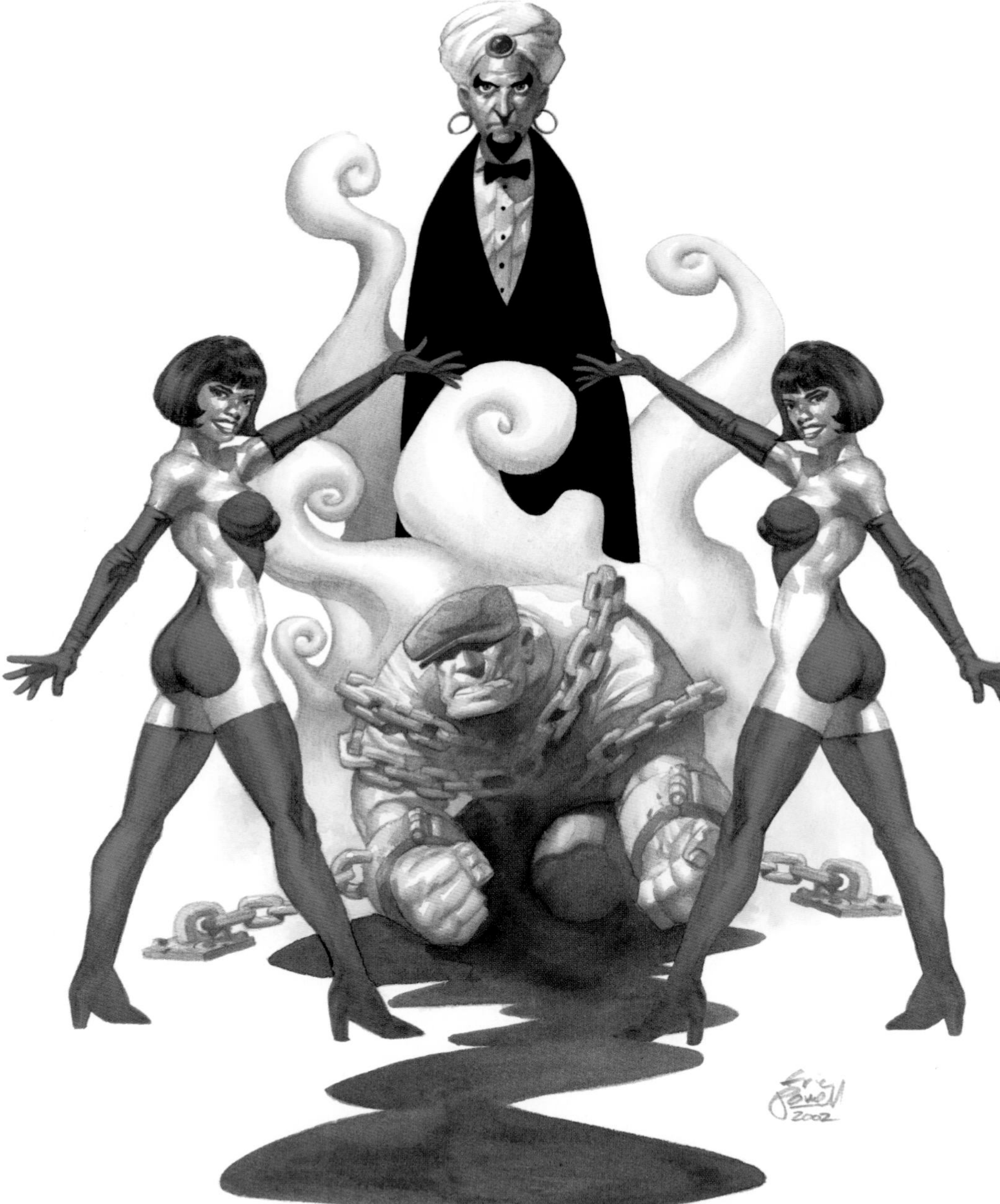

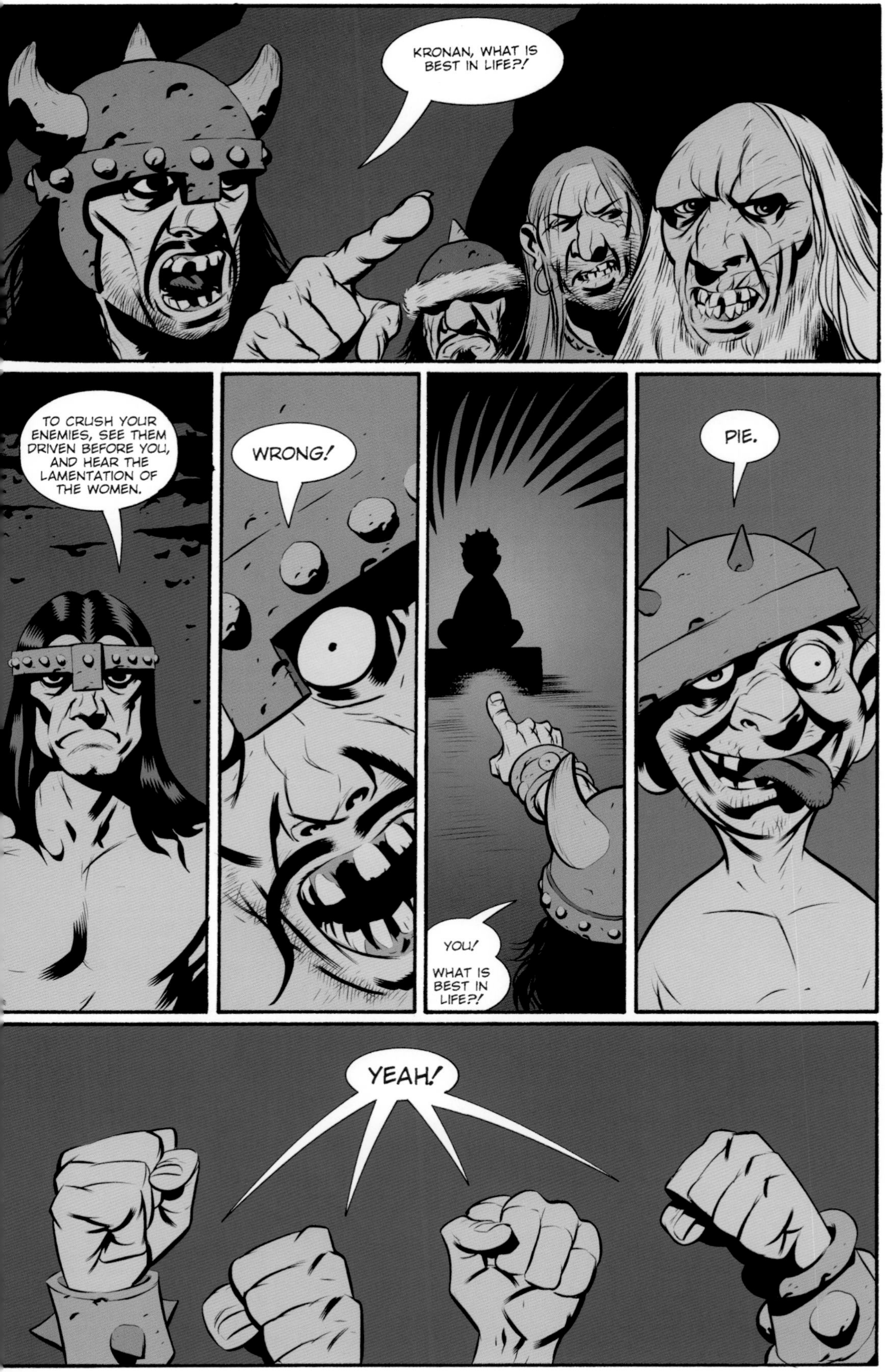
KRONAN, WHAT IS BEST IN LIFE?!
TO CRUSH YOUR ENEMIES, SEE THEM DRIVEN BEFORE YOU, AND HEAR THE LAMENTATION OF THE WOMEN.
WRONG!
YOU! WHAT IS BEST IN LIFE?!
PIE.
YEAH!

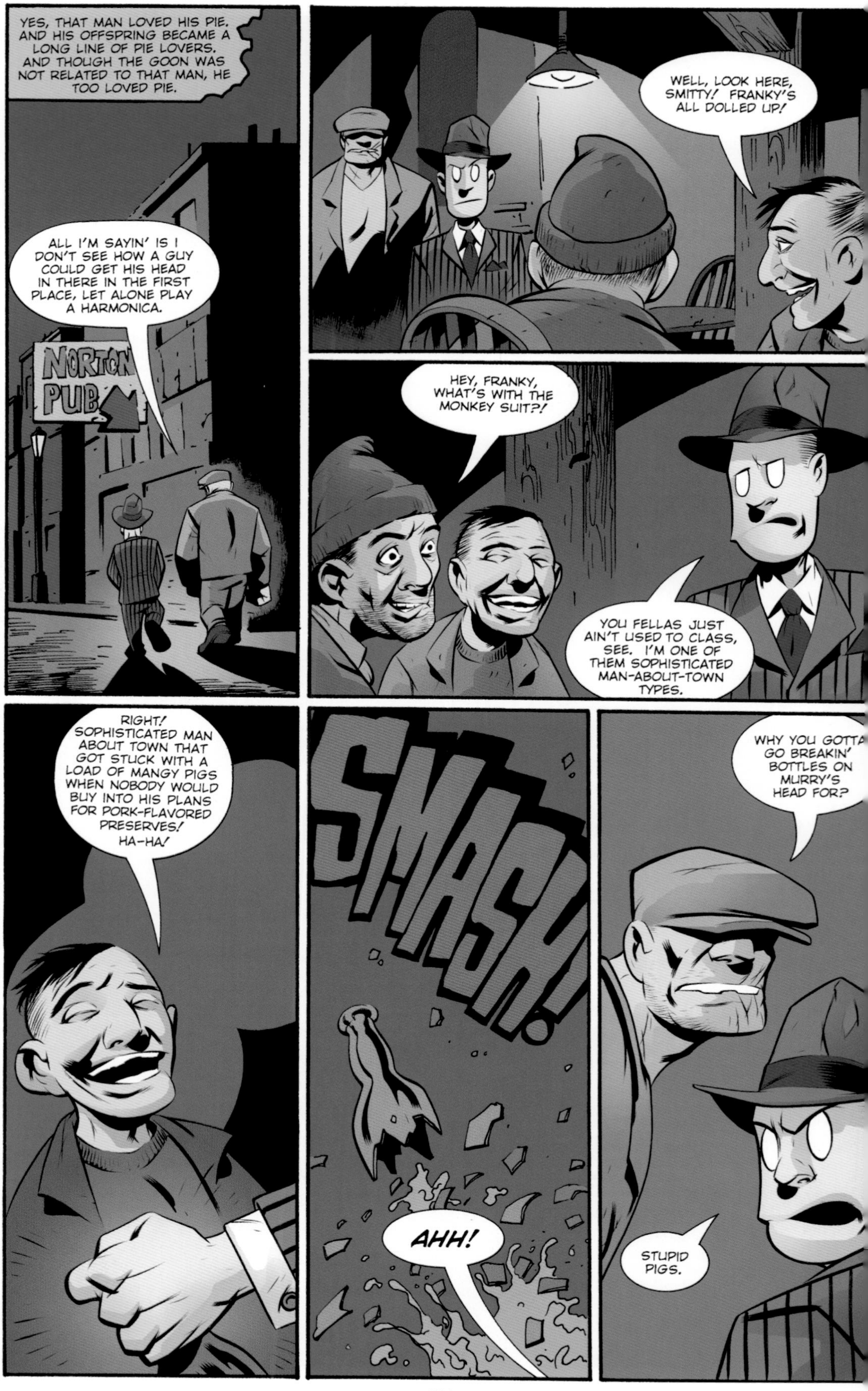

YES, THAT MAN LOVED HIS PIE. AND HIS OFFSPRING BECAME A LONG LINE OF PIE LOVERS. AND THOUGH THE GOON WAS NOT RELATED TO THAT MAN, HE TOO LOVED PIE.
ALL I'M SAYIN' IS I DON'T SEE HOW A GUY COULD GET HIS HEAD IN THERE IN THE FIRST PLACE, LET ALONE PLAY A HARMONICA.
NORTON PUB
WELL, LOOK HERE, SMITTY! FRANKY'S ALL DOLLED UP!
HEY, FRANKY, WHAT'S WITH THE MONKEY SUIT?!
YOU FELLAS JUST AIN'T USED TO CLASS, SEE. I'M ONE OF THEM SOPHISTICATED MAN-ABOUT-TOWN TYPES.
RIGHT! SOPHISTICATED MAN ABOUT TOWN THAT GOT STUCK WITH A LOAD OF MANGY PIGS WHEN NOBODY WOULD BUY INTO HIS PLANS FOR PORK-FLAVORED PRESERVES! HA-HA!
SMASH!
AHH!
WHY YOU GOTTA GO BREAKIN' BOTTLES ON MURRY'S HEAD FOR?
STUPID PIGS.

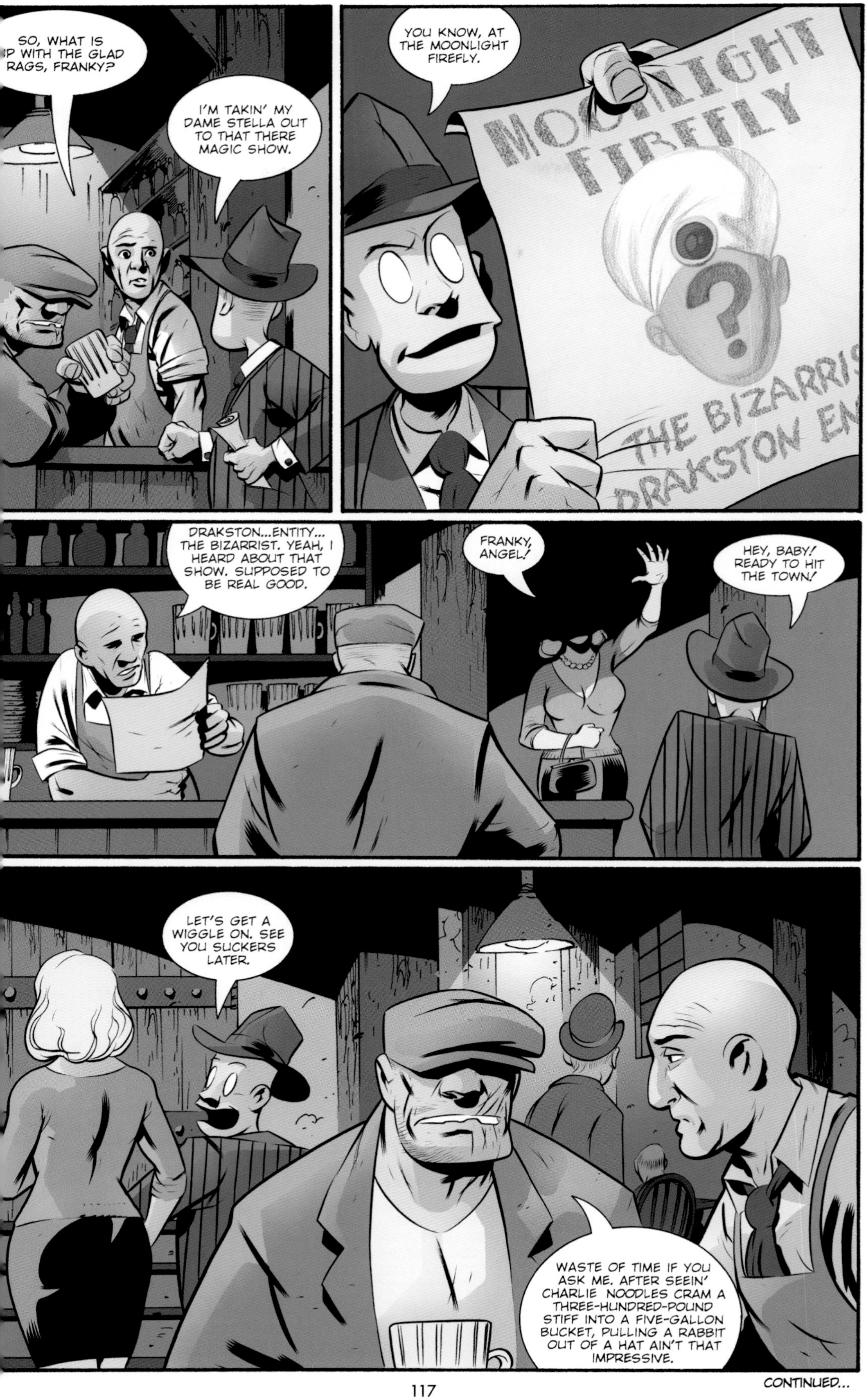
SO, WHAT IS
P WITH THE GLAD RAGS, FRANKY?
I'M TAKIN' MY DAME STELLA OUT TO THAT THERE MAGIC SHOW.
YOU KNOW, AT THE MOONLIGHT FIREFLY.
FIREFLY
THE BIZARRIS
DRAKSTON EN
DRAKSTON...ENTITY... THE BIZARRIST. YEAH, I HEARD ABOUT THAT SHOW. SUPPOSED TO BE REAL GOOD.
FRANKY, ANGEL!
HEY, BABY! READY TO HIT THE TOWN!
LET'S GET A WIGGLE ON. SEE YOU SUCKERS LATER.
WASTE OF TIME IF YOU ASK ME. AFTER SEEIN' CHARLIE NOODLES CRAM A THREE-HUNDRED-POUND STIFF INTO A FIVE-GALLON BUCKET, PULLING A RABBIT OUT OF A HAT AIN'T THAT IMPRESSIVE.

CONTINUED...

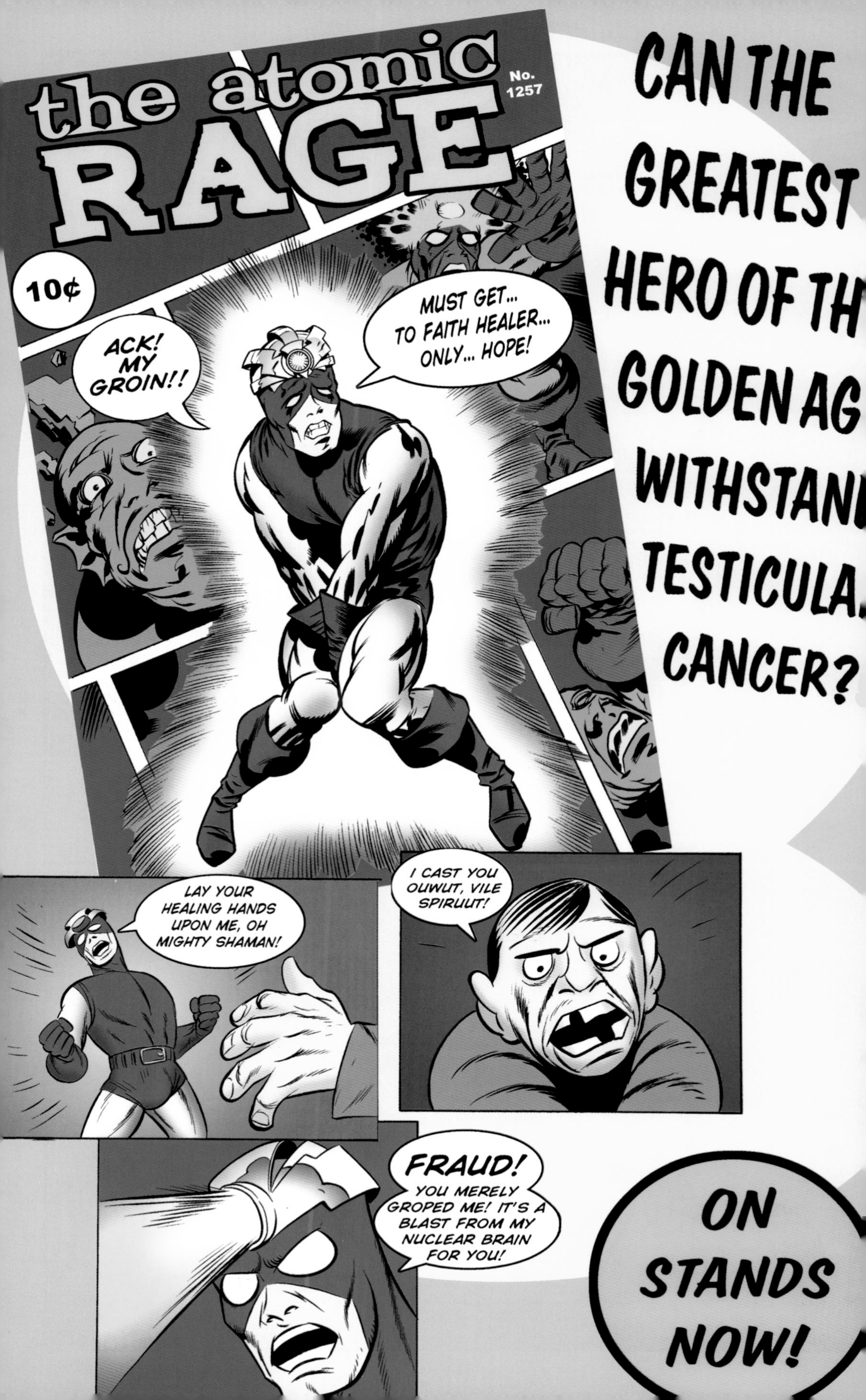

the atomic RAGE
No. 1257
10¢
ACK! MY GROIN!!
MUST GET... TO FAITH HEALER... ONLY... HOPE!
CAN THE GREATEST HERO OF TH GOLDEN AG WITHSTAN TESTICULA CANCER?
LAY YOUR HEALING HANDS UPON ME, OH MIGHTY SHAMAN!
I CAST YOU OUWUT, VILE SPIRUUT!
FRAUD! YOU MERELY GROPED ME! IT'S A BLAST FROM MY NUCLEAR BRAIN FOR YOU!
ON STANDS NOW!

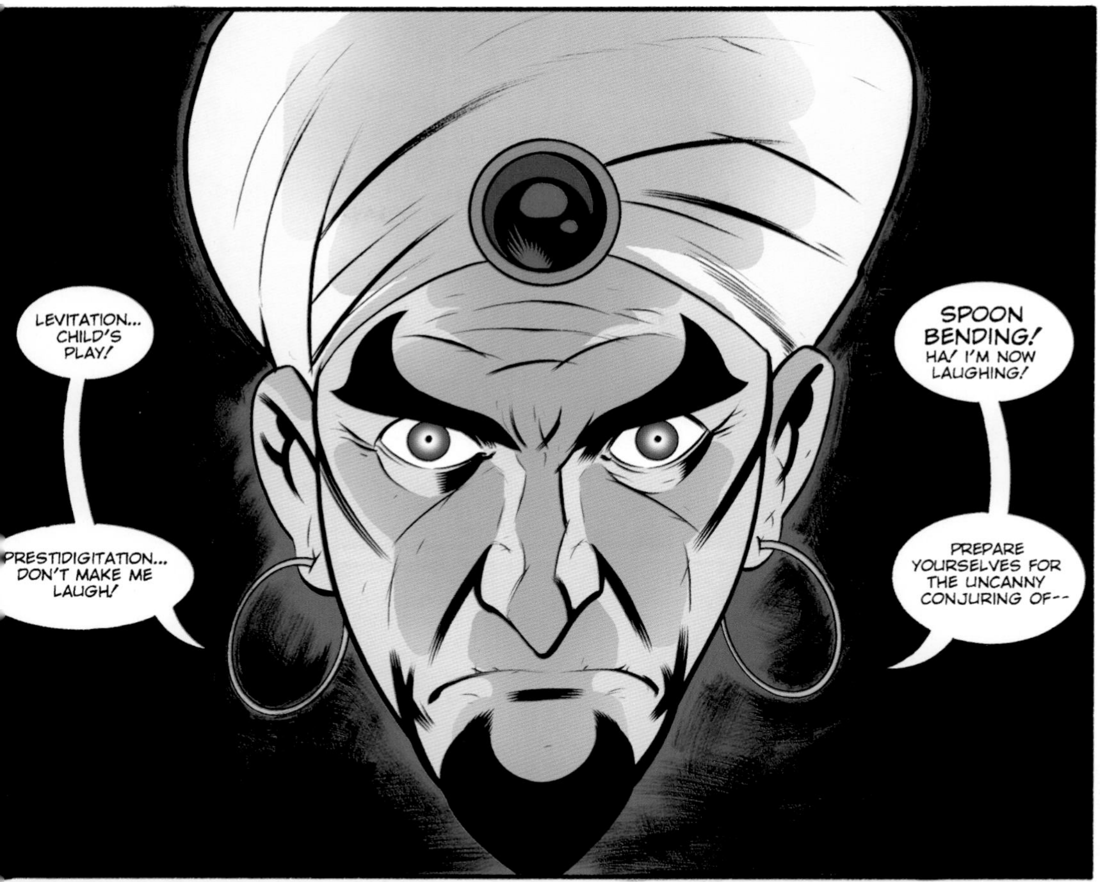
LEVITATION... CHILD'S PLAY!
PRESTIDIGITATION... DON'T MAKE ME LAUGH!
SPOON BENDING! HA! I'M NOW LAUGHING!
PREPARE YOURSELVES FOR THE UNCANNY CONJURING OF--

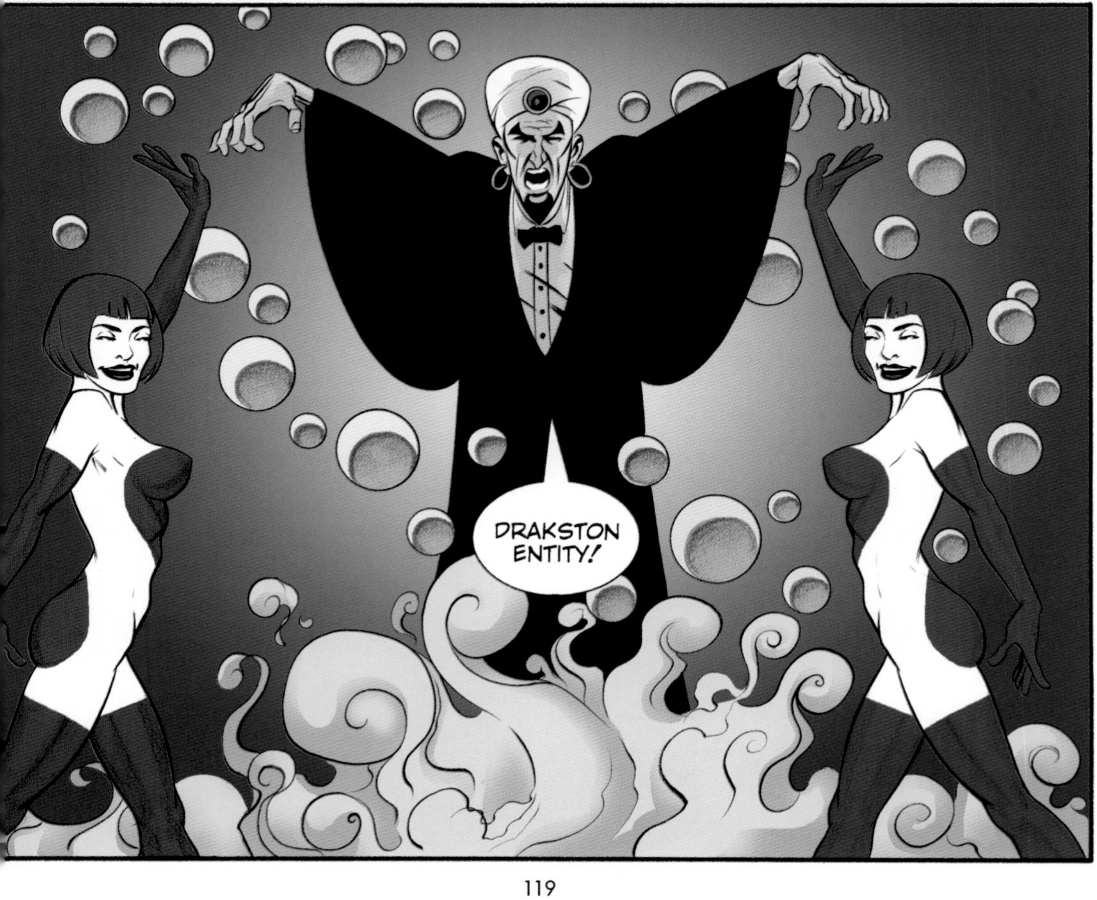
DRAKSTON ENTITY!

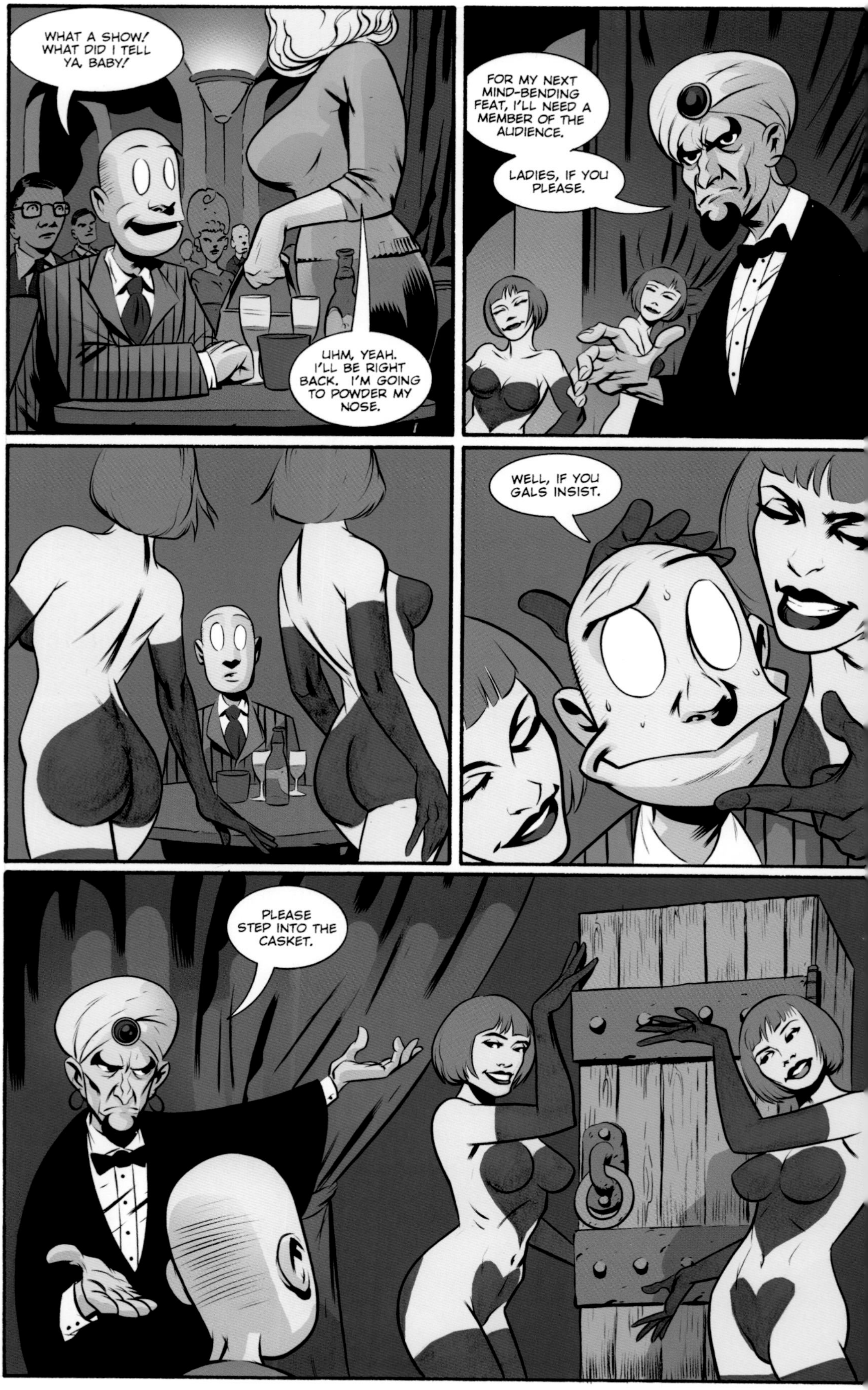
WHAT A SHOW! WHAT DID I TELL YA, BABY!
UHM, YEAH. I'LL BE RIGHT BACK. I'M GOING TO POWDER MY NOSE.
FOR MY NEXT MIND-BENDING FEAT, I'LL NEED A MEMBER OF THE AUDIENCE.
LADIES, IF YOU PLEASE.
WELL, IF YOU GALS INSIST.
PLEASE STEP INTO THE CASKET.

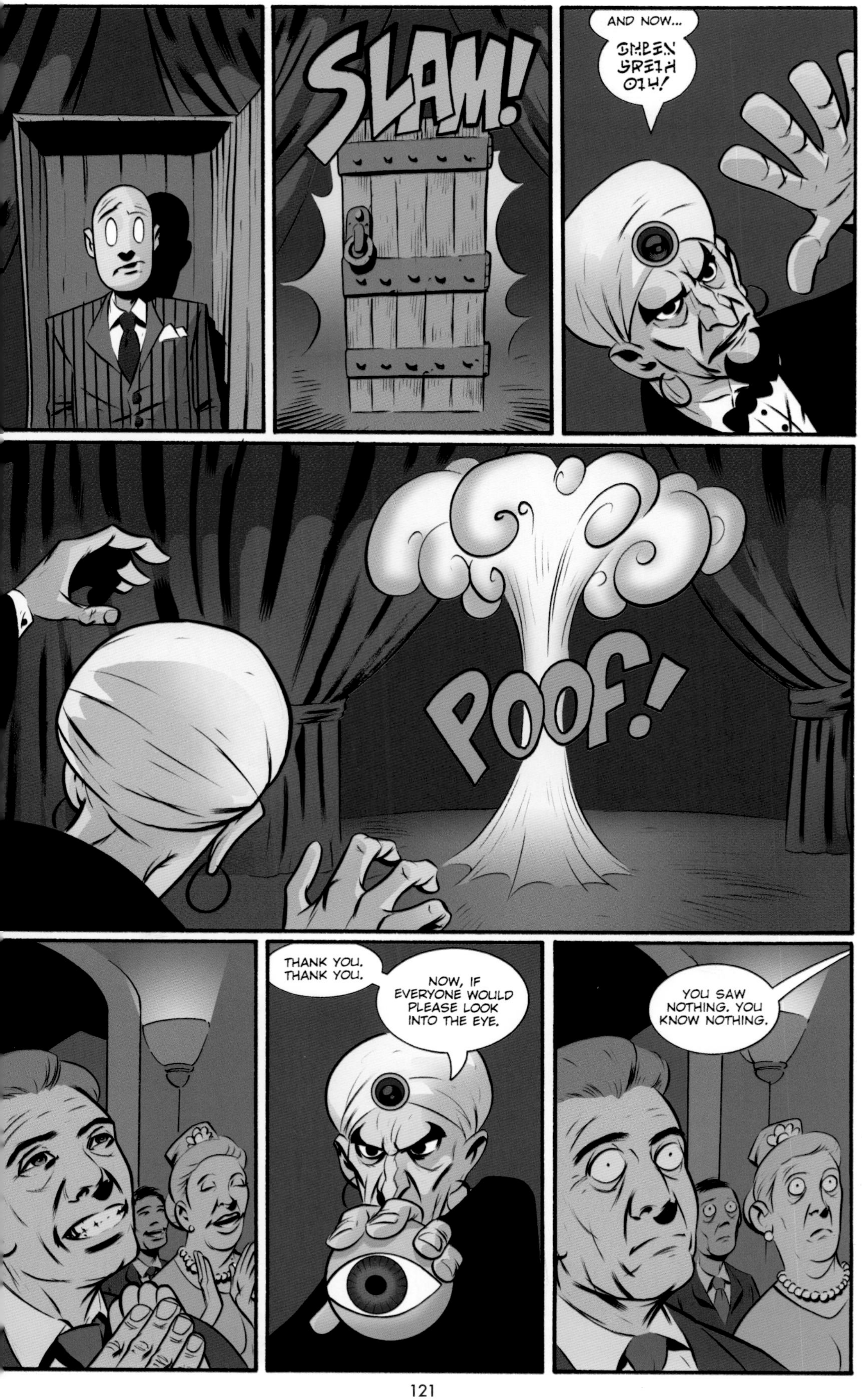
SLAM!
AND NOW...
POOF!
THANK YOU. THANK YOU.
NOW, IF EVERYONE WOULD PLEASE LOOK INTO THE EYE.
YOU SAW NOTHING. YOU KNOW NOTHING.

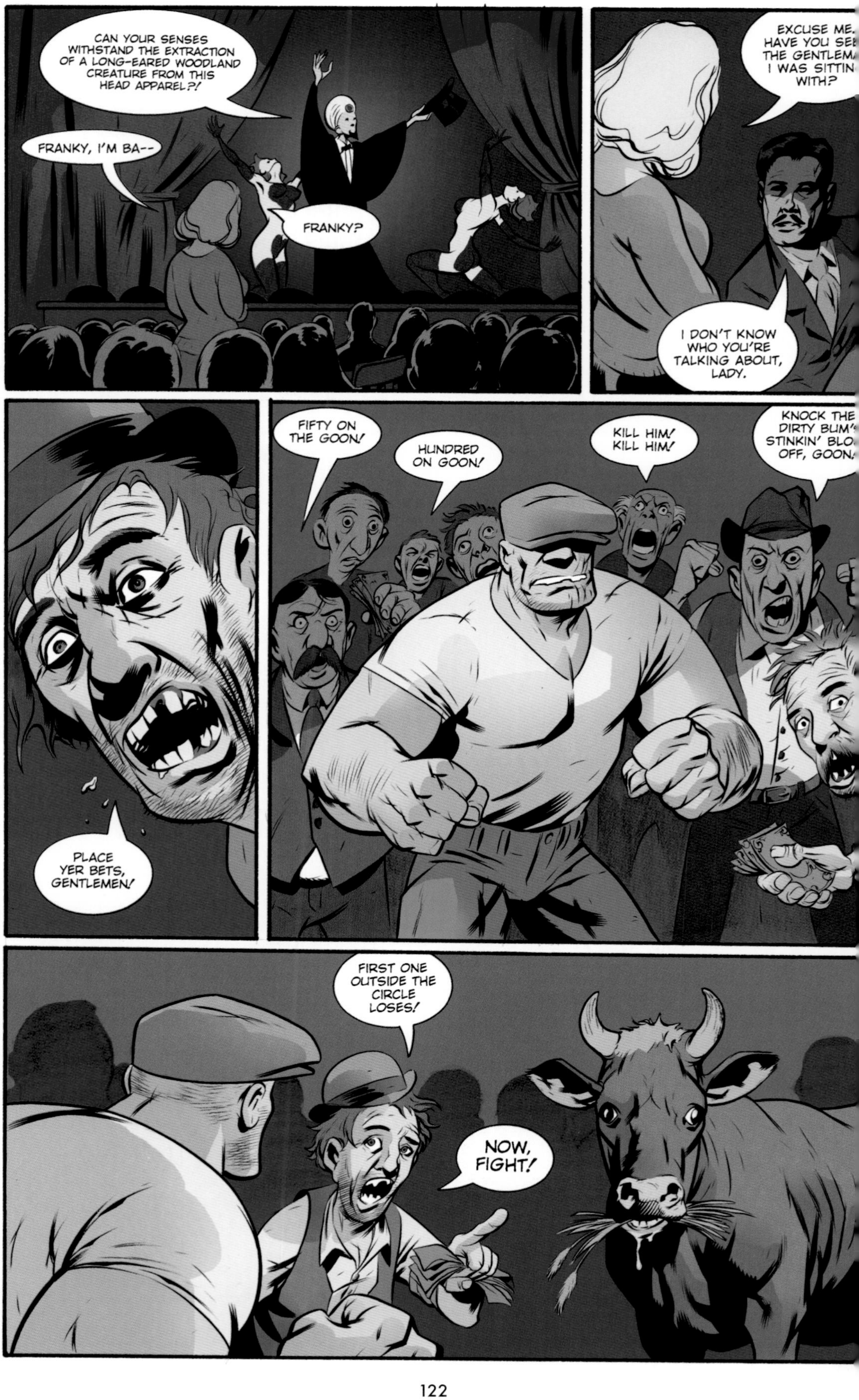

CAN YOUR SENSES WITHSTAND THE EXTRACTION OF A LONG-EARED WOODLAND CREATURE FROM THIS HEAD APPAREL?!
FRANKY, I'M BA--
FRANKY?
EXCUSE ME. HAVE YOU SE THE GENTLEMA I WAS SITTIN WITH?
I DON'T KNOW WHO YOU'RE TALKING ABOUT, LADY.
PLACE YER BETS, GENTLEMEN!
FIFTY ON THE GOON!
HUNDRED ON GOON!
KILL HIM! KILL HIM!
KNOCK THE DIRTY BUM' STINKIN' BLO OFF, GOON
FIRST ONE OUTSIDE THE CIRCLE LOSES!
NOW, FIGHT!

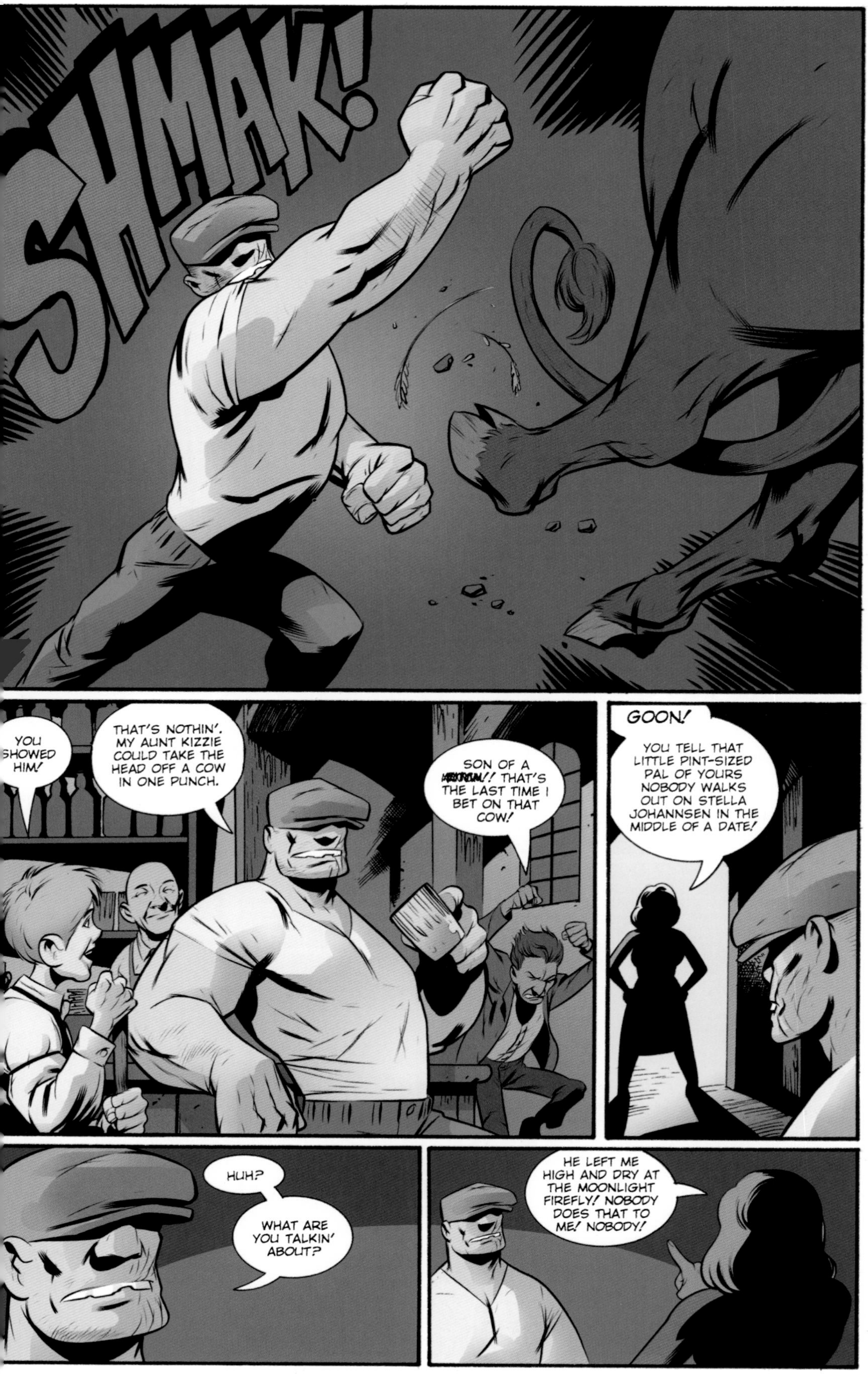
SHMAK!
YOU SHOWED HIM!
THAT'S NOTHIN'. MY AUNT KIZZIE COULD TAKE THE HEAD OFF A COW IN ONE PUNCH.
SON OF A [redacted]!! THAT'S THE LAST TIME I BET ON THAT COW!
GOON!
YOU TELL THAT LITTLE PINT-SIZED PAL OF YOURS NOBODY WALKS OUT ON STELLA JOHANNSEN IN THE MIDDLE OF A DATE!
HUH?
WHAT ARE YOU TALKIN' ABOUT?
HE LEFT ME HIGH AND DRY AT THE MOONLIGHT FIREFLY! NOBODY DOES THAT TO ME! NOBODY!

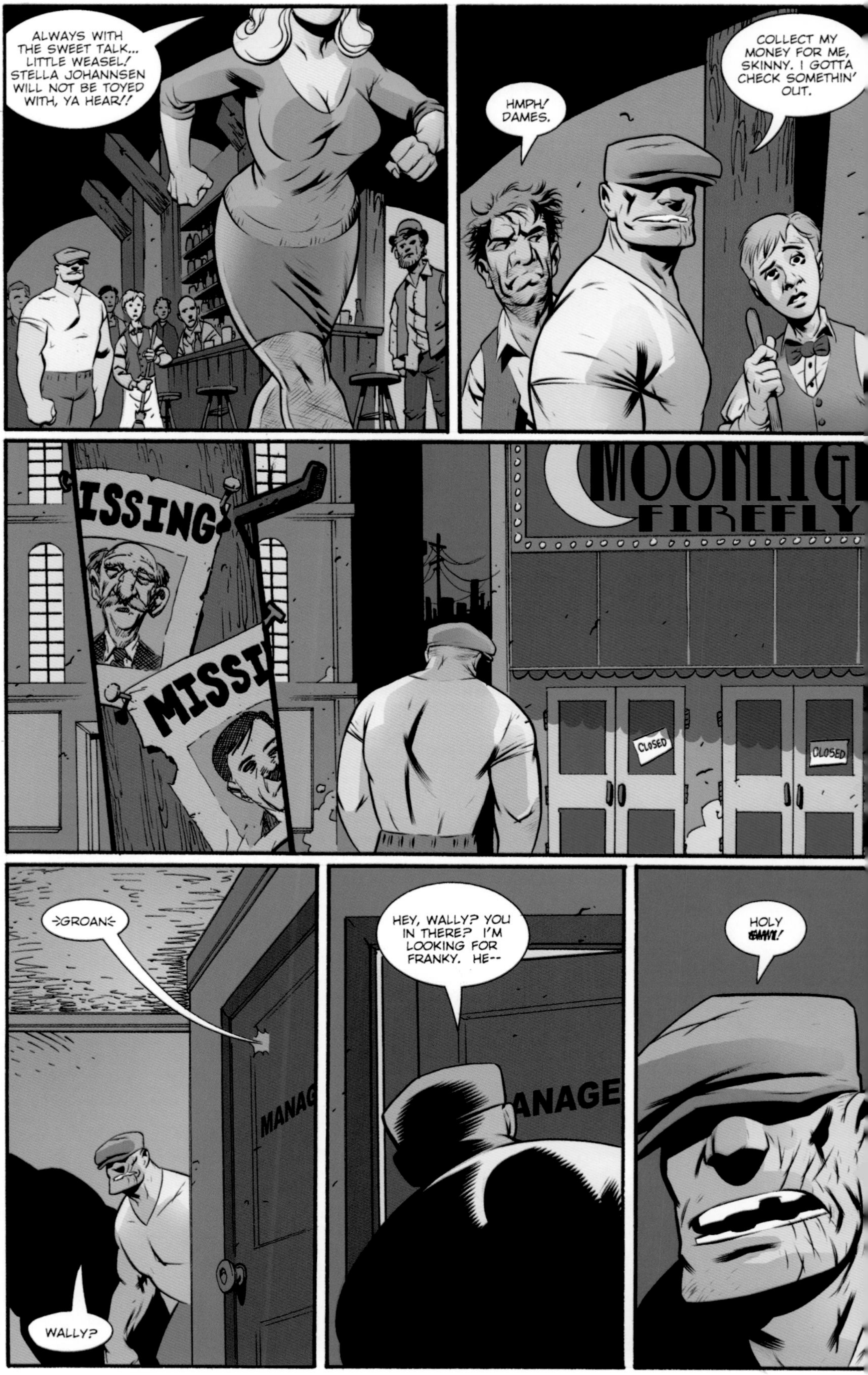
ALWAYS WITH THE SWEET TALK... LITTLE WEASEL! STELLA JOHANNSEN WILL NOT BE TOYED WITH, YA HEAR?!
HMPH! DAMES.
COLLECT MY MONEY FOR ME, SKINNY. I GOTTA CHECK SOMETHIN' OUT.
ISSING!
MISSI
MOONLIG
FIREFLY
CLOSED
CLOSED
GROAN
MANAG
WALLY?
HEY, WALLY? YOU IN THERE? I'M LOOKING FOR FRANKY. HE--
ANAGE
HOLY

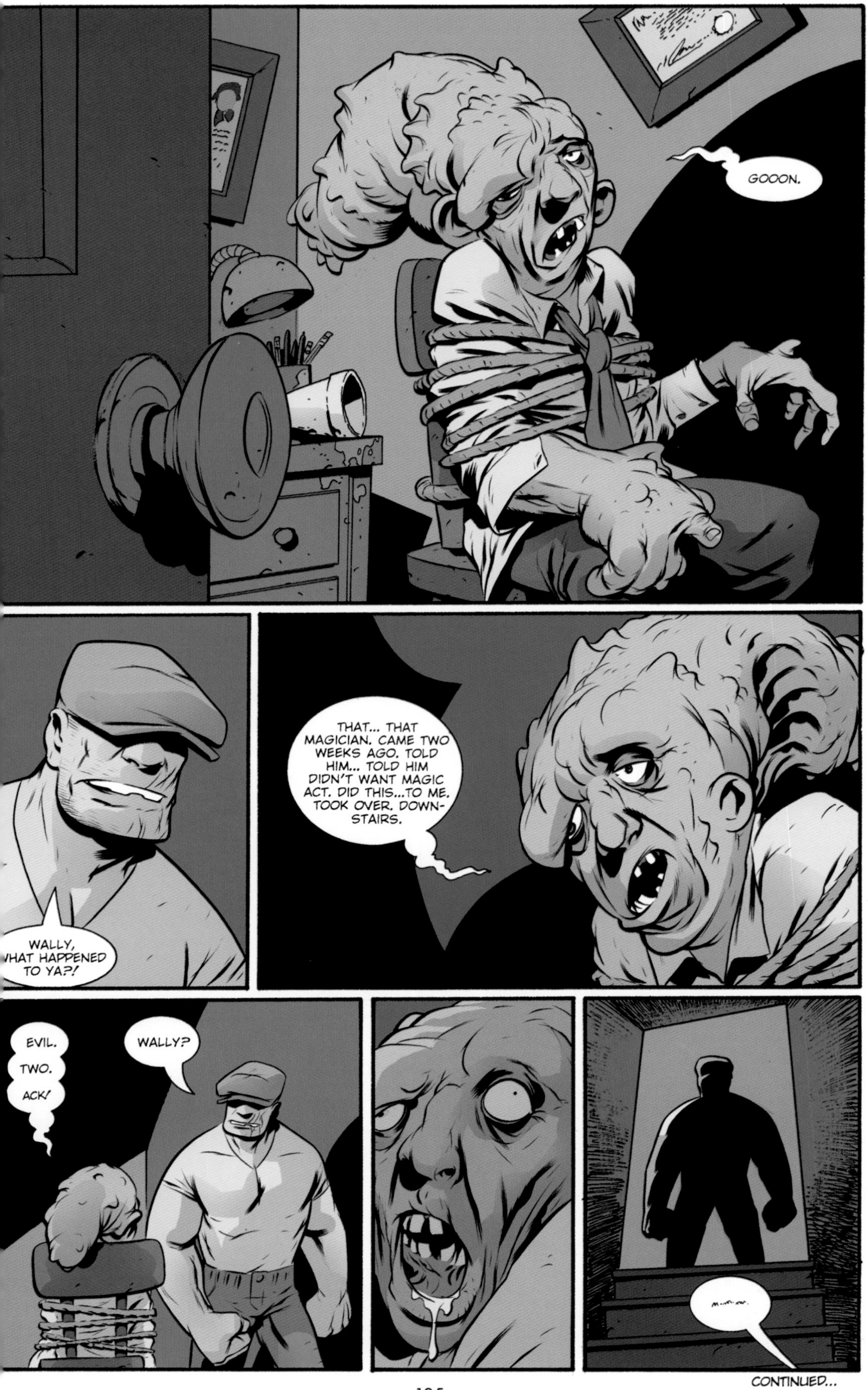
GOOON.
WALLY, WHAT HAPPENED TO YA?!
THAT... THAT MAGICIAN. CAME TWO WEEKS AGO. TOLD HIM... TOLD HIM DIDN'T WANT MAGIC ACT. DID THIS...TO ME. TOOK OVER. DOWN-STAIRS.
EVIL.
TWO.
ACK!
WALLY?

CONTINUED...

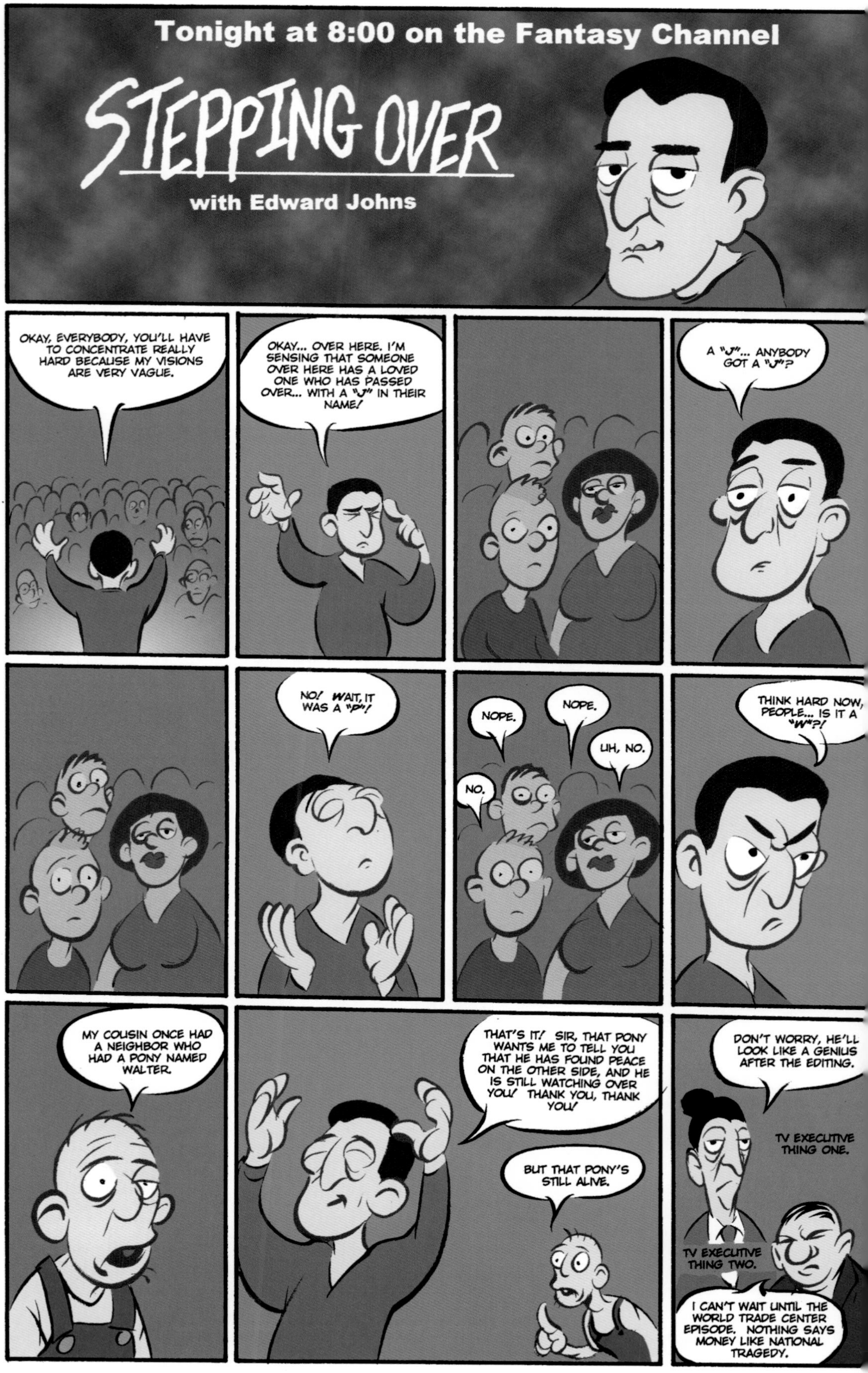
Tonight at 8:00 on the Fantasy Channel
STEPPING OVER
with Edward Johns
OKAY, EVERYBODY, YOU'LL HAVE TO CONCENTRATE REALLY HARD BECAUSE MY VISIONS ARE VERY VAGUE.
OKAY... OVER HERE. I'M SENSING THAT SOMEONE OVER HERE HAS A LOVED ONE WHO HAS PASSED OVER... WITH A "J" IN THEIR NAME!
A "J"... ANYBODY GOT A "J"?
NO! WAIT, IT WAS A "P"!
NOPE.
NOPE.
UH, NO.
NO.
THINK HARD NOW, PEOPLE... IS IT A "W"?!
MY COUSIN ONCE HAD A NEIGHBOR WHO HAD A PONY NAMED WALTER.
THAT'S IT! SIR, THAT PONY WANTS ME TO TELL YOU THAT HE HAS FOUND PEACE ON THE OTHER SIDE, AND HE IS STILL WATCHING OVER YOU! THANK YOU, THANK YOU!
BUT THAT PONY'S STILL ALIVE.
DON'T WORRY, HE'LL LOOK LIKE A GENIUS AFTER THE EDITING.
TV EXECUTIVE THING ONE.
TV EXECUTIVE THING TWO.
I CAN'T WAIT UNTIL THE WORLD TRADE CENTER EPISODE. NOTHING SAYS MONEY LIKE NATIONAL TRAGEDY.

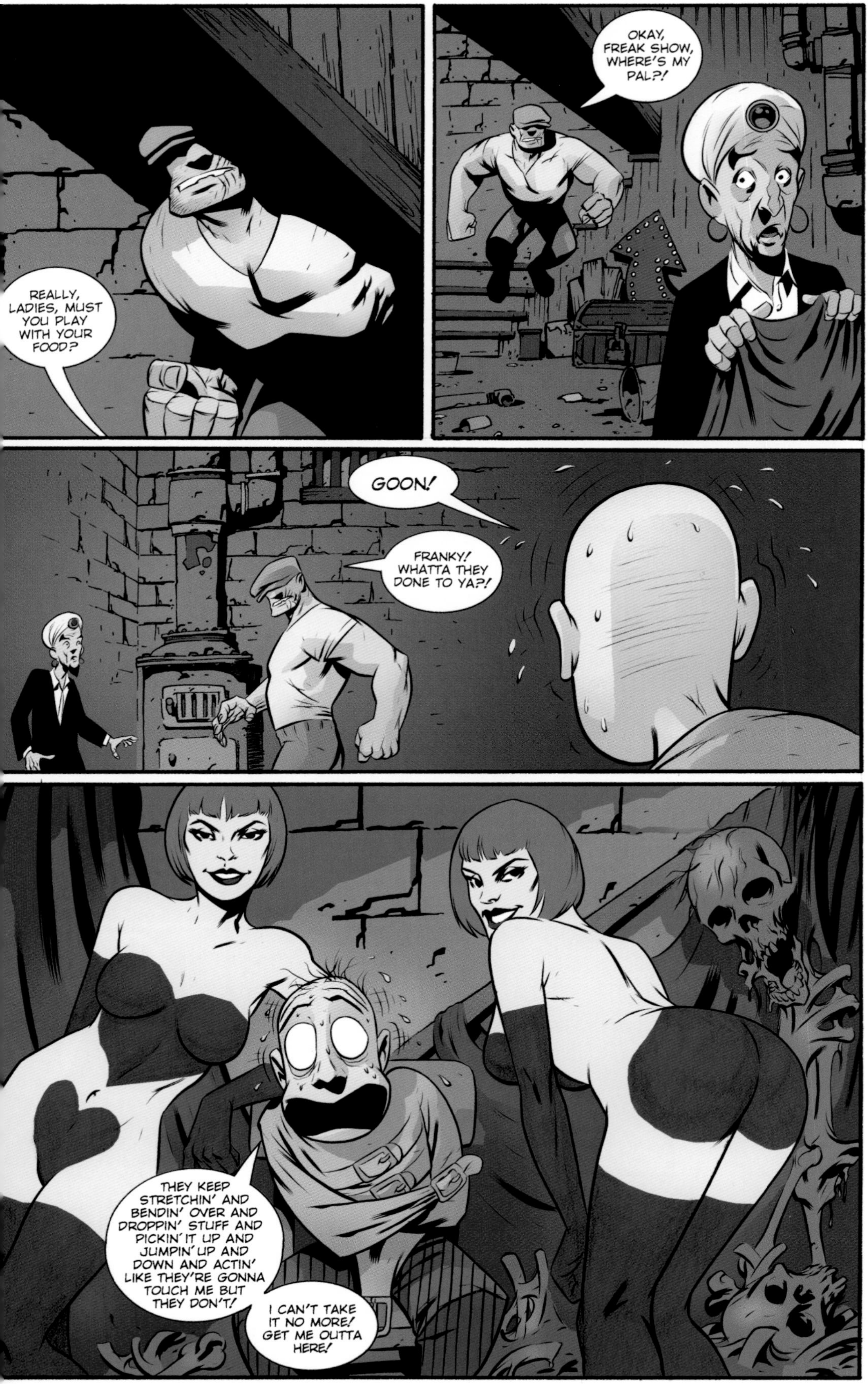
REALLY, LADIES, MUST YOU PLAY WITH YOUR FOOD?
OKAY, FREAK SHOW, WHERE'S MY PAL?!
GOON!
FRANKY! WHATTA THEY DONE TO YA?!
THEY KEEP STRETCHIN' AND BENDIN' OVER AND DROPPIN' STUFF AND PICKIN' IT UP AND JUMPIN' UP AND DOWN AND ACTIN' LIKE THEY'RE GONNA TOUCH ME BUT THEY DON'T!
I CAN'T TAKE IT NO MORE! GET ME OUTTA HERE!

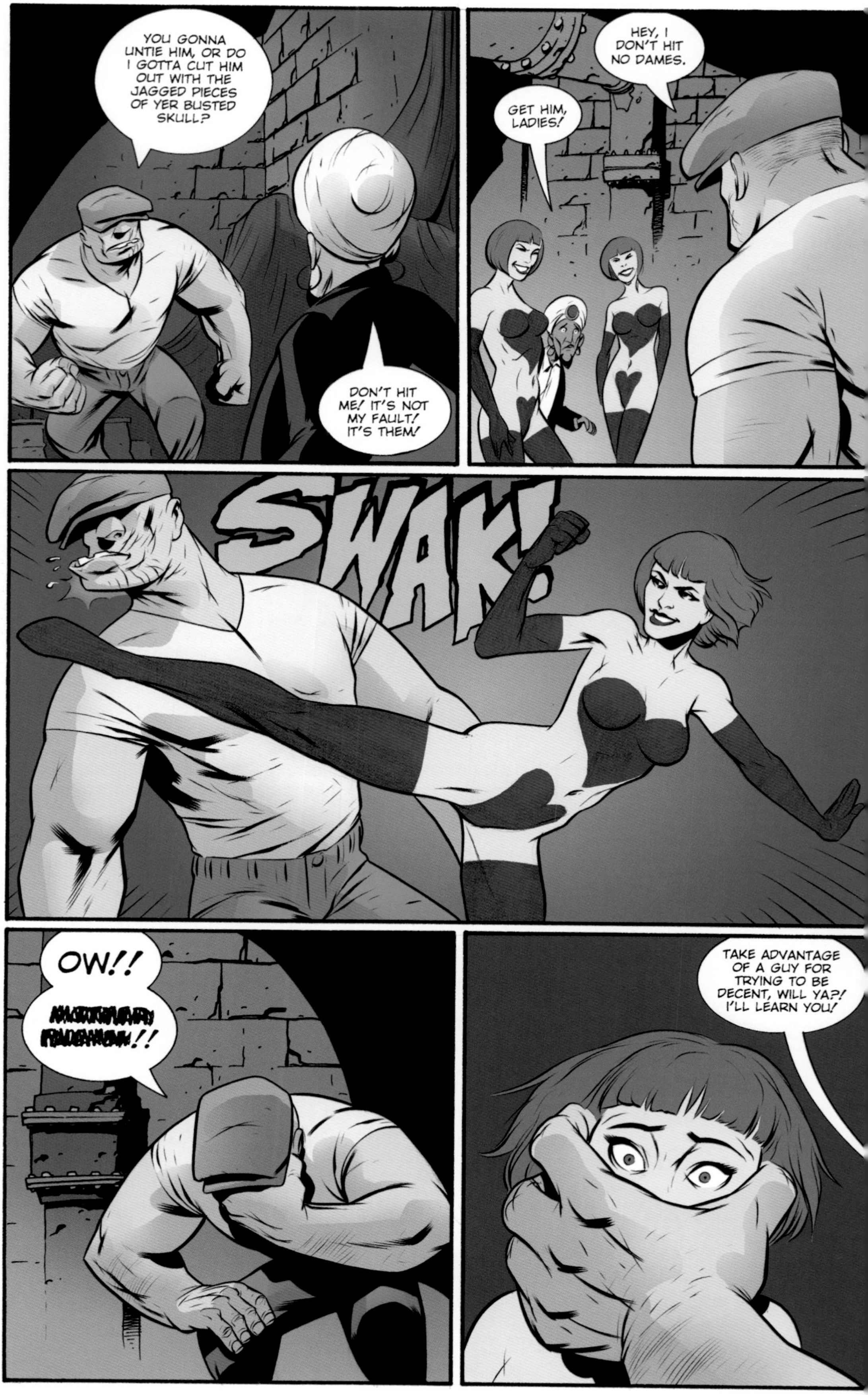
YOU GONNA UNTIE HIM, OR DO I GOTTA CUT HIM OUT WITH THE JAGGED PIECES OF YER BUSTED SKULL?
DON'T HIT ME! IT'S NOT MY FAULT! IT'S THEM!
HEY, I DON'T HIT NO DAMES.
GET HIM, LADIES!
SWAK!
OW!!
TAKE ADVANTAGE OF A GUY FOR TRYING TO BE DECENT, WILL YA?! I'LL LEARN YOU!

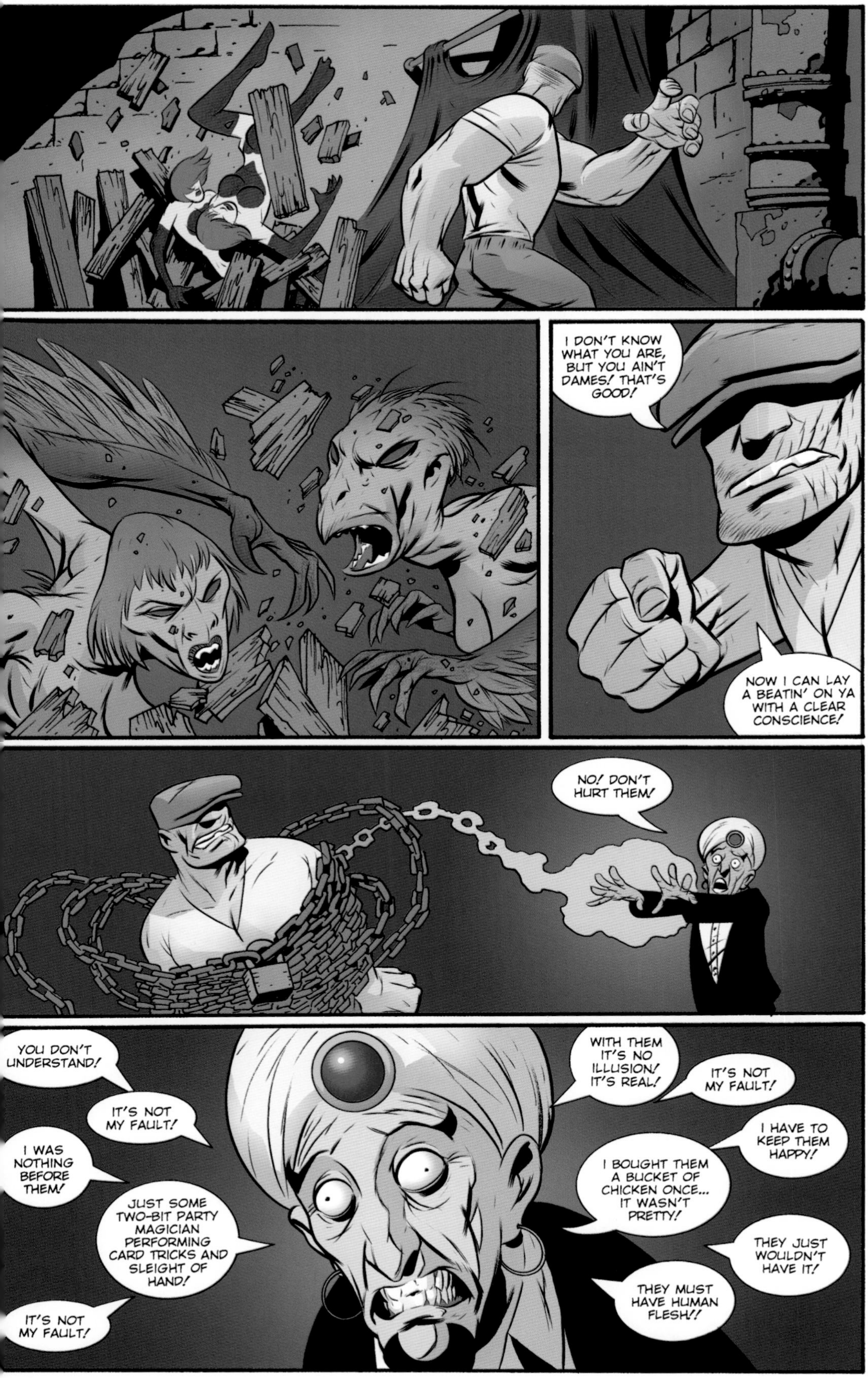

I DON'T KNOW WHAT YOU ARE, BUT YOU AIN'T DAMES! THAT'S GOOD!
NOW I CAN LAY A BEATIN' ON YA WITH A CLEAR CONSCIENCE!
NO! DON'T HURT THEM!
YOU DON'T UNDERSTAND!
IT'S NOT MY FAULT!
I WAS NOTHING BEFORE THEM!
JUST SOME TWO-BIT PARTY MAGICIAN PERFORMING CARD TRICKS AND SLEIGHT OF HAND!
IT'S NOT MY FAULT!
WITH THEM IT'S NO ILLUSION! IT'S REAL!
IT'S NOT MY FAULT!
I HAVE TO KEEP THEM HAPPY!
I BOUGHT THEM A BUCKET OF CHICKEN ONCE... IT WASN'T PRETTY!
THEY JUST WOULDN'T HAVE IT!
THEY MUST HAVE HUMAN FLESH!!

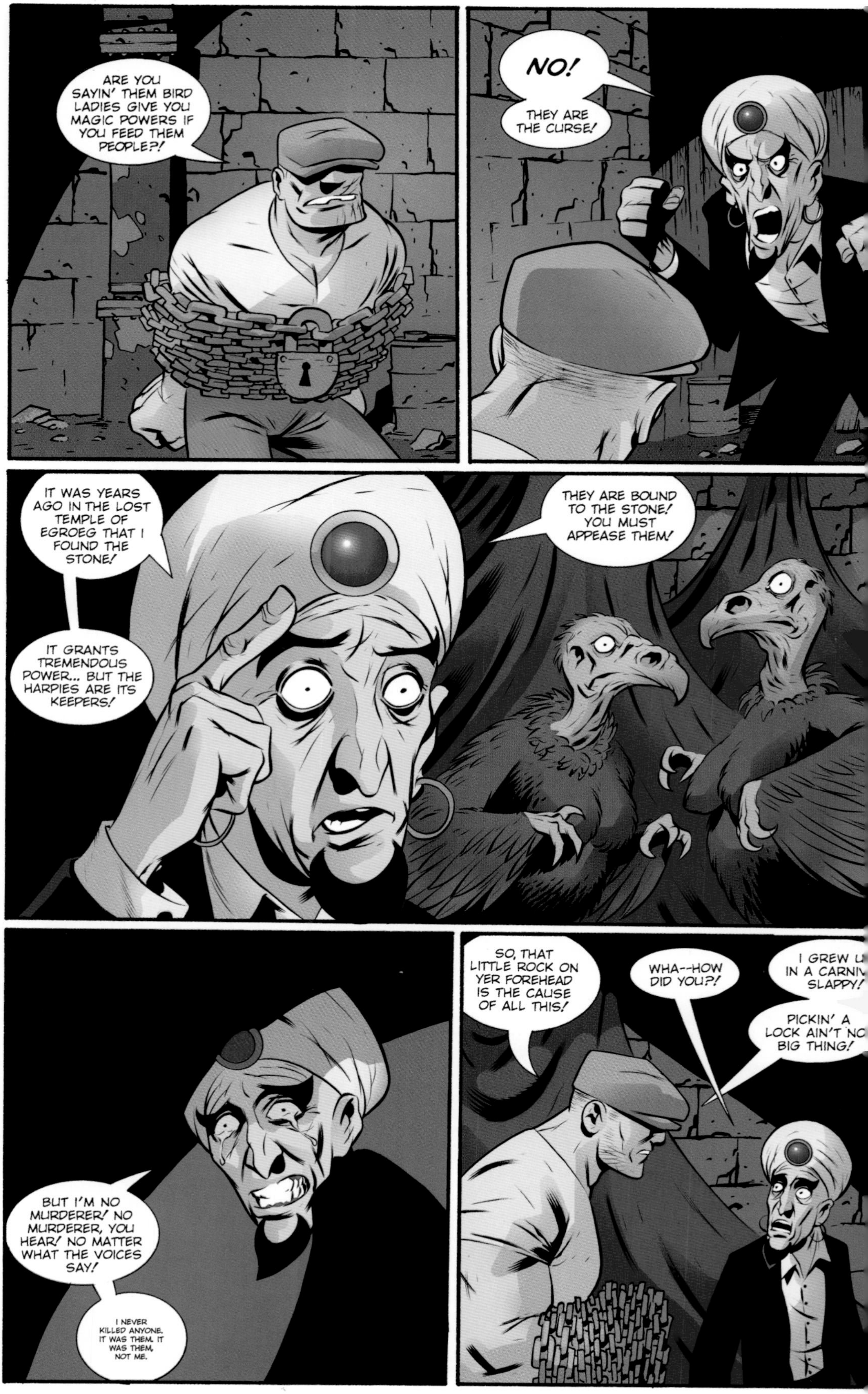
ARE YOU SAYIN' THEM BIRD LADIES GIVE YOU MAGIC POWERS IF YOU FEED THEM PEOPLE?!
NO!
THEY ARE THE CURSE!
IT WAS YEARS AGO IN THE LOST TEMPLE OF EGROEG THAT I FOUND THE STONE!
IT GRANTS TREMENDOUS POWER... BUT THE HARPIES ARE ITS KEEPERS!
THEY ARE BOUND TO THE STONE! YOU MUST APPEASE THEM!
BUT I'M NO MURDERER! NO MURDERER, YOU HEAR! NO MATTER WHAT THE VOICES SAY!
I NEVER KILLED ANYONE. IT WAS THEM. IT WAS THEM, NOT ME.
SO, THAT LITTLE ROCK ON YER FOREHEAD IS THE CAUSE OF ALL THIS!
WHA--HOW DID YOU?!
I GREW IN A CARNI SLAPPY!
PICKIN' A LOCK AIN'T BIG THING!

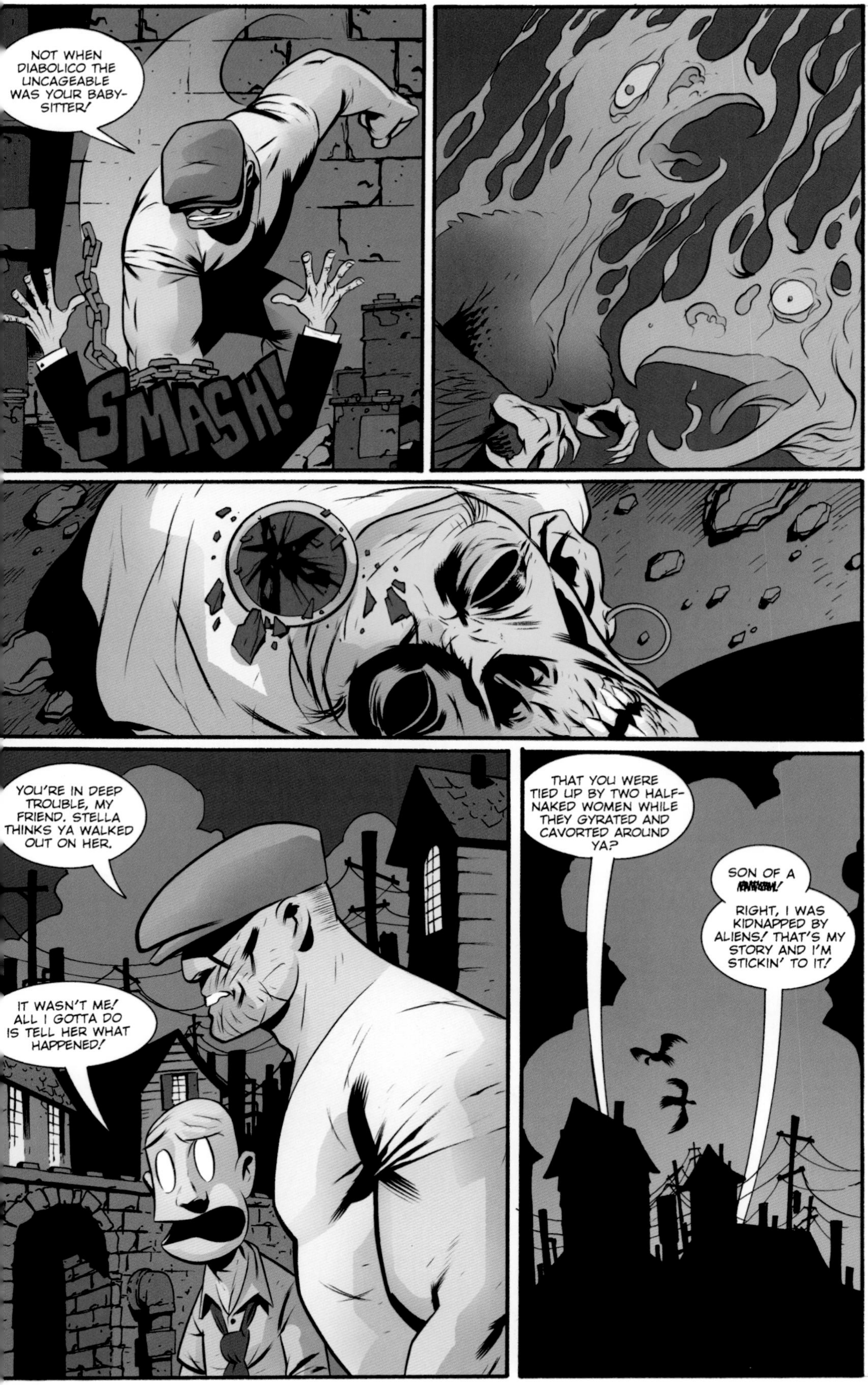
NOT WHEN DIABOLICO THE UNCAGEABLE WAS YOUR BABY-SITTER!
SMASH!
YOU'RE IN DEEP TROUBLE, MY FRIEND. STELLA THINKS YA WALKED OUT ON HER.
IT WASN'T ME! ALL I GOTTA DO IS TELL HER WHAT HAPPENED!
THAT YOU WERE TIED UP BY TWO HALF-NAKED WOMEN WHILE THEY GYRATED AND CAVORTED AROUND YA?
SON OF A
RIGHT, I WAS KIDNAPPED BY ALIENS! THAT'S MY STORY AND I'M STICKIN' TO IT!

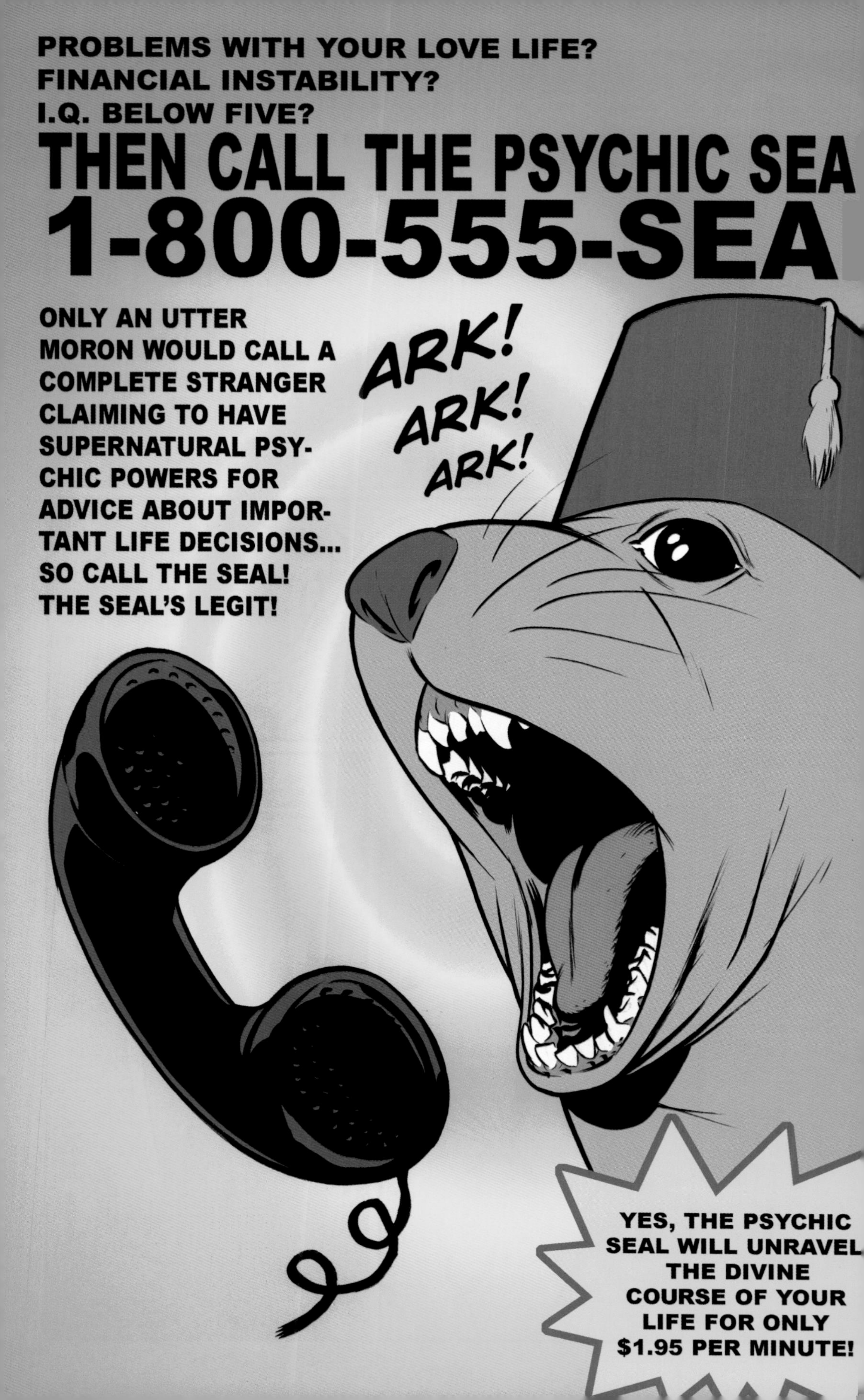
PROBLEMS WITH YOUR LOVE LIFE?
FINANCIAL INSTABILITY?
I.Q. BELOW FIVE?
THEN CALL THE PSYCHIC SEA
1-800-555-SEA
ONLY AN UTTER MORON WOULD CALL A COMPLETE STRANGER CLAIMING TO HAVE SUPERNATURAL PSYCHIC POWERS FOR ADVICE ABOUT IMPORTANT LIFE DECISIONS... SO CALL THE SEAL! THE SEAL'S LEGIT!
ARK!
ARK!
ARK!
YES, THE PSYCHIC SEAL WILL UNRAVEL THE DIVINE COURSE OF YOUR LIFE FOR ONLY $1.95 PER MINUTE!

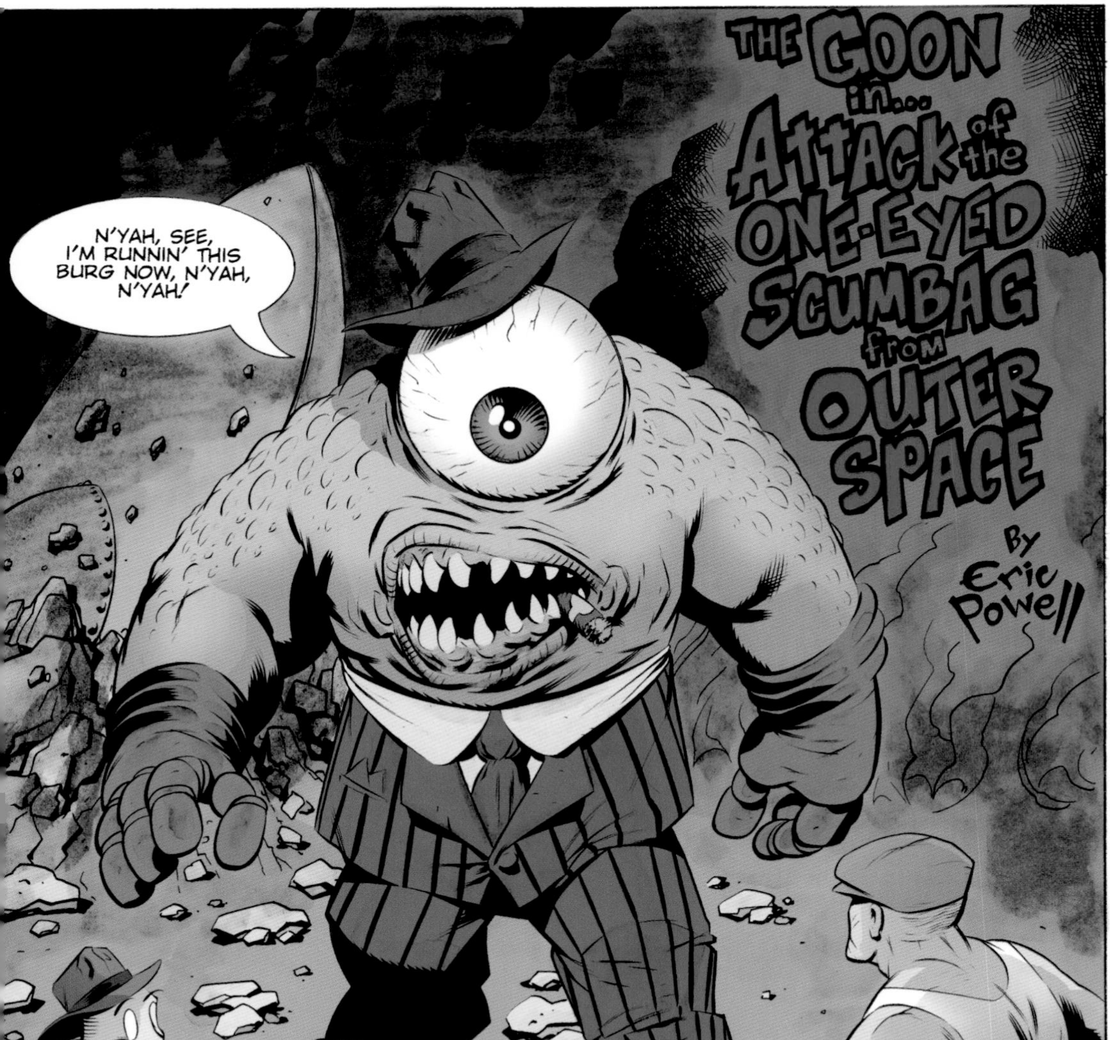
THE GOON in... Attack of the ONE-EYED SCUMBAG from OUTER SPACE
By Eric Powell
N'YAH, SEE, I'M RUNNIN' THIS BURG NOW, N'YAH, N'YAH!

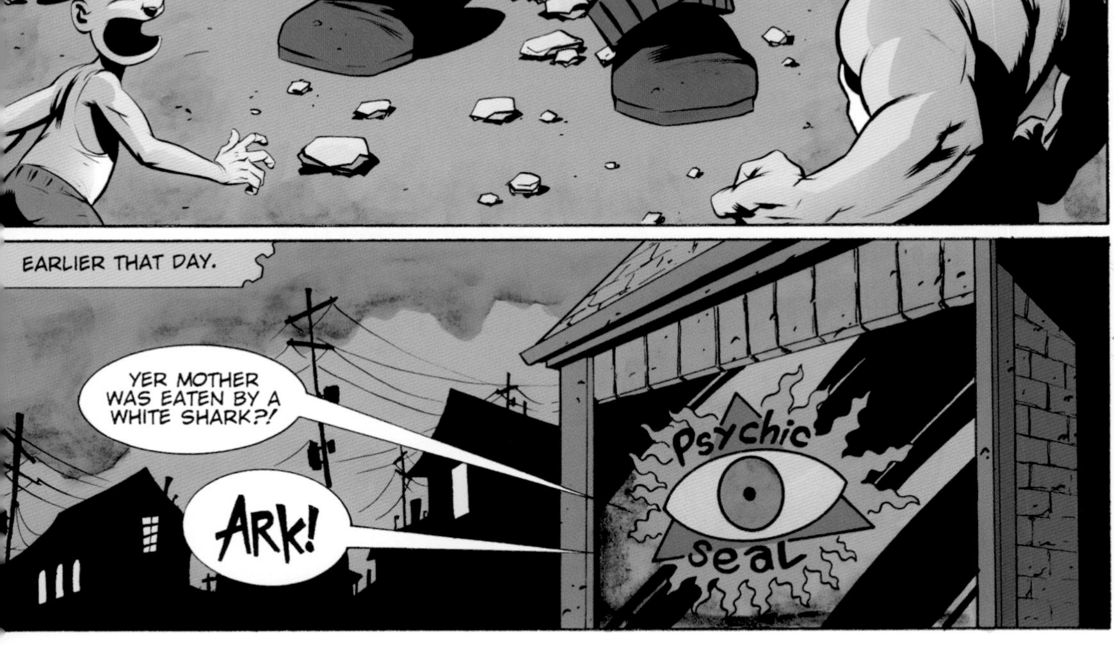
EARLIER THAT DAY.
YER MOTHER WAS EATEN BY A WHITE SHARK?!
ARK!
Psychic seal

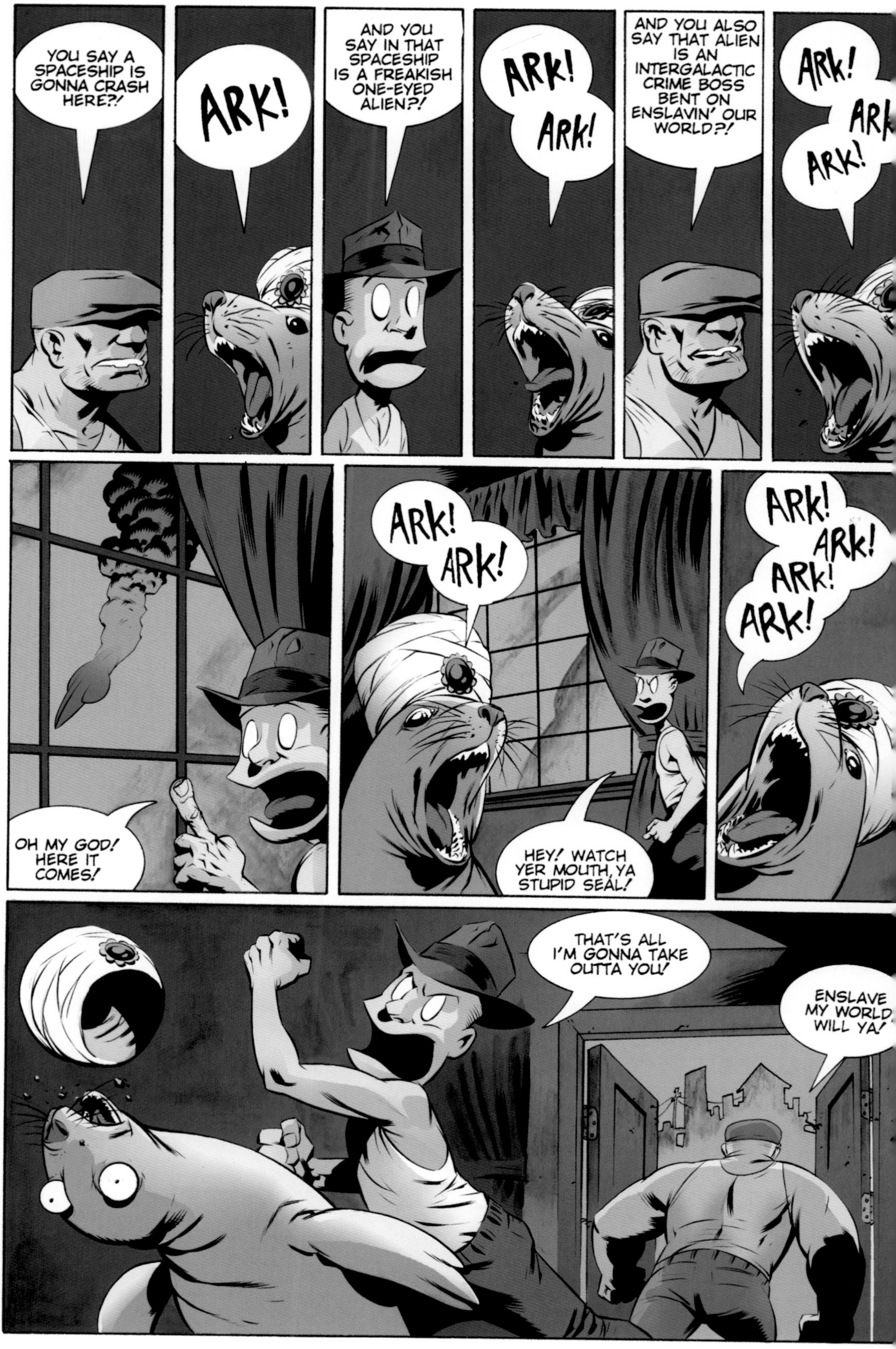
YOU SAY A SPACESHIP IS GONNA CRASH HERE?!
ARK!
AND YOU SAY IN THAT SPACESHIP IS A FREAKISH ONE-EYED ALIEN?!
ARK!
ARK!
AND YOU ALSO SAY THAT ALIEN IS AN INTERGALACTIC CRIME BOSS BENT ON ENSLAVIN' OUR WORLD?!
ARK!
ARK!
OH MY GOD! HERE IT COMES!
ARK!
ARK!
HEY! WATCH YER MOUTH, YA STUPID SEAL!
ARK!
ARK!
ARK!
ARK!
THAT'S ALL I'M GONNA TAKE OUTTA YOU!
ENSLAVE MY WORLD WILL YA!

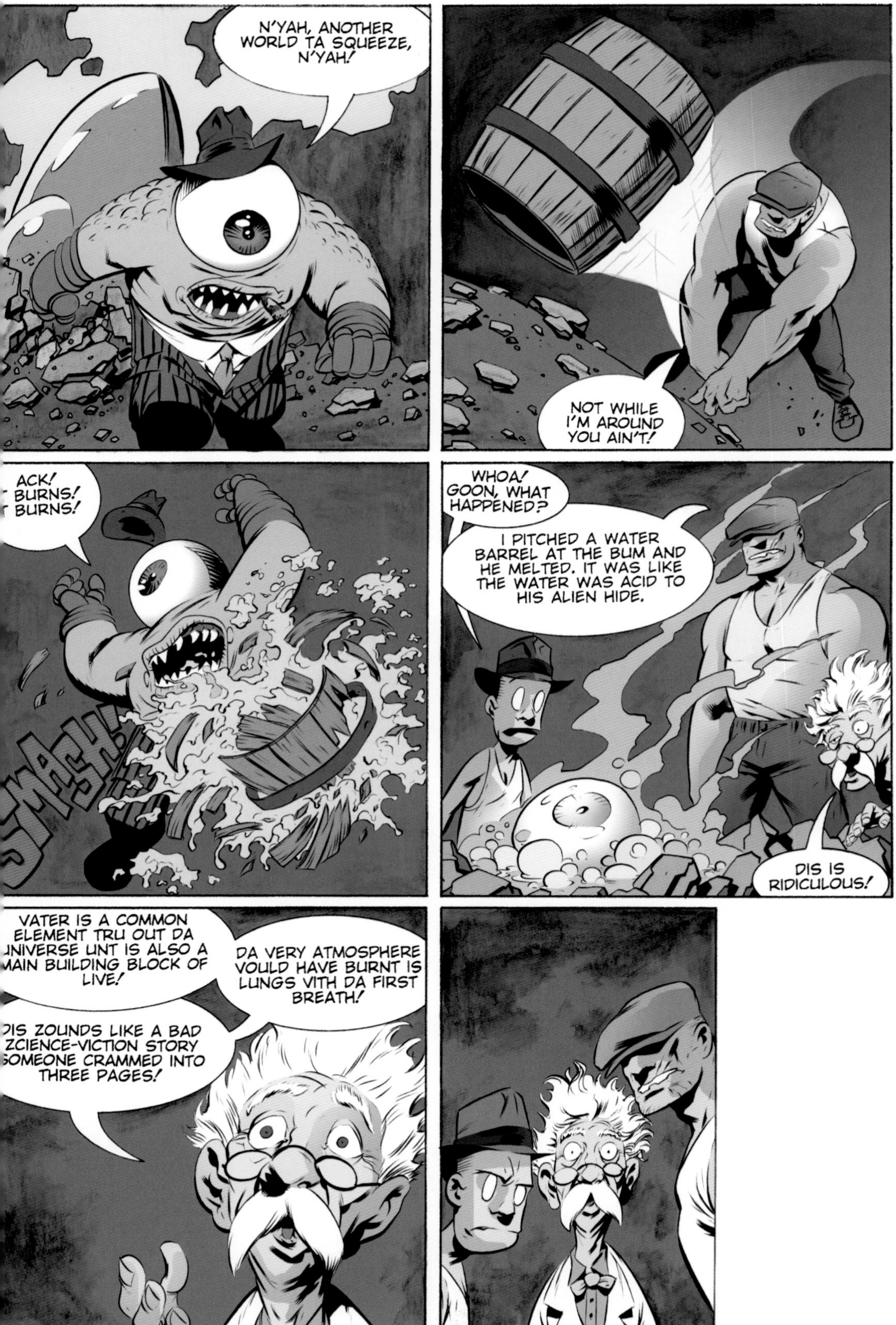
N'YAH, ANOTHER WORLD TA SQUEEZE, N'YAH!
NOT WHILE I'M AROUND YOU AIN'T!
ACK! BURNS! BURNS!
SMASH!
WHOA! GOON, WHAT HAPPENED?
I PITCHED A WATER BARREL AT THE BUM AND HE MELTED. IT WAS LIKE THE WATER WAS ACID TO HIS ALIEN HIDE.
DIS IS RIDICULOUS!
VATER IS A COMMON ELEMENT TRU OUT DA UNIVERSE UNT IS ALSO A MAIN BUILDING BLOCK OF LIVE!
DA VERY ATMOSPHERE VOULD HAVE BURNT IS LUNGS VITH DA FIRST BREATH!
DIS ZOUNDS LIKE A BAD ZCIENCE-VICTION STORY SOMEONE CRAMMED INTO THREE PAGES!

THE GOON™

GALLERY

Featuring:

MICHAEL AVON OEMING

GUY DAVIS

MIKE HAWTHORNE

KYLE HOTZ

CHRISTOPHE QUET

colors by **ERIC POWELL**

except **GUY DAVIS**, *colored by* **DAN JACKSON**

and **CHRISTOPHE QUET**, *colored by* **STÉPHANE PERU**

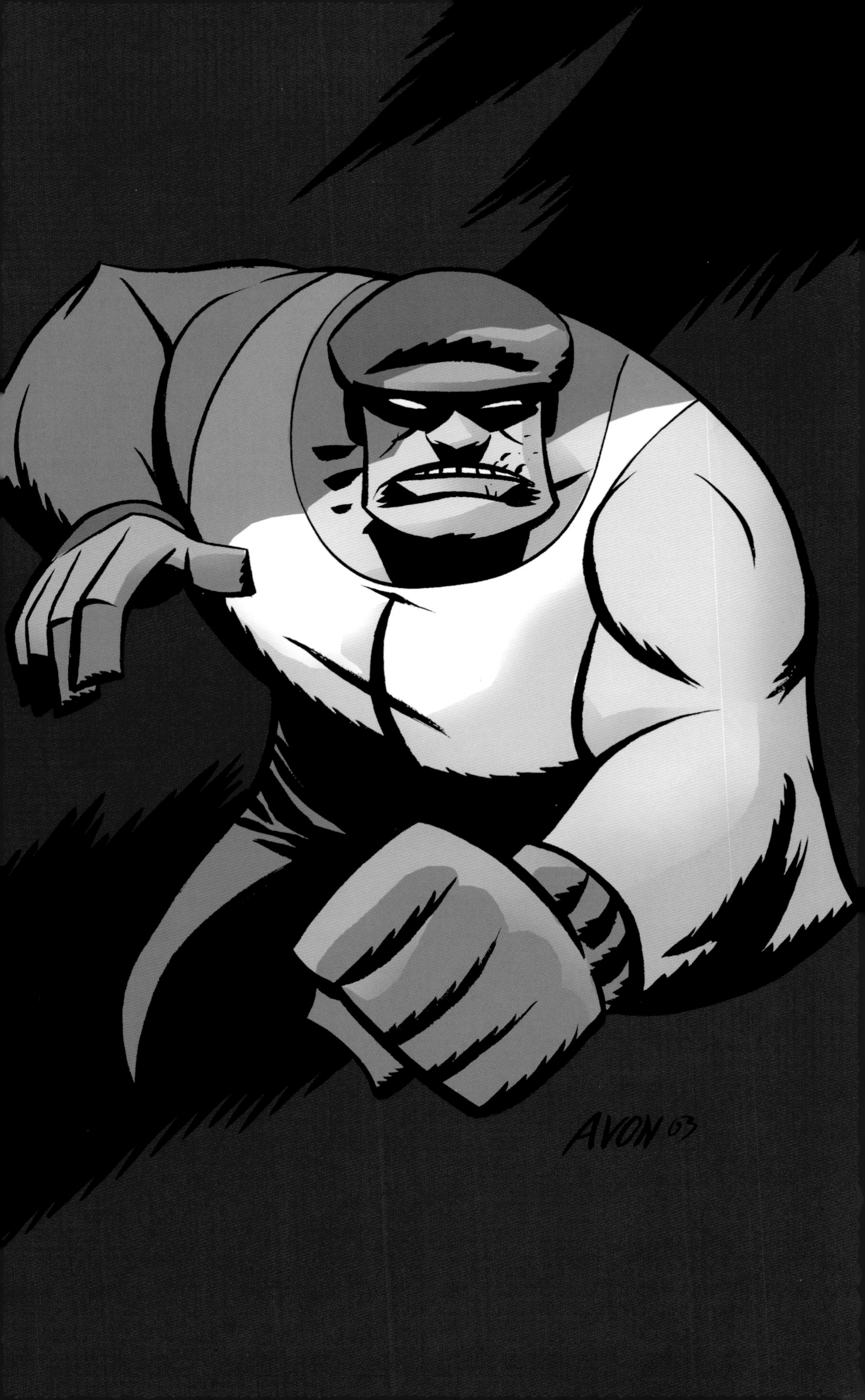
AVON 03

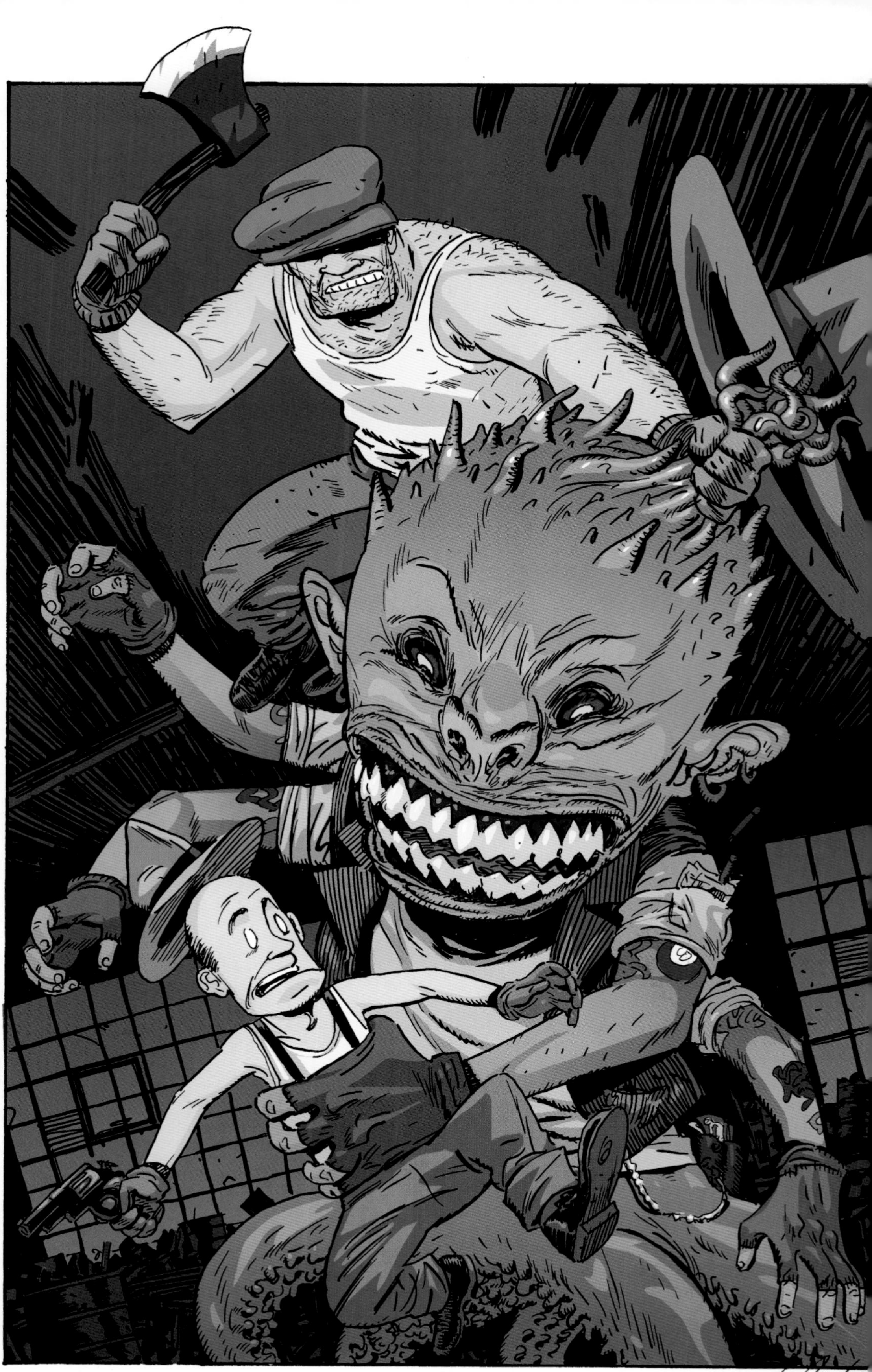

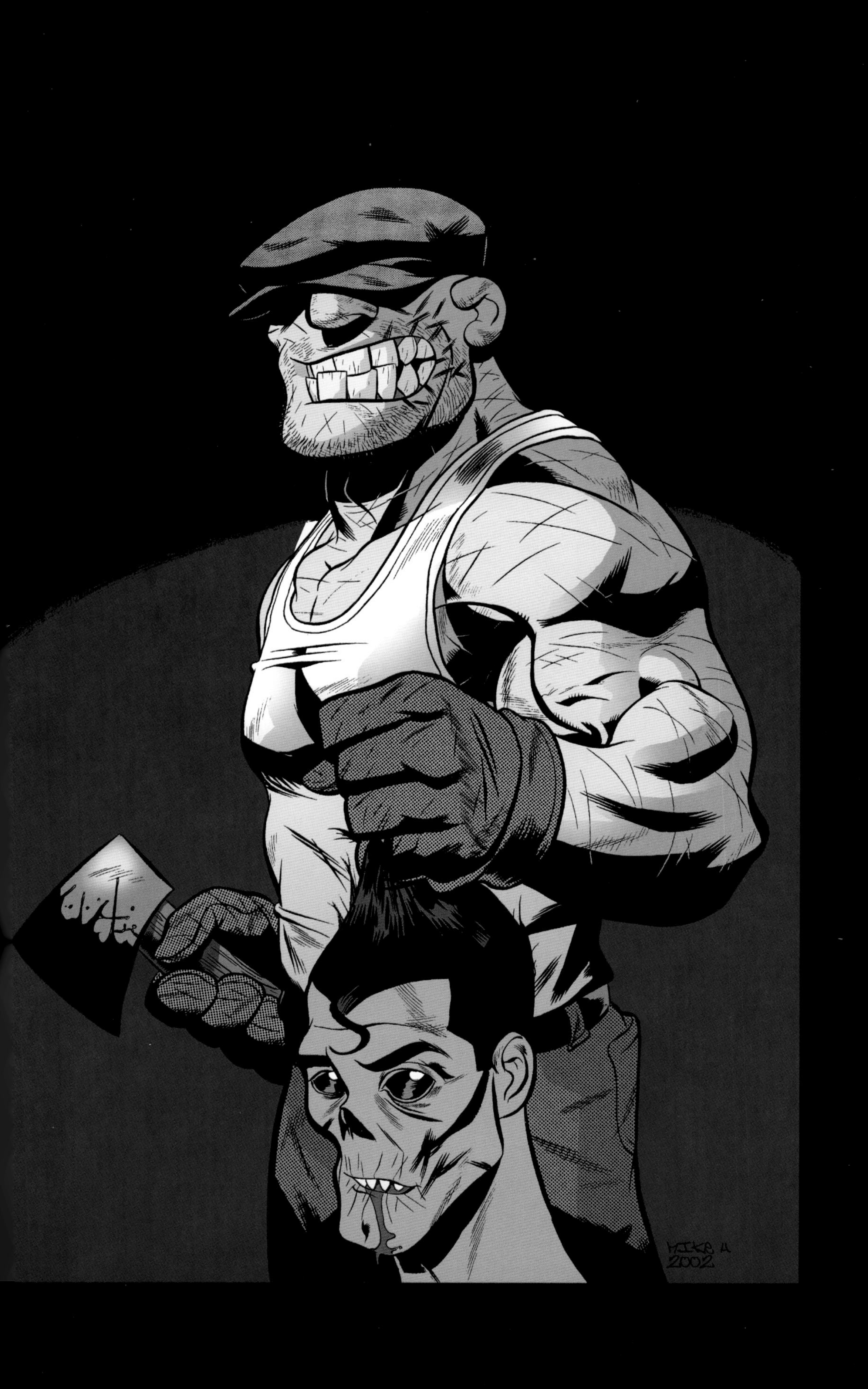
MIKE M
2002

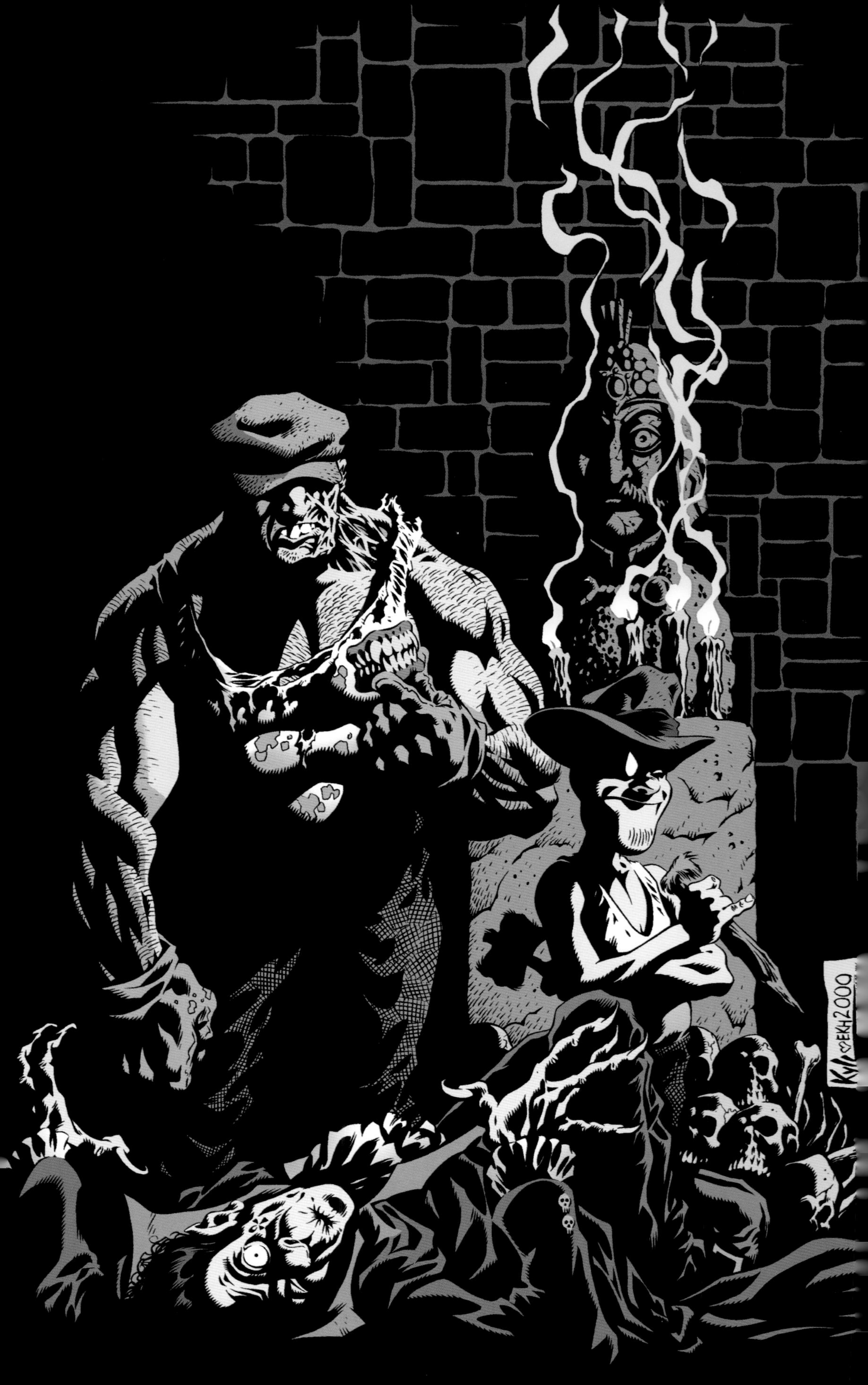

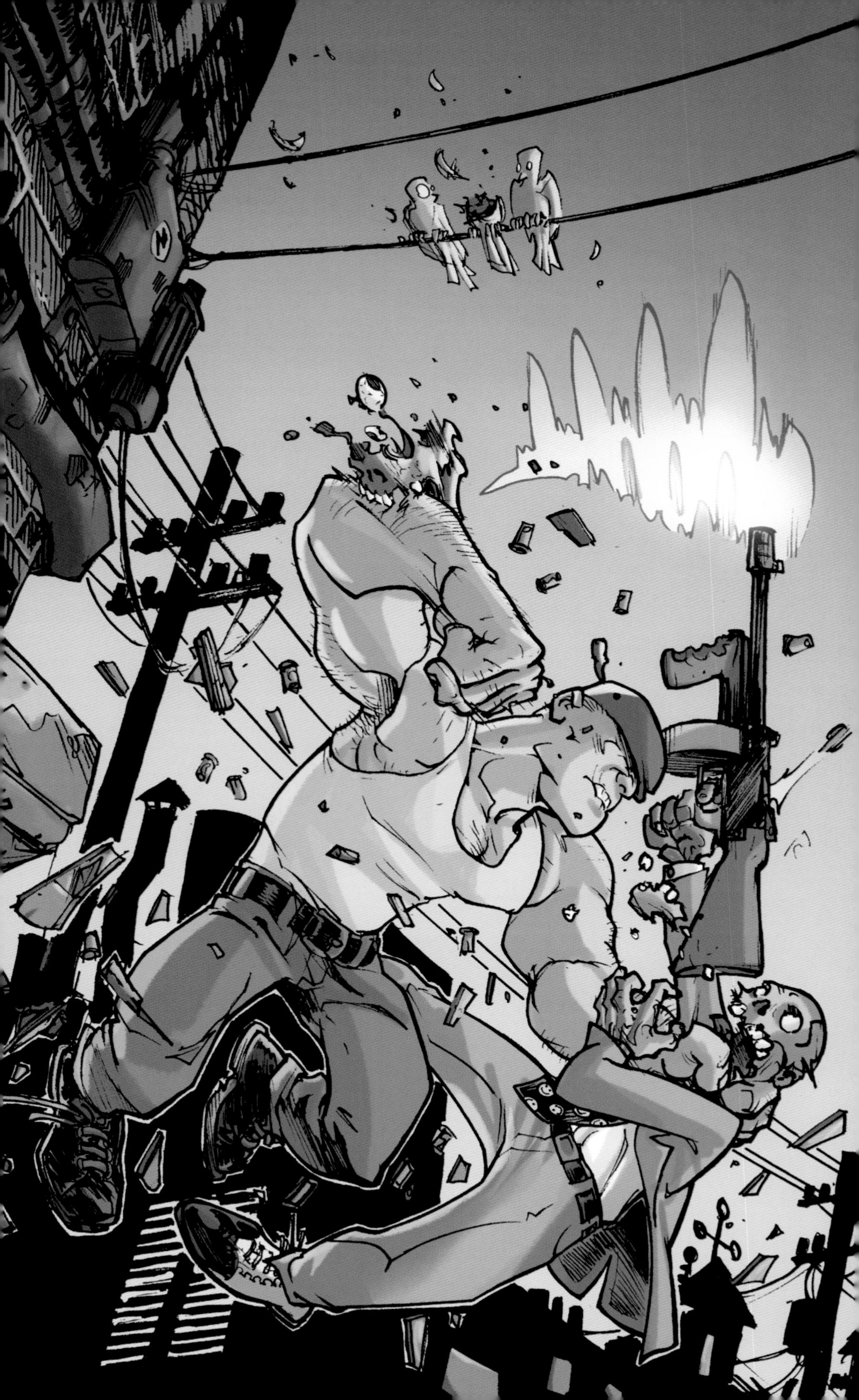

RECOMMENDED DARK HORSE READING

TAKI SOMA + MICHAEL AVON OEMING
RAPTURE

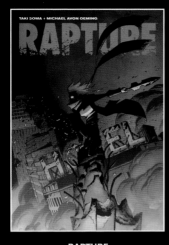

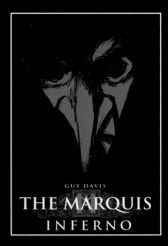

RAPTURE

Taki Soma and Michael Avon Oeming

After warring for a century, Earth's greatest champions and villains suddenly disappear, leaving the planet decimated. Amongst this wreckage, two lovers find themselves separated by a continent and will do anything to find each other again.

$19.99 | ISBN 978-1-59582-460-8

GUY DAVIS
THE MARQUIS
INFERNO

THE MARQUIS VOLUME 1: INFERNO

Guy Davis

In eighteenth-century Venisalle, faith governs life and death, the guilty hide their shame behind masks, and the souls of Hell have escaped to possess the living. One man is blessed with the clarity to recognize the demons—and the means to return them to Hell.

$24.99 | ISBN 978-1-59582-368-7

THE FINEST IN ILLUSTRATED HORROR!
CREEPY

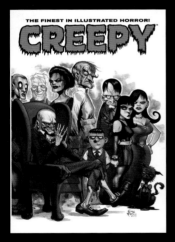

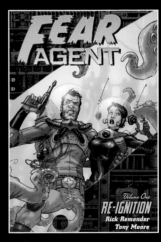

CREEPY COMICS VOLUME 1

Joe R. Lansdale, Doug Moench, Jason Shawn Alexander, Greg Ruth, Eric Powell, and others

It's the biggest, bloodiest, most creepy collection of new terror tales you'll find this year! *Creepy Comics* Volume 1 gathers all of the new material from the first two years of Dark Horse's celebrated new *Creepy* series into one gargantuan book!

$19.99 | ISBN 978-1-59582-750-0

FEAR AGENT
Volume One
RE-IGNITION
Rick Remender
Tony Moore

FEAR AGENT VOLUME 1: RE-IGNITION

Rick Remender and Tony Moore

When down-and-out alien exterminator Heath Huston stumbles upon an extraterrestrial legion of amoebas preparing to annihilate the Earth, he's forced to choose between the bottle and resuming his role as a peacekeeper, as the last Fear Agent.

$14.99 | ISBN 978-1-59307-764-8

THE GOON ™

by Eric Powell

DARK HORSE BOOKS®
darkhorse.com

To find a comics shop in your area, call 1-888-266-4226 For more information
order direct: • On the web: darkhorse.com • E-mail: mailorder@darkhorse.com • P
1-800-862-0052 Mon.–Fri. 9 AM to 5 PM Pacific Time